Perception and Organization

Perception and Organization

Art, Music, Media

Alexander Styhre

palgrave
macmillan

Palgrave Macmillan in the UK is an imprint of Macmillan Publishers Limited, registered in England, company number 785998, of Houndmills, Basingstoke, Hampshire RG21 6XS.

Palgrave Macmillan in the US is a division of St Martin's Press LLC, 175 Fifth Avenue, New York, NY 10010.

Palgrave Macmillan is the global academic imprint of the above companies and has companies and representatives throughout the world.

Palgrave® and Macmillan® are registered trademarks in the United States, the United Kingdom, Europe and other countries.

ISBN-13: 978–0–230–51615–1
ISBN-10: 0–230–51615–7

This book is printed on paper suitable for recycling and made from fully managed and sustained forest sources. Logging, pulping and manufacturing processes are expected to conform to the environmental regulations of the country of origin.

A catalogue record for this book is available from the British Library.

Library of Congress Cataloging-in-Publication Data

Styhre, Alexander.
  Perception and organization : art, music, media / Alexander Styhre.
      p. cm.
  Includes bibliographical references and index.
  ISBN-13: 978–0–230–51615–1 (hardback : alk. paper)
  ISBN-10: 0–230–51615–7 (hardback : alk. paper) 1. Attention.   2.
Perception.   3. Organizational behavior.   4. Art.
  5. Music.   6. Mass media.   I. Title.
  BF321.S79   2008
  153.7—dc22

                                                                          2008027560

10   9   8   7   6   5   4   3   2   1
17   16   15   14   13   12   11   10   09   08
Printed and bound in Great Britain by
CPI Antony Rowe, Chippenham and Eastbourne

Contents

Preface and Acknowledgements

In *Delirious New York*, Rem Koolhaas tells an intriguing story of how the great Mexican mural painter Diego Rivera painted a small portrait of Lenin on a mural commissioned for the Rockefeller Center in New York City. Rivera, a widely acclaimed artist with socialist sympathies, clearly saw the value of symbolism and visuality, and without doubt could foresee the controversy emerging when bringing the Bolshevik leader into the very heart of capitalism (in the end, after long negotiations following Rivera's refusal to remove the image, the painting was demolished by workmen on 10 February 1934, but was eventually recreated by Rivera in the Palace of Fine Arts in Mexico City). This piece of Rivera's work is a telling example of how perception, ideology, and power are always intersecting and thereby a major source of interest for organization theorists and students of management practice. While many scholars, also in the field of organization theory and management studies, writing about perception have a background in the liberal arts (aesthetics, art theory, musicology, etc.), my take on perception instead derives from the science and technology literature. In this literature, science is what is produced through the integration of theory, the technical instruments and laboratory apparatus, and actual practices and elaborations. This assemblage of theory/technology/practices also, at the bottom line, one may say, relies on human perception, that is, the ability to visually identify, detect and sort out what counts as 'normal' and 'deviant' within enacted frameworks of analysis. It was perhaps Michael Lynch (1985) who first called my attention to the matter of perception in his discussion of how microbiologists not only inspected images (e.g. photographs) generated in the laboratory work to identify what had been predicted (in the conventional positivist manner) but also to find 'absences' in the images. These absences could be regarded as being 'real' or 'artifactual'. Says Lynch (1985: 86): 'The failure of an expected phenomenon to appear was of interest here for the way in which the absence could be formulated under different conditions as an artifactual absence or as a "real" absence. Under actual absence research conditions, such absences were troublesome since they were necessarily definitive of any real worldly absences, but could be taken as "failures" in the technical ways of making a phenomenon appear.' In Lynch's (1985) view, perception is here of necessity laden with expectations and theoretical assumptions on what to expect and what to hope for, and, consequently, what to see. This 'way of seeing' is an example of what Daston and Galison (2007) call the 'trained judgment' of the practising researcher. Such trained judgment is in turn embedded in certain – again with Daston and Galison's (2007) term – 'epistemologies of the eye'. The practising scientist is then not only theorist or a laboratory technology operator but is also an *inspector*, a specialist trained in reviewing means of representation to identify interesting and noteworthy occurrences or, on the contrary, their very absence. In this book, the interest for perception is examined more broadly as what is underlying many organizational activities and processes, but the very foundation of the concept of perception derives from the science and technology literature. What both Rem Koolhaas and Michael Lynch in their own particular ways illustrate is that organizing is what is always already embedded in perception. Deviances from norms and expectations – 'Isn't that Lenin on the wall, right?' or 'Shouldn't we expect to see something more, given such and such conditions, on the print?' – are identified by visual inspection and thereafter articulated. Perception is what makes organizing continue because what is rendered 'problematic' (i.e. what is abnormal or 'pathological', to use Georges Canguilhem's term) is dealt with in productive ways or eliminated *tout court*.

Substantial parts of this book were written and restructured during a sabbatical semester as a visiting scholar at SCANCOR at Stanford University in the fall of 2007. I greatly appreciated the ability to focus on writing while at the same time having the opportunity to speak to other visiting scholars and members of the Stanford faculty. Some of the ideas presented in Chapter 4 were presented at the EGOS Colloquium in Vienna in July 2007 and I am grateful for the comments on the paper from the participants and the stream convenors Jannis Kallinikos and Giovan Francesco Lanzara. I am also indebted to Mats Sundgren and Sofia Börjesson for collaborating with me in various research works. Katja Lindqvist and Emma Stenström have been helpful in recommending literature pertaining to arts management. I would also like to thank the interviewees participating in the study from which parts are presented in Chapter 2.

ALEXANDER STYHRE

Note: The quotations on pages 141–2 from the IBM Songbook are published with the kind permission of the IBM Corporation.

Introduction

The social problem of attention

Martin Jay (1988, 1996, 2002) has at a number of occasions defended what he calls the 'visual turn' in the social sciences and humanities. Speaking against the much-debated 'linguistic turn' and its emphasis on *logos*, on speech and writing, Jay suggests that there is a growing interest in what has been called 'visual cultures' (see e.g. Schwartz and Przyblyski, 2004), that is, a concern for social and cultural representations that are figural or symbolic and are '[r]esisting subsumption under the rubric of discursivity; the image is demanding its own unique mode of analysis' (Jay, 1996: 1). The merits but also potential shortcomings of such analysis of forms of visuality are addressed shortly. More specifically, the relationship between the new theories of vision emerging in the first half of the nineteenth century, carefully examined by Jonathan Crary (1990, 1999), and the concomitant emergence of both organizations and managerial doctrines (Shenhav, 1999; Guillén, 1994; Chandler, 1977; Wren, 1972; Pollard, 1965) demonstrate an intriguing co-evolution of thought and practice. Crary (1999) argues convincingly that the location of vision to the body, rendering it a subjective and somatic matter, paves the way for a new concept, that of *attention*. Crary (1999) explains:

> At the moment when the dynamic logic of capital began to dramatically undermine any stable or enduring structure of perception, this logic simultaneously attempted to impose a disciplinary regime of attentiveness. For it is in the late nineteenth century, within the human sciences and particularly the nascent field of scientific psychology, that the problem of *attention* becomes a fundamental issue. It was a problem whose centrality was directly related to the emergence of a social urban, psychic, and industrial field increasingly saturated with sensory input. Inattention, especially within the context of new forms of large-scale industrialized production, began to be treated as a danger and a serious problem, even though it was often the very modernized arrangements of labor that produced as an ongoing inattention. (Crary, 1999: 13)

Speaking of another, later period of time, Hansen (1995: 367) says that the concept of 'Americanization' was used in Weimar Germany to denote a range of social and technological changes including Fordist-Taylorist principles of production (relying on 'mechanization, standardization, efficiency, the assembly line'), mass consumption, new forms of social organization, freedom from tradition, social mobility, mass democracy, and 'the cultural symbols of the new era – skyscrapers, jazz (*Negermusik*), boxing, revues, radio, and cinema' (Hansen, 1995: 367). Managerial principles, social changes, and perception and its specific form operationalized as attention, were again interrelated concepts. However, rather than arguing for a causal linearity between theories of vision, research on attention, emerging social organization, and new modalities of power, Crary (1999) suggests that these different changes in, with a Foucaultian term, regimes of power/knowledge are entangled and interrelated in intricate ways: 'Attention was not part of a particular regime of power but rather part of a space in which effects of power operated and circulated' (Crary, 1999: 24). Moreover, attention is always, Crary (1990: 5) argues, embedded in wider social conditions: 'Vision and its effects are always inseparable from the possibilities of an observing subject who is both the historical product and the site of certain practices, techniques, institutions, and procedures of subjectification.'

This brings us to the central arguments in the book: (1) both theories of vision and consequently theories of perception at large, and theories of social organization and practices of day-to-day management emerge at the same time, have their roots in the period 1820–1840 but are becoming more immediately visible in the last thirty years of the nineteenth century; (2) the 'problem of attention', an aggregate of potentialities and concerns derived from the concept of perception, first identified and formulated by psychologists and physiologists in the mid-nineteenth century, has always been at the centre of interest for organizations theories and management practice, from F.W. Taylor and human relations researchers to contemporary forms of managerial and leadership practice.[1] Hugo Münsterberg, 'the father of industrial psychology' (Guillén, 2006: 26) sharing – albeit he in places expresses

---

[1] The human capacity of attention has been of central interest for a long range of organization theories. For instance, the behavioural theory of the firm and theories of decision-making formulated by James March and a number of colleagues (Cyert and March, 1963; March and Olsen, 1976; Cohen, March and Olsen, 1972) strongly emphasize the contingent and selective nature of human attention. March (1994: 10) even claims that '[t]heories of decision making are often better described as theories of attention of search than a theory of choice. They are concerned with the way in which attention is allocated'. Recently, a number of organization and management researchers have used the concept of attention when theorizing organizations; Ocasio (1997) calls for an 'attention-based view

some scepticism (e.g. Münsterberg, 1913: 49) – many objectives and beliefs with the scientific management movement, emphasizes the central role of the concept of attention:

> The problem of attention, indeed, seems to stand quite in the centre of the field of industrial efficiency. This conviction has grown upon me in my observations of industrial life. The peculiar kind of attention decides more than any mental trait for which economic activity the individual is adapted. The essential point is that such differences in attention cannot be characterized as good or bad; it is not a question of the attentive and of the inattentive mind. One type is not better than another, but is simply different. Two workingmen, not only equally industrious and capable, but also equally attentive, may yet occupy two positions in which they are both complete failures because their attention does not fit the places, and both may become highly efficient as soon as they exchange positions. Their particular types of attention have now found the right places. (Münsterberg, 1913: 136)

Similar to Taylor's rhetoric, Münsterberg's proposed model does not aim at judging 'good or bad' but rather to optimize the efficiency and the use of available resources. Such optimization is accomplished through experimental research and careful analysis. Münsterberg (1913) emphasizes the external sources of distraction and points at the practical applicability of his theories:

> [B]y far the more important cause of distraction of attention lies in those disturbances which come in from without ... In a great printing-shop a woman who was occupied with work which demanded her fullest attention was seated at her task in an aisle where trucking was done. Removing this operator to a quiet corner caused an increase of 25 per cent in her work. (Münsterberg, 1913: 210)

Today, almost a hundred years after Münsterberg and the scientific management movement, writers such as Lanham (2006) advance the

---

of the firm'; Cho and Hambrick (2006) show that the deregulation of the American airplane industry directed the attention of the corporate boards in airplane companies to more entrepreneurial concerns; Weick and Sutcliffe (2006) theorize attention as a central feature of what they refer to as 'mindfulness' in organizations. These studies suggest that attention is limited (Oscasio, 1997), scarce (March, 1994), and costly to use (Weick and Sutcliffe, 2006). In other words, the concept of attention is at the centre of a series of managerial and organizational problems and challenges to be resolved.

argument that attention is in fact the single most important scarce resource in today's economy and thus calls for a 'political economy of attention': '[I]nformation is not in short supply in the new information economy. We're drowning in it. What we lack is the human attention needed to make sense of it all. It will be easier to find our place in the new regime if we think of it as an economist of attention. Attention is the commodity in short supply', Lanham (2006: xi) argues (see also Hansen and Haas, 2001; Davenport and Beck, 2001). Furthermore, Jonathan Beller argues in his intriguing book *The cinematic mode of production* (2006) that contemporary capitalism is characterized by an 'expropriation of the visual' – the Marxist vocabulary abounds in Beller's text – enabling new forms of 'value-productive labour' which Beller (2006: 108) names 'the production value of attention'. While capitalist production used to operate on the plane of materiality, the 'cinematic mode of production' is primarily visual, operating through 'sensual labor' and on the 'visual register' – 'perception is increasingly bound to production', Beller (2006: 3) claims. He continues: 'The cinematization of the visual, the fusion of the visual and with a set of socio-technical institutions and apparatuses, gives rise to the advanced form of network expropriation characteristic of the present period. Capitalized machine interfaces prey on visuality.' This operation is instantaneous because the image, as a technology, 'extracts sensual labor (attention) directly in the moment of its apprehension', Beller (2006: 78) says. For Beller (2006: 8), it is the development of cinema, a precursor to media such as television, computing, email, and the World Wide Web, that is the driver behind the – to use Aglietta's (1979) term – new regime of accumulation. 'Cinema is the development of a new medium for the production and circulation of value, as important in the reorganization of production and consciousness as the railroad track and the highway', Beller (2006: 207) claims. Moreover, Beller (2006: 8) argues that cinema can be seen as being as part of an 'emerging cybernetic complex' which functions as a 'technology for the capture and redirection of global labor's revolutionary social agency and potentiality'. Furthermore, the cinematic image is in opposition to the linearity of the written text and therefore radically restructures human perception and consciousness:

> [C]inema underscores the historico-material shattering of the linguistic alongside the rise of the visual, the displacement of ontological categories, and the reconfiguration of the imaginary and the subject in the logic of the spectacle ... attention makes clear the baseline

functioning of consciousness/bodies (labor) in relation to all forms of social machinery, and allows for a consideration of input, output, and throughput at intellectual and corporeal levels. (Beller, 2006: 295)

The use of new media is part of an emergent 'calculus of the visible' that is representative of the move from material to visual production. Beller quotes a Google[2] representative speaking of the strategies of Google to navigate in the 'attention economy' where the aggregate of perception-visuality-attention is of central importance:

> For Google, being in the attention business means it's of utmost importance for Google to find out what people are paying attention to. To do that, Google has made a history of giving away services that other companies charge an arm and a leg for. Even more amazingly, the services that Google gives away is usually better than the services that other people are charging for ... In exchange for that free services and software, Google wants to look over your shoulder and take note on what you are paying attention to and what you are ignoring. (Mitch Wagner, Google, cited in Beller, 2006: 303)

The intensification of visuality, centered on the term and social practice of attention, is 'essential to capital's expansion and valorization' (Beller, 2006: 8). Not only does the cinematic mode of production have implications for organizations and the economy, the very consciousness of social actors is at stake, Beller argues. The restructuring of perception, consciousness and production in the cinematic society leads to a gradually

---

[2] It is noteworthy that the IT company Google, primarily known for its innovative search engine and located in Mountain View, California, is today playing a central role as what is representing the future of the economy. For instance, *New York Times* reported in December 2007 that while previous presidential candidates have been careful to pay visits to General Motor assembly plants, today a visit to the so-called Googleplex in Silicon Valley is playing a similar role: 'In terms of theatrical symbolism, the trip to Google is similar to the G.M. [General Motors] plant visit. In both cases, the visits gave the candidates the chance for a photo opportunity at the most technologically advanced edge of the economy, "signalling identification with the future", said Kathleen Hall Jamieson, a professor at the University of Pennsylvania's Annenberg School of Communication' (Stross, 2007). Google is then not seen as any Silicon Valley based information technology company but as the most prominent representative of an entire 'economic-cultural aggregate' comprising industries, technologies, innovation work practices, and a broader set of life styles developed in the San Francisco Bay Area (see Saxenian, 1994, for an account of the Silicon Valley IT cluster).

dematerialized society, embedded in sensual and abstract categories and experiences (Beller, 2006: 295).

Perception and organization

Following Crary's (1999) recommendation to not subscribe to linear causality schemes, it will not be argued that new theories of vision and perception as such leads to new managerial doctrines and practices; instead, the two domains of thought appear at the same period of time, at the verge of the modern society in the mid-nineteenth century. They are both part of a broad reconfiguration of the modern subject, anchored in wide-ranging scientific, economic, cultural, and social changes taking place in the nineteenth century. This enfolding of vision and perception and organizing – effectively intersecting in the very concept of attention – produced new methods and practices. For instance, Frank and Lillian Gilbreth, early proponents of scientific management, 'made extensive use of photographs in micromotion study and the cyclegraphic technique' (Reeves, Duncan and Ginter, 2001: 146) and made references to for instance Eadward Muybridge's ground-breaking photographic analysis of movement. Theories of perception and organizing both derive from a tradition of thinking that may be further explored.

At a few times in history, managerial thinking and doctrines and aesthetic and visual work have been folded into one another, thus producing new hybrid forms of visuality and management. For instance, the scientific principles in the Taylorist program did not only influence industrial and social organization but also found its way into the arts, architecture, and social planning (Guillén, 1997). Reeves, Duncan and Ginter (2001) show that the interest for motion study demonstrated by Frank and Lillian Gilbreth was shared by a number of persons in the liberal arts. In theatre, François Delsarte and later Emile-Henri Jaques-Dalcroze used motion studies to eliminate unnecessary movement in plays. In Germany, Rudolf von Laban applied motion study to dance and he eventually formulated a method for recording human movement called *labanotation*. Reeves, Duncan and Ginter (2001) argue that this interest in the detailed analysis of elementary components and their relations derived from a new scientific paradigm developed since the middle of the nineteenth century. In both the arts and in management, these novel ideas were gradually adapted and were applied in terms of motion study:

> Like the Gilbreths, Delsarte, Dalcroze, and von Laban were all strongly predisposed toward atomistic views [the paradigm examining parts

and their relations]. All focused on the scientific study of movement. Their approaches were attuned to the times in which they
lived and were scientific in outlook and attitude, Movement was anal-
ysed, labeled, and combined into laws or rules. Movement elements
were then synthesized into various notation systems by each of these
people. (Reeves, Duncan and Ginter, 2001: 148).

Furthermore, Van Delinder (2005) examines how Taylorist thinking
came to influence the joint work of the choreographer George Balanchine and composer Igor Stravinsky in the 1910s. After the Russian
revolution, Taylorist thinking became fashionable and represented the
new emerging socialist society structured in accordance with rational
principles. Also avant-garde artists adapted Taylorism in their work. For
instance, art theoretician Nikolai Chuzhal used time and motion studies to 'improve' drama performance skills by 'eliminating redundant or
inefficient emotions, gestures, and expressions' (Van Delinder, 2005:
1443) and the Russian theatre director and producer Vsevolod Meyer-
hold experimented with applying Taylorist to the theatre by developing
'a science of movement based on the science of "biomechanics" '; Meyer-
hold here used ' "Taylorist work rhythms and military tempi" to "discover
those movements of work which facilitate the maximum use of work
time" so as to improve acting skills and reduce play duration from 4
hours to 1 "without lessening aesthetic content or form" ' (Sites, 1989:
161) (Van Delinder, 2005: 1443). Balanchine's two collaborations with
Stravinsky, the ballets *Apollo* (1910) and *Agon* (1911), reflected the ideals of modernism: 'fast paced, realistic, and always aspiring to imitate
the technological precision of machinery' (Van Delinder, 2005: 1445).
These aesthetic effects were accomplished through a detailed monitoring and control over the dancers' bodies and their movement in space;
for Balanchine efficiency comes when 'everyone understands their place
in their hierarchy, taking orders from someone above them, not below'
(Van Delinder, 2005: 1448). Expressed differently, 'truth in movement
meant precision, not a moral code of conduct', Van Delinder (2005:
1448) argues. She (2005) concludes:

> Like Taylor, Balanchine and Stravinsky thought it was to the mutual
> advantage of everyone to determine the best way to perform any
> task ... Balanchine perfected an abstract form of ballet that was based
> entirely on the movement of the body in space rather than on dancers
> using their bodily movement to convey emotions or a character in a
> story ... In this way, the choreographer as manager now becomes

more important than the individual dancer, just as in industrial production professional managers now planned every move of the work
done on the shop floor. (Van Delinder, 2005: 1449)

In the collaborative work of Balanchine and Stravinsky, visuality, aesthetics and managerial principles and practices constitute a seamless web;
the arts and the perception it invokes are not detached form broader
social arrangements or ideologies. Perception and organizing are mutually constitutive, producing 'ways of perceiving' through the various
arrangements of social resources.

Taken together, organizations are not only carefully structured and
monitored social configurations operating on basis of bureaucratic and
Taylorist principles. They are also arenas where visuality and other forms
of perception are engaged and mobilized. Organizations are not only
maintained through speech, written documents, and formalized standard operation procedures, but are also social formations embedded in
the use of the five senses. This brings us back to Martin Jay's (1988) declaration, underlining the 'ocularcentrism' in Western thinking. When
examining organizations or any other entity or process in social fields,
visuality is by tradition a privileged human faculty – vision is after all,
needless to say, the most widely recognized human sense – but there is
no reason to exclude other means of perception. For instance, to use
an example from the service economy, restaurant chefs engage their
taste, smell, vision, tactile capacities, and even hearing in their day-
to-day work (Fine, 1996); when cooking, restaurants chefs do not only
taste, smell and look at the food (as most of us would believe), they
do in fact also touch the food (e.g. when frying a steak) and listen to
sounds (e.g. when putting the steak into the frying pan to determine the
adequate temperature). In organizations and firms, a variety of expert
groups and professions engage their five senses on a daily basis in their
examination of the object of investigation. Wine tasters taste wine, tea
importers smell and taste different qualities, music studio technicians
arrange microphones to accomplish certain sounds, and medical doctors
diagnose on basis of tactile examinations. Thus, rather than accepting
Jay's (1988) emphasis on visuality offhand, it may be argued that there is
a need for speaking more broadly of perception than vision. Perception
here includes all the five senses and does not of necessity give privilege
to vision *vis-à-vis* other perceptual capacities. However, while Jay (1988)
is participating in a theoretical debate, seeking to advance certain epistemological and methodological positions in a politicised field concerned
with authority and the enactment of legitimate perspectives, this book is

more concerned with practical and organizational matters. For instance, the relatively undertheorized concept of perception in organization studies; in comparison to the totality of linguistic, discursive and narrative studies of organization, the literature on perception and organizing is scattered and marginal. As a consequence, this book aims to address two specific forms of perception, visual and auditory capacities, here represented by the categories of art and music. These two groups of concepts are not synonymous – not all vision is directed towards art, neither is all we hear music – but they are overlapping. One may say that art and music are metonymic to these to modes of perception. When mentioning art, vision is implied; when making reference to music, the capacity of hearing is assumed to be involved in the process. In the fourth chapter of this book, the concept of media will be addressed as what is in fact capable of 'remediating' art and music, enabling new and complementary forms of perception. The subtitle of the book is thus *Art, Music, Media* emphasizing the importance of these three 'perception-based' bodies of resources in day-to-day organizing. What we learn from Jay's (1988, 1996, 2002) thinking is that not everything is to be examined on the level of discursivity and *logos*, being reduced to a system of representations constituted by utterance and written texts. Art, music and media are social and organizational resources, embedded in the human capacity of perception, mobilized and employed as what are complementary or additional to speech and text in organizations. More specifically, they are resources embedded in – when alluding to Martin Jay – 'regimes of perception' that deserve a proper analysis in their own right and not only as being merely conceived of as a specific form of 'reading' of a 'text' constituted by (with Deleuze and Guattari's, 1994, term) *percepts*. Perception is a central component of organizing and therefore it must be carefully examined in term of its social, cultural, political, and economic significance and consequences.

Outline of the book

In Chapter 1, *The concept of perception*, the concept of perception is examined both as an historical and philosophical concept and related to the concept of organizing and the emerging doctrine of organization theory. Perception is discussed as what was radically shaped by a new epistemology, leading to new theories of vision, emerging in the middle of the nineteenth century. Rather than suggesting that organizations and theories of organizations and management are the effects of such new epistemologies, it is suggested that there are two ideas or 'tendencies', the new images of perception and organization theory, developed in tandem and drawing on shared social interests and epistemologies. For instance, the concept of *attention*, central to the new research on perception, is also of central importance for the new doctrine of management, very much concerned with the development of practices shaping workers' attention and aspirations. In addition, the concept of perception is discussed as being a philosophical term, discussed in detail by for instance Henri Bergson and later on Maurice Merleau-Ponty.

Chapter 2, *Art: Visual perception and the aesthetic*, discusses the concept of art and conceives of art as a social and aesthetic category in many ways influencing social life. In addition, art is related to discourses on gender, ethnicity, and power and the underlying ideologies of regimes or schools of art are emphasized. One section of the chapter reviews the literature on art and perception, suggesting that the 'art of seeing' is by no means an uncomplicated or socially unmarked practice but is instead strongly influenced by personal, collective, and class-based preferences and beliefs. In the latter half of the chapter, the use of art and images in organizations are discussed. In this section, there is a division between the use of art in organizations and organizations working with art. In the one case, art is serving a decorative or practical function; in the other case, art is what is developed, produced, distributed, and exhibited on professional day-to-day basis in organizations.

In Chapter 3, *Music: Auditory perception and organized sound*, the concept of music, a social and human resource embedded in the manipulation and organization of intangible but immediately perceivable sound waves, is examined. The body of literature commonly referred to as the 'new musicology' addressing music as a social category embedded in ideologies, material conditions, and social relations is given special attention. While much musicology of the *ancien regime* is positivist and among other things concerned with the identification of mathematical patterns in great composers' work, the new musicology literature renders music a human accomplishment open to interpretations and meaning. In the latter half of the chapter, the use of music in organizations is examined. Here, there is a decisive difference between, on the one hand, the use of music to influence organizational settings and milieus, and organizations and individuals working with music as a professional occupation on the other. In the first category, music is a tool in the hands of managers and other organization members, and in the category music is what is the common lowest denominator for a series of professionals and experts such as opera house directors, sound engineering technicians, and instrument builders.

In Chapter 4, *Media: The remediation of image and sound*, the concept of media is examined in some detail. While art and music are, notwithstanding the innate heterogeneity of these two concepts, operating on (in generic terms) images and sounds, media are assemblages of technology, inscription practices, and information resources capable of remediating – repackaging and render open to endless manipulation – images and sounds produced in artistic work. Media are therefore what in contemporary society but actually since the emergence of media strongly affect and shape perception in organizations. In this chapter, the media theory and media studies literature is reviewed addressing central terms such as hypertext, inscription, code, interface but also more speculative topics of discussion such as posthumanist theories and ideas. In the latter half of the chapter, the use of media in organizations is discussed.

In the final chapter, Chapter 5, *Perception and organizing: Beyond the text*, some concluding remarks on the relationship between perception and organizing are presented. The chapter provides a summary of the arguments of the previous chapters and contends that the intersection between perception and organizing is of great interest when understanding contemporary organizations. More and more organizations are relying on the use of means of control that mobilized images and sounds (e.g., in marketing and in the branding of the firm name) and media is increasingly influencing day-to-day work in organizations. Therefore, rather than conceiving of organizations as social units to be examined as integrated by texts and utterances, for instance written documents and shared storytelling reiterating ready-made plots and morals, perception and its reliance on the more epistemologically frail resources of images and sounds deserves its proper analysis.

1
The Concept of Perception

Introduction

The purpose of this book is to discuss the concept of perception as an organizational resource being mobilized in many organizational activities and processes. The concept of perception is undertheorized in organization theory and management studies for a number of reasons. In the recent research interests derived from the so-called linguistic turn in the social sciences, organizations and companies are essentially portrayed as products of the use of various forms of language in written and spoken form. Even though this stream of research – positioned into a number of theoretical frameworks such as discourse analysis, narrative studies, organizational storytelling and conversation analysis – has provided new and in many cases interesting views of organization, it envisages organization as a cognitively founded entity, derived from the use of linguistic and symbolic resources. Such a view to some extent downplays or even overlooks the material and embodied features of organization. The concept of perception is, similar to the use of language, a human faculty that is bordering between the self and the other, inner and outer, the body and the environment. Perception is embodied, yet it is grounded in cognition that in itself is socially embedded. Theorizing perception then does not imply a flight into the interiority of the body or a denial of the socially embedded constitution of organization but is instead an attempt at bridging ready-made binary terms such as self and other, mind and body, individual and society. Speaking in more practical and mundane terms, perception is a human faculty that is constantly used in day-to-day organizing; in meetings, in embodied performances, in leadership work, in internal and external communication and so forth, seeing, smelling, tasting, hearing and touching are

1

bound up with organizational endeavours. Therefore, organization and perception need to be properly theorized to fully make sense of a range of organizational processes and activities, many socially unmarked and therefore at times passing unnoticed.

In the following, the concept of perception will be theorized on the basis of a transdisciplinary corpus of texts. In this chapter, the concept of perception will be examined from historical, sociological and philosophical terms. In the three following chapters, the concepts of art, music and media, all inextricably entangled with the concept of perception, will be discussed and related to organizational practice. In the final chapter, the contributions from this analysis will be discussed. The intended outcome from this discussion is then not to formulate a theory about perception in organization but rather to show how the concept of perception has been used to constitute and influence a range of organizational activities.

The ocularcentrism thesis

A point of departure for this book is the assumption that perception plays a central role in the day-to-day management of organizations. Perception is here used to denote essentially the five senses but in practical terms, it is vision, hearing and tactile capacities that are examined. In order to underline the broader sense of the term, what has been called the 'ideology of ocularcentrism' is examined as what gives privilege to vision and denigrates other senses.

As Levin (1993) points out, already in the fragments of Heraclitus, vision is the privileged human faculty: 'The eyes are more exact witnesses than the ears,' Heraclitus says (fragment 101a, cited in Levin, 1993: 1). The ancients formulated theories of vision emphasizing sight as being a privileged connection between the human subject's perception and mind and the external world (Goldhill, 1996). Pliny (cited in Leppert, 1996: 6) argued that 'the mind is the real instrument of sight and observations, the eye acts as a sort of vessel receiving and transmitting the visible portions of the consciousness'. The entire history of Western thinking has emphasized vision and metaphors derived from vision. In Blumenberg's (1993) treatment of the history of philosophy, light is a predominant metaphor for truth. Moreover, a theorist like Martin Jay (1988; 1996; 2002) has carefully examined what he calls the *ocularcentrism* of the Western epistemology. Warneke (1993: 287) explicates the concept:

> By ocularcentrism, Jay means the epistemological privileging of vision that begins at least as early as Plato's notion that ethical universals must be accessible to the mind's eye and continues with

the Renaissance, the invention of printing, and the development of modern science.

Jay (1996) defends what he calls the 'pictorial turn' – and later, in Jay (2002), 'the visual turn' – in social theory and the humanities:

> The new fascination with modes of seeing and the enigmas of visual experience in a wide variety of fields may well betoken a paradigm shift in the cultural imaginary of our age. What has been called 'the pictorial turn' bids fair to succeed the earlier 'linguistic turn' so loudly trumpeted by twentieth-century philosophers. The model of 'reading texts', which served productively as the master metaphor for postobjectivist interpretations in many different phenomena, is now giving way to models of spectatorship and visuality, which refuse to be described in entirely linguistic terms. The figural is resisting subsumption under the rubric of discursivity; the image is demanding its own unique mode of analysis. (Jay, 1996: 1)

Jay (1996) argues that vision is culturally embedded and that various 'scoptic regimes' (to use the French film critic Christian Metz's term) are examined in scientific disciplines: 'Now attention has been paid to scientifically and technologically generated "techniques of observation", which are shown to be dependent on culturally inflected visual practices and able to turn to influence later on,' Jay (1996: 1) argues. 'We work under the epistemological regime of the eye,' Corbett (2003: 265) contends. Anthropological and historical studies suggest that the Western preference for vision, visuality, observation and inspection is a historically and culturally determined preference (Goody, 1997). For instance, in cultures influenced by the religious teachings of Islam, there is a negative attitude towards images and instead intricate and sophisticated patterns are used to decorate such things as carpets and buildings. The Western belief in perception and visuality is reaching its heights in technoscience, where the much-praised concept of objectivity serves as a form of 'vision without subject' – a de-contextualized and disembodied mode of vision that Daston (1999) calls 'aperspectival objectivity' (see also Porter, 1995). In many cases, such as in Jeremy Bentham's (1995) panopticon writings, brought into wider attention in the social sciences by Foucault (1977), vision is associated with power and the ability to control individuals. However, as Žižek (1995) persuasively suggests, vision can also be a source of helplessness and alienation, an idea illustrated by Žižek (1995) with reference to Alfred Hitchcock's *Rear Window*, where the observer, a disabled man (played by James Stewart) stuck in his wheelchair, witnesses a murder and has few opportunities to intervene in the act. Thus vision is always dual and comprises both power and its opposite, the sense of powerlessness.

In the following, a series of theories, models, technologies, artefacts and procedures for enabling, shaping and informing perception pertaining to the practice of organizing will be examined. In this endeavour, it must be kept in mind that perception does not solely denote the faculty of vision and visuality but the whole spectra of human perceptual capacities. This stands in contrast to the single-minded focus on the use of language, symbolism and narrative and discursive practices in organizing.

Organizing, language, text

In this section, the concept of perception will be positioned as diverging from the various frameworks of analysis derived from the so-called linguistic turn in the social sciences and organization theory and management studies more specifically. Before defending a perception-based view of organization – emphasizing that organizations are not only the sum of the use of language in written and verbal form but are actually affected by what is heard, seen and smelled – some of the predominant theoretical frameworks drawing on language will be reviewed.

The linguistic turn: organization as discourse and narrative

At the most generic level, the use of linguistic resources in organizations is referred to as 'talk' (Boden, 1994; Donnellon, 1996). Boden (1994) relies on Harold Garfinkel's ethnomethodology framework in her analysis of talk in an organization. In her view, organization members constitute the organizations as 'a real and practical place' through their timing, placing, pacing and patterning of 'verbal interaction' (p. 15). Contrary to more functionalist or rationalist views of organization, Boden emphasizes that the circulation of information and the joint constitution of knowledge rest not so much on 'hard facts' and unambiguous conditions, but such information is instead 'soft', incomplete, fuzzy and flexible (p. 152). Such 'weak signals' need to be amplified, classified, interpreted and enacted through talk among organization members. Seen in this view, the small talk and gossiping in corridors and cafeterias are by no means wasteful or without function but are instead what constitute the fabric of everyday life in organizations. Boden (1994) examines how individuals communicate in everyday situations and notices that even though verbal communication (talk) is never capable of being wholly conclusive and self-contained – talk always presupposes what Garfinkel calls the 'etcetera principle', that the listener is capable of 'filling in the blanks' in any message – organizations operate fairly effectively on basis of talk.

Another theoretical framework examining the use of verbal and written statements and utterances in organizations is discourse analysis and critical discourse analysis (for an overview, see Keenoy, Oswick and Grant, 1997; Oswick, Keenoy and Grant, 2000; Hardy, 2001). The etymology of discourse derives from the Latin, *discurrere*, suggesting 'a movement "back and forth", or a "running to and fro" ' (White, 1978: 3). In French, the concept has connotations similar to that of 'thesis' or 'treatise', that is, a scholarly work presenting a series of interconnected statements. Discourse analysis was popularized in organization theory by the writings of Michel Foucault (1972), speaking of discourses as a texture of statements and claims on a particular subject, capable of producing non-discursive, material effects. In organization theory, there is a range of definitions of the term. For instance, Hassard and Parker define discourse thus:

> Discourses emerge as regulated systems of statement ... which have both ideational content and implications for social practice, and cannot be reduced to either. Discourse produces 'rules' which systematically 'delimits' what can be said, whilst providing the spaces – the concepts, metaphors, models, analogies – for making new statements within any specific discourses' and for articulating with other discourses. (Hassard and Parker, 1993: 63)

For Du Gay (2000: 67), a discourse is a 'group of statements that provide a way of talking about and acting upon a particular object'. Such statements also make it 'possible to construct that object in a particular way'. Hardy and Philips (1999: 2) define discourse as a 'system of texts that brings an object into being'. Discourses are thus a delimited domain wherein statements can be articulated. Such statements are legitimate on the basis of the spokesman's institutional affiliation, individual biographies and former discursive activities. Once a discursive formation has been established, it may produce material effects. For instance, the discourse on mental illness in the nineteenth century produced a narrower domain of expertise referred to as psychoanalysis, fundamentally dependent on the work of Sigmund Freud. Psychoanalysis theory then enacted a set of material and procedural practices used in psychoanalytic work. Psychoanalysis also produced broader institutional changes such as new health care procedures to treat mental disorders and the development of psychopharmacological drugs. The discourse on mental illness and the discourse on psychoanalysis are then serving to make certain social practices legitimate.

Some contributors also prefer to speak of *critical discourse analysis* (CDA) as a means for, in Treleaven's (2004: 159) account, 'foregrounding for examination of the taken-for-granted factors (historical, social, cultural, educational and political) that shape the language people use'. While discourse analysis is by no means uncritical of the objects of study, critical discourse analysis makes the notion of power a central object of enquiry. For instance, Wodak (1997: 7) declares that 'critical discourse analysis in my view, is an instrument whose purpose is precisely to expose power structures and "disorders of discourse"'. Elsewhere, Weiss and Wodak (2003) further develop this position:

> [C]DA might be defined as fundamentally interested in analyzing opaque as well as transparent structural relationships of dominance, discrimination, power and control as manifested in language. In other words, CDA aims to investigate critically social inequality as it is expressed, constituted, legitimized, and so on, by language use (or in discourse). (Weiss and Wodak, 2003: 15)

Although the discourse analysis perspective bridges the domain of linguistic production (i.e. the totality of written and verbal statement, formal documents, images and illustrations), and the domains of institutions and practices, the social world wherein discursive ideas are manifested in actual activities, it is not very explicitly addressed how perception plays a role in the social fabric. Even though Foucault, one of the principal references for discourse analysis, says a great deal about perception, vision and inspection – most notably in his panopticon writings – the human faculties of perception are rendered rather marginal in the discourse and critical discourse analysis perspective.

A third perspective advocating the verbal and written interaction of individuals inside and outside of organizations is narrative studies (Boje, 1991; Czarniawska, 1997; Gabriel, 2000). The concept of narrative was first developed in literature theory and was first brought into the social sciences through the domain of cognitive psychology as a conceptdenoting how human cognition structures social and psychic reality into series of events (Bruner, 1986). Polkinghorne (1988: 13) represents this school and defines narrative accordingly:

> 'Narrative' can refer to the process of making a story, to the cognitive scheme of the story, or to the result of the process – also called 'stories', 'tales', or 'histories'. I will be using 'narratives' and its cognates to refer to both the process and the results; the context should clarify which meaning is intended.

Bruner (1990), another psychologist representing the cognitive orientation in the field, speaks of narrative in similar terms but emphasizes in particular the *plot* of the narrative:

> [A] narrative is composed of a unique sequence of events, mental states, happenings involving human beings as characters or actors. These are its constituents. But these constituents do not, as it were, have a life or meaning of their own. Their meaning is given by their place in the overall configuration of the sequence as a whole – its plot or *fabula*. The act of grasping a narrative, then, is a dual one: the interpreter has to grasp the narrative's configuring plot in order to make sense of its constituents, which he must relate to that plot. But the plot configuration must itself be extracted from the succession of events. (Bruner, 1990: 43–4)

In organization theory, a discipline derived from the zones inbetween disciplines such as sociology, political science and economics, traditionally laden with the burden to qualify as a quantitative science capable of presenting numerical facts on how to manage and lead organizations and firms, the concept of narrative has often been dismissed or tarnished as 'mere hearsay, opinion, or invention' (Gabriel, 2004: 2). Narratives have then been regarded as suffering from inaccuracy, exaggeration, omission and other liberties of the *fabula* and – to use a concept from Russian formalists in literature theory – the *sjuzet*, the very telling of the story. However, the value of a narrative lies not in its ability to truthfully capture existing conditions but in its ability to constitute meaning in social communities: 'the truth of the story lies not in its accurate depiction of facts but in its meaning' (Gabriel, 2004: 20). Boje (2001) even claims that the very value of storytelling is its incompleteness and its transient status as what is open towards the future. Boje (2001) speaks of 'antenarratives', describing what can be reiterated over and over, thus reproducing certain values, norms, ideologies, or myths: 'Antenarrative is never final; it is improper,' Boje contends (2001: 2).

However, the ability to make sense and produce meaning is central to narratives and storytelling. Cunliffe, Luhman and Boje (2004: 276) emphasize the meaning-making function of narratives and storytelling: 'Meaning unfolds in narrative performance, in time and context, as storytellers and listeners discuss their experiences, interweave their own narratives: a polyphony of competing narrative voices and stories told by many voices within different historical, cultural, and relational contexts.' Since narratives are meaningful, they have a 'mnemonic value' (Tsoukas, 2005: 84) because they are capable of bringing together and ordering sets of prepositional statements. Tsoukas (2005) explicates his position:

> Narratives are indeed an important category of organizational knowledge and discourse, and are constructed around memorable episodes derived from participating in practice. Unlike prepositional statements, narratives are contingently linked to individual action, thus facilitating individual adaptation to a large number of unforeseeable circumstances. Furthermore, narration facilitates social interaction, preserves a community's collective memory, enhances a group's sense of shared identity as participants in a practice, and serves as a repository of tacit organizational knowledge. (Tsoukas, 2005: 87)

Much of the mnemonic value derives from what Hayden White (1987) calls 'emplotment', the constructing of a credible and intelligible storyline wherein events unfold in a meaningful manner. The concept of emplotment has been used in organization theory by Patriotta (2003), for instance, in his study of factory work at a Fiat plant in southern Italy. Patriotta (2003: 353) writes: 'Emplotment is the process whereby actors impose a logical structure (a beginning, a middle and an end) upon a flow of equivocal happenings through processes of ordering and sequencing'. He continues:

> [N]arratives show how knowledge in organizations is mobilized through discourse, and therefore highlight a distinctive mode of knowing related to the everyday coping with the world. Because of their connection to experience, narratives display common-sense wisdom – in the form of anecdotes, jokes, and war stories – in

organizational discourse. Common sense is based on unspoken premises and therefore underscores the tacit aspects of knowledge in organizations. Narratives, articulated in plots, are the carriers of such deep-seated, sticky, common sensical stock of knowledge. (Patriotta, 2003: 353–4)

The narrative is thus, similar to what Boden (1994) refers to as 'talk', capable of making sense out of what is in essence ambiguous, fluid and poorly integrated and operates through the mechanism of emplotment, wherein events are ordered into a meaningful whole that individuals can easily grasp and understand. In addition, certain narratives can be reiterated and told over and over to reproduce social norms and values in a community or to draw a line of demarcation between competing communities. Similar to discourse analysis, theories of narrative point at the social production of meaning inherent in the continuous declarations, statements and utterances in organizations. Organizations are here constituted by jointly produced systems of meaning derived from such strategic and active use of oral and written communication. In addition to ethnomethodological studies of talk, discourse analyses of organizations and narrative and storytelling perspectives, some researchers have emphasized the use of scripts and written documents as being of central importance in the functioning of organizations. Cooren (2004) speaks of *textual agency* in organization when signs, memos, contracts, written instructions, power point presentations and so forth influence everyday undertakings. Textual agency, especially in its written form, Cooren (2004: 388) argues, 'enables delegation through *tele-action* and *tele-communication*'. He continues: 'By remaining, these textual agents fabricate relatively fixed spaces and times; they define objectives; they forbid specific behaviors; and they invite or enforce humans to follow specific organizational pathways'. Written documents are then not innocent or detached from everyday practice but are in fact capable of orchestrating rather complex interactions on everyday basis, in many cases over great distances, for example, when the head office submits new declarations on how to proceed in the regional offices or subsidiaries. Similarly, Callon (2002) has examined *scripts* as being the tools for collecting, constructing, processing and calculating information. Without such tools, '[a]gents would be unable to plan, decide or control. In short, organized action would be impossible' (Callon, 2002: 191). Scripts are what Cooren (2004) calls *textual agents*, written documents capable of making 'systems of action' manageable and controllable without reducing practice to a mere recipe but allowing for individual performances.

Scripts thus draw on Garfinkel's (1967) 'etcetera clause', stating that no written document can provide all information or instructions needed for a thoughtful performance of a task, but that there are always some activities that the agent is expected to figure out on his or her own. Cooren (2004) and Callon's (2002) contributions to organization theory underline the importance of written documents, while the other perspectives are more concerned with verbal interaction. They do still share the strong belief in language and regimes of representation and inscription as the single most powerful socal practice in the everyday work of organizations.

Organizing and the organization of perception

Contrary to the linguistic or symbolic view of organization, emphasizing verbal and written communication as the principal constitutive process of organizing, a perception-based view of organization underlines that organizational realities are not only verbalized or inscribed but are also what are constituted on the level of vision and other forms of perception prior to the use of language (Kavanaugh, 2004). Edenius and Yakhlef (2007), examining organization learning in open office spaces, advocate a perception-based view of organization:

> Most previous research assumes that spatial orderings of things and people are merely part of the background that does not intervene in the learning process. Rather, the concern has been with the relation between learning and processes of interacting, working together, sharing tools, story-telling and narrating ... This relationship is framed in ideological terms, overlooking the centrality of the (prediscursive) visual, perceptual, bodily incorporations, and how discursive and cognitive practices are contingent upon incorporating practices. (Edenius and Yakhlef, 2007: 207)

In addition, Belova (2006: 94) says that while it is hard to deny that organizations are sites of olfactory (Fitzgerald and Ellen, 1999), tactile, kinaesthetic (Prentice, 2005) and auditory (Porcello, 2004) experiences, 'organizational artefacts' have a 'stong appeal' to the visual senses. Documents, uniforms, interiors, architecture are some examples where organizational visuality is manifested. In addition, outside of the organization, the visual remains the principal way to communicate with the broader public, for instance through logos, TV advertisements, visual displays, billboards and glossy brochures communicating values and aesthetics that are subscribed to. There is a great number of examples and illustrations of these tendencies, brought together under the banner 'the visual turn' noted by Jay (1988; 1996; 2002). Alan Bryman (2004) examines what he calls the 'Disneyization of society' leading to new forms of spectacles, performative labour and new modes of consumption. Similarly, Ritzer (1998; 2005) debates what he calls the 'McDonaldization of society', the increased reliance on services and the standardization of both services and products. Wolf (1999) is, contrary to Bryman (2004) and Ritzer (1998; 2005), enthusiastic over the emerging 'entertainment economy', which is characterized by the implosion of shopping, entertainment and leisure time and the emergence of new events, services and spectacle. McNair (2002) explores what he calls the growth of 'striptease culture', a social ideology raising the tolerance for sexuality and nudity in the public sphere and where what McNair calls the 'pornosphere', the totality of images, representations and texts of nude bodies and sexual acts, colonialize (in Habermas's [1987] sense of the term) the everyday life world. Nixon (2005) examines what he calls advertisement culture in the metropolitan London area; individuals working in advertisement agencies and public relations bureaus to produce images and campaigns promoting certain goods and services. Guillén (1997) argues that the entire system of managerial thought that is referred to as Taylorism is representative of a broader social ideology brought about by modernity. In Guillén's view, politics, managerial practices and aesthetics are modalities of the same underlying social beliefs. Taylorism is then not solely a set of principles for managerial practice but also engenders specific forms of visuality, manifested in, for instance, architecture and design. Julier (2000) examines the increased interest in design and its political and managerial use as a means for shaping and structuring social life. Chung *et al.* (2001) offer an extensive and richly illustrated overview of recent tendencies in the design and architecture of spaces dedicated to shopping and entertainment. Theoretically, a variety of authors draw on what Guy Debord (1977) and the situationists called the *la societé du spectacle*, and Baudrillard's (1998) concept of the *consumer society*, heavily indebted to Debord's seminal analysis. In addition, Mikhail Bakhtin's (1968) concept of the carnival (Lock, 2003) has been drawn on to capture the intensification of perception in contemporary society. Boje (2001) speaks, for example, of 'carnivalesque resistance' in organizations, and Rhodes (2001) identifies similar tendencies in popular culture, and more specifically in the American cartoon *The Simpsons*.

In addition to the broader changes in how perception is influencing social and organizational life, on the more practical level, research shows that communication is strongly influenced by visuality and perception; bodily gestures, movements, facial expressions and other embodied and visual practices strongly affect communication in organizations. In 1967, Mehrabian studied non-verbal communication and found that '[n]on-verbal channels such as facial expressions, body movements, and voice tone contributed 93 per cent of the "attitudinal" message of the receiver' (Graham, Unruh and Jennings, 1990: 46).

To draw a broad line of demarcation for the sake of simplicity, one may separate the literature into *seeing and perceiving in organizations* and *being seen and perceived*. The former literature focuses on the organizational subject's ability to make use of perceptual skills and capacities in day-to-day work. The literature on being seen and perceived includes a range of studies emphasizing the embodied, visual and symbolic practices, procedures, rituals, rites and ceremonies in organizations.

The first group of literature includes a great range of studies. Cuff (1991) shows that architectural work is based on the ability to conceive of the connections between the demands and expectations of a number of diverging interests. Architectural work is embedded in visuality and the ability to give shape to buildings that operate in the intersection between social, technical, aesthetic and political interests (see also Pinnington and Morris, 2002). Fine's (1996) study of restaurant chefs in the St Paul-Minneapolis area, Minnesota, USA, emphasizes the chefs' use of a range of perceptual skills including taste, vision, smell, but also touch when cooking. Foucault (1973) shows that medical practice as diagnosing and prescription of treatment derives from the ability to undertake visual inspections and to draw on a variety of documented symptoms. Martin (2005) similarly emphasizes the need for skilful inspection on the part of medical doctors in the investigation of rape crimes. Moreover, the entire discipline of accounting and auditing is based on metaphors and models of vision expressed in terms of inspection, review, auditing, counting and calculation (McGivern and Ferlie, 2007; Moore *et al.*, 2006; Pentland, 2000; Hopper and Macintosh, 1998; Porter, 1995; Power, 2004, 1994). In the predominant accounting culture, accountants are capable of detecting deviances from plan through their training and expertise in decoding facts and figures provided by the various accounting procedures. Accounting is a specific form of what Goodwin (1994) calls 'professional vision'. Professional vision is for Goodwin a vision that is trained and embedded in professional expertise and authority. In practical terms, it is based on a series of operations that Goodwin (1994: 606) refers to as (1) coding, (2) highlighting and (3) producing and articulating material representations. This process enables certain ways of seeing: 'Central to the social and cognitive organization of a profession is its ability to shape events in the domain of scrutiny into the phenomenal objects around which the discourse of the profession is organized,' Goodwin (1994: 626) suggests. Examining the Rodney King trial, a much-debated case where the violation and abuse of an Afro-American motorist by four Los Angeles Police Department officers was video-recorded by a witness, an event that triggered substantial unrest in the Los Angeles metropolitan area in 1994, reveals an example of how professional vision is mobilized. For the defence, various professional experts testified in favour of the police officers' behaviour, denying they were using excessive violence. However, the asymmetry of interpretative authority between professional experts and victims and is complicated to handle:

> Insofar as the perceptual structures that organize interpretation of the tape are lodged within the profession and not an isolated individual, there is a tremendous asymmetry about who can speak as an expert about the event on the tape and thus structure interpretation of it ... While administrating a beating like this is recognized within the courtroom as part of the work of the police profession, no equivalent social group exists for the suspect. Victims do not constitute a profession. Thus no expert witnesses are available to interpret these events and animate the images on the tape from King's perspective, In the second trial, King was called a witness, but he could not testify about whether the police officers beating him were using unreasonable force since he lacked 'expertise on the constitution or the use of force'. (Goodwin, 1994: 625)

This asymmetry is an example of what Lyotard (1988) calls *a differend*, a dispute that cannot be properly resolved by using the means at hand; professional expertise is capable of undermining the actual experience of the victim, and since there is no community of victims serving as professional experts capable of testifying in favour of specific cases, there are no adequate strategies available on part of the victim. The defence of the four police officers effectively exploits this differend, thereby making the victim the aggressor and portraying the abuse of King as being more or less justified given the specific conditions.

Another form of professional vision is the use of visual representations in architect work (Whyte *et al.*, 2007; Ewenstein and Whyte, 2007a).

The visual representations serve a series of functions in the work: they can communicate meaning symbolically; they serve as boundary-objects for a number of stakeholders such as designers, architects, clients and end-users; they help stabilize the use of both individual and collective knowledge in the community of architects; they are a means of power when negotiating alternative decisions (Ewenstein and Whyte, 2007a: 82). In addition, the production, use and dissemination of visual representations are central processes in the architect's professional identity. Following Nicolini (2007: 578), visual representations or 'visual artefacts' are meaningful only when located in complex and 'messy' everyday practice: 'Visual artefacts emerge and express their performative power only when they are used within a specific activity and in conjunction with other elements.' As a consequence, much of the expertise and experience involved in the process, Nicolini suggests:

> In order to function ... visual artefacts require a certain amount of work that often remains hidden, what could be called the 'non-visual work' necessary for making visual artefacts work. Put differently, while it is undeniable that a picture is often worth 'a thousand words', it is also true that pictures and words work together according to a subtle and often unnoticed division of labour. (2007: 578)

The use of visual representations in architectural work is therefore a special practice that needs to be carefully examined and whose elements are strongly interrelated and mutually supportive.

Scientific work in laboratories and in fieldwork is another specific form of social practice heavily dependent on perception and 'professional vision'. Historical studies (e.g. Shapin, 1994) show that the emphasis on empirical experiments and systematic observations is a scientific ideal that emerged in the seventeenth century and was very much in conflict with scholastic medieval thinking wherein deductive reasoning, based on few canonical works, was regarded as the only legitimate source of scientific knowledge (Eisenstein, 1983; Alexander, 2002. See Chapter 4 for a more detailed discussion). The development of modern science rested on sense-perception and the use of experiments: 'Central to the development of this experimental philosophy were debates about the limits of knowledge, and the validity of sense experience or perception. Francis Bacon argued in *Novum organum* (1620) that nature should be interpreted through the senses, aided by experiments 'fit and apposite', Hackman (1989: 35) writes. Today, modern technoscience is inextricably entangled with a substantial body of what Gaston Bachelard called *phenomenotech-niques*, machines for observing phenomena (see e.g. Traweek [1988], on the work of particle physicians, and Pasveer [2006], on the use of X-ray in medicine). Recent studies of scientific practice have emphasized the reliance on mathematical representations (e.g. Lynch, 1988) or gendered (Jordanova, 1989) or cultural assumptions (Haraway, 1989) inherent to the scientific gaze. Scientific work is, similar to accounting, based on the idea of inspection and observation, the ability to 'see' events and entities (in many cases mediated by various technologies), what may be called *epistemic things* (Rheinberger, 1997) in scientific practice. For instance, Nightingale (1998) argues that skilled medicinal chemists, experienced from working in new drug development, develop what Nightingale calls 'chemical intuition', the ability to identify promising molecules:

> The medicinal chemist uses this built up knowledge to select molecules that are potentially similar to the desired molecule. This sense of similarity is termed 'chemical intuition' and is a form of tacit knowledge that allows some medicinal chemists to recognize potential drug-like molecules for testing. While the novice might see a simple molecule, a medicinal chemist with years of experience and built up tacit 'chemical intuition' can recognize the same molecule as more or less drug-less, and therefore as a more or less likely candidate for testing. Just as the electronic engineer can see components 'as' things, the tacit knowledge allows the medicinal chemist to relate to function. (Nightingale, 1998: 704)

For the medicinal chemist, visuality is a central component of the scientific work. In addition to vision, Mody (2005) emphasizes auditory abilities when using advanced technoscientific equipment in laboratory work in the material sciences: '[s]ound is an integral (if often overlooked) ingredient in tacit knowledge. Surface scientists carefully manage auditory (as well as visual and haptic) cues to liberate different kinds of information from the experiments', he suggests (p. 177). Mody exemplifies:

> Many instruments in surface science and materials science have parts and mechanisms that make specific sounds – the whirr of micrograph plates being moved inside a TEM [Transmission Electron Microscope], the chuk-chuk of a probe being lowered on an atomic force microscope (AFM), the spring and click of a coil being shoved into place on a microscope. (Mody, 2005: 186)

A long series of professions and trades are dependent on the ability to use the human senses; the five senses are mobilized on an everyday basis. However, such skills and capacities are in most cases intimately entangled with the use of language. For instance, a food-taster in, say, a coffee-roasting laboratory must be able to account for his or her verdict of the tasted specimen and individual tasters must be calibrated against some standard to safeguard a procedure that provides the best possible results. Here perception and taste and cognition and language form a seamless web enabling the identification of a satisfying blend of various tastes in the coffee. A great many professionals and working individuals are thus dependent on their perceptual skills and their ability to express their impressions.

In addition, organizations are also dependent on their ability to structure and orchestrate impressions in their everyday functioning.* All organizations have their own idiosyncratic ceremonies, rituals and events wherein organizational objectives, values, norms, or cultures are reproduced or manifested for individuals inside as well as outside of the organization (Meyer and Rowan, 1992). Such events and procedures are based on perception in the second sense of the term, that is, in terms of *being seen*. Michael Rosen (1985; 2000) has reported two excellent studies of how semi-formal rituals in organizations (a Christmas party and an annual business breakfast meeting) serve to legitimize the instituted social order. Rosen also shows that it is most complicated to break through the chimera of camaraderie and sense of shared objectives and

---

* It is here useful to distinguish between actual perception (i.e. perception through the senses) and the concept of perception as a general category denoting the beliefs and assumptions regarding a matter. For instance, Elsbach (2006) advocates what she calls *organizational perception management*; various procedures and practices designed to '[i]nfluence audience perception of the organization as an entity or a whole' (Elsbach, 2006: 12). Such procedures and practices include a concern for organizational *images*, *reputation* and *identities* and aim at increasing the legitimacy and trustworthiness of the organization. In Elsbach's account, *organizational perception management* serves as a supplement to business ethics; while business ethics addresses how decision-making and organizational practices can be embedded in ethical consideration, organizational perception management appears to be primarily engaging in the shaping and influencing of how various stakeholders and the broader community is perceiving the organization, notwithstanding its ethical standing. What Elsbach (2006) calls *organizational perception management* is thus in the first place the strategic shaping of the public image of the organization. However, the following perception is invoked to denote actual sense-impression and not a general worldview or set of enacted assumptions.

goals produced at such ceremonies because they are carefully designed to make the participants feel they belong to a privileged group and that they are deemed trustworthy in the eyes of top management. In general, the entire domain of dramaturgical sociology, first formulated by Erwin Goffman (1959), emphasizes the mechanisms identified and laid bare by Rosen (1985; 2000), that is, the strong emphasis on formal symbols and carefully rehearsed performances as what holds the social fabric together. Rituals and ceremonies are events wherein the totality – or at least a substantial part – of the organization becomes visible for the individual member. Another body of literature examines the embodied performance of individual organization members at work. Tyler and Abbott (1998) report from their study of flight attendants that female air stewardesses were expected to carefully monitor their bodies and guard against putting on weight or in any other way failing to present a neat and tidy bodily appearance. Tyler and Taylor (1998) here speak of the role of female co-workers in certain organizations as serving a 'decorative' and 'aesthetic' function, underlining the values and norms of the employing organization. Seen in this view, the primary role of air stewardesses is to become visible *qua* a symbol of organizational excellence; their role is to be decorative. Similarly, Rafaeli *et al.* (1997) examine how the use of business attire is becoming a central concern for the female administrative personnel in an organization. Female employees have to be able to navigate in a domain wherein the wrong choice of dress may lead to undesirable consequences, for example, either being regarded as 'unfeminine' or being accused of exploiting their sexuality. In general, feminist organization theory has contributed substantially to the embodied view of organization, not only emphasizing the choice of dress but also making the entire bodily performance a source of concern and controversy (Trethewey, 1999). Entwhistle and Racamora (2006) studied a major event in the British fashion industry, London Fashion Week, and identified carefully monitored and controlled embodied performances of participants as a major mechanism for reproducing the social hierarchy of the fashion industry. '[I]n the field of fashion, it is critical that one's body articulates fashion capital, position and status in the field,' Entwhistle and Racamora (2006: 748) suggest. In order to accomplish or maintain a certain position in the industry, that is, to accumulate or defend one's 'fashion capital', 'being seen' at the right events is imperative:

> To be spotted by buyers and journalists outside a show waiting to go in – holding the precious ticket prominently – or seated in the catwalk theatre itself undoubtedly signalled our social and symbolic capitals

and thereby helped lend some weight to our research and our position in the field. (Entwhistle and Racamora, 2006: 740–1)

Since status, reputation and recognition are central to the fashion capital, in turn generating economic capital, the field of fashion is saturated with symbolism and procedures that are complicated to decode for the neophyte or outsider. For instance, Entwhistle and Racamora (2006: 74) dedicate some space to examine the significance of the 'air kiss' (that is when two individuals, female or male, touching one another's cheek and 'kissing into the air'), how it is performed and what role it plays in forging associations and alliances. During central and semi-public events such as London Fashion Week, perception and visuality are central organizational categories determining social positions and relations between individuals or groups. For instance, the very presence of some authority (e.g. the editor of *Vogue* magazine or some widely recognized designer) automatically generates a 'buzz' around a certain fashion house or brand.

In leadership studies, Ropo and Parviainen (2001) have advocated an embodied view of how leaders perform their role in formal meetings and in everyday work. In this view, leadership skills are not an innate quality but what is actively entrenched through training and thoughtful performances. Leaders are therefore informed that they need to be concerned about their dress, their bodily posture and other embodied features that may affect their performance. Similarly, Leidner (1993), studying fast-food restaurant work and sales work, reports that in both occupations, the ability to orchestrate a performance that complied with the customer's expectation enhanced the interaction. Both restaurant clerks and salesmen were expected to act with confidence and to be able to take a professional and friendly attitude towards the clients, no matter how they were treated by the clients. Needless to say, such an attitude does not come for free, but demands significant emotional labour on part of the worker. Hochschild's (1983) classic study of air stewardesses accounts faithfully for the human and emotional costs of repressing natural responses and for performing what Hochschild calls *surface acting*. Another domain wherein vision, inspection and bodily performance are central is the sex trade, examined by Brewis and Linstead (2000) and Sanders (2004). Sex workers exploit the faculty of vision in their services (for example, in so-called peepshows, where women expose themselves for customers) but need to draw a clear line of demarcation between vision and 'non-vision' (e.g. touching) so that they do not end up in difficult situations. Yet another example of how organizations make use of vision is the work of museums, wherein objects are not merely on display but are brought into broader discursive formations and are located in specific positions where they can, perhaps, attain a new meaning. Harrison's (1997) study of an exhibition in a Canadian museum shows that although the intentions to provide a new form of experience for the visitors were justified, the final exhibition was fundamentally shaped by what Harrison (1997) calls neocolonialist thinking. In Harrison's account, museums are not value-neutral media for the dissemination of exhibitions but are instead anchored in predominant beliefs and assumptions. Another domain wherein instituted beliefs and assumptions are reproduced is the internet where, for instance, gendered images of society reappear in new shapes. Gustavsson and Czarniawska (2004) demonstrate that avatars on internet homepages, aimed at helping newcomers to the site or individuals unfamiliar with internet services, tend to take on a female persona. The image of femininity as what is servile, helpful and representing the unrestrained patience to be able to listen to any enquiry, no matter how trivial or stupid, is thereby projected onto the computer homepage interface. Again, visuality and perception is a constituent component of organization.

One domain of research that bridges the perception of seeing and being seen is the literature on surveillance in organizations (examined in greater detail in Chapter 4). Writers like Lyon (1994), Bogard (1996) and Davis (1990) suggest that we are living in an emerging surveillance society wherein individuals' lives become increasingly monitored and controlled by authorities. In organizations, several contributors (e.g. Sewell and Barker, 2006; Ball, 2005; Mason *et al.*, 2002; McGail, 2002) point at the new emphasis on scrutinizing employees' behaviours, both at work and outside of it (for example, in the case of drug testing, Cavanaugh and Prasad, 1994). In this literature, the individual is subject to monitoring but it is also the role of certain members of the organization to serve as inspectors watching the employees. Such a role is, the literature suggests, riddled by juridical, ethical and economical concerns that are not yet resolved.

Taken together, there are a substantial number of theoretical perspectives, studies and concepts advocated and put forth underlining the perceptual aspects of organizations. Organizations employ individuals making use of their perceptual skills as an integral part of their day-to-day work; organizations structure and shape perception for both customers and clients but also for the general public; organizations are mobilizing practices and technologies for perception in their daily functioning (e.g. accounting procedures and surveillance technology). In brief, organizations are domains wherein perception plays a central and decisive role.

The modern concept of perception

New theories of perception

The first management books and the first more systematic reflections on management derive from the first half of the nineteenth century. Writers like Andrew Ure (1835) and Charles Babbage (1833) formulated the first modern accounts of how corporations and enterprises are to be managed. Speaking from an historical perspective, it is interesting to notice that the modern conceptualization of organization and what may be regarded as the modern view of perception emerges at the same moment in history, during the first half of the nineteenth century. Prior to any more detailed engagement with the concepts of perception and sense-perception, the modern view of perception will be examined in greater detail.

Among the great social changes brought by the industrial revolution, first noticeable in the UK and in Flanders, urbanization was significant. Gay (1984: 49–50) points at the remarkable growth of several European cities: by 1800, 21 per cent of the population in England and Wales lived in towns of 10,000 or more inhabitants; by 1850 40 per cent; and in 1890 the figure had risen to 61 per cent. In 1800, Paris had 600,000 inhabitants; in 1900, 2.5 million people lived in the French capital; Berlin had 420,000 inhabitants in 1850 and 2 million in 1900. A comparatively small town such as Middlesbrough in the UK had 581 inhabitants in 1801; in 1891, 76,135. In the USA, urban population quadrupled between 1870 and 1910 (Singer, 1995: 73). London had seven times as many inhabitants in 1910 as in 1800 (Davis, 2006). Such a significant movement of people and steady growth of European and American cities opened up new ways of living and provided new opportunities but also brought a variety of social problems. It also provided new grist to the mill for social commentators and thinkers. By the middle of the first half of the twentieth century, a number of theorists such as George Simmel, Siegfried Kracauer and Walter Benjamin had formulated a range of perspectives on how the modern, urbanized human being perceived his or her life world. They were, to use Singer's (1995) phrase, formulating a 'neurological conception of modernity':

> These theorists focused on what might be called a *neurological* conception of modernity. They insisted that modernity must also be understood in terms of a fundamentally different register of subjective experience, characterized by the physical and perceptual shocks of the modern urban environment . . . Modernity implied a phenomenal world – specifically an urban one – that was markedly quicker,

more chaotic, fragmented and disorienting than in previous phases of human culture. (Singer, 1995: 72–3)

Even though the Weimar republic produced eminent theorists of the urban modern experience, the interest for perception *qua* modern phenomena started much earlier. Leppert (1996: 103) suggests that in the early seventeenth century, there developed an:

> intense humanistic and scientific interest in the human senses (sight, hearing, smell, touch, taste). The visual arts, literature, and philosophy, as well as the new sciences of anatomy, biology, and medicine delved into the subject. In humanistic and philosophical inquiry, the senses were studied as keys to human identity, principally as vehicles of our embodied 'apparatus' of knowing.

Crary (1990), on the other hand, locates this increased interest to the period from the 1810s to the 1840s. For instance, in his path-breaking and massive three-volume work *Treatise on Physiological Optics* (first published in 1859–66), Hermann von Helmholtz defined his scientific pursuit thus:

> *Physiological Optics* is the science of the visual perception by the sense of sight. The objects around us are made visible through the agency of light proceeding thence and falling on our eyes. The light, reaching the retina, which is a sensitive portion of the nervous system, stimulates certain sensation therein. These are conveyed to the brain by the optic nerve, the result being that the mind becomes conscious of the perception of certain objects disposed in space. (2004: 42)

Helmholtz (2004: 43) is generally credited with rendering perception a cognitive phenomenon and he explicitly states that '[t]he theory of perception belongs properly to the domain of psychology'. For Helmholtz, there is no 'direct perception'; instead, all perception (*Anschauungen*) is embedded in 'experience and training' (Helmholtz, 1968: 179). Helmholtz emphasizes that the ability to control one's perception is an effect of long practice:

> Steady fixation of a point for a long time while observations are being made in indirect vision; controlling the attention; taking the mind away from sense-impression; estimation of difference of colour and

of difference of space in the visual field – all those things take much practice. (1968: 185)

Helmholtz's foundational and empiricist work turned perception from what was essentially an unproblematic act of observing the world to a complex psychological process based on the dynamic exhange between memory and the human eye; for Helmholtz, cognition and perception are, rather than being detached or isolated, mutually constitutive.

Perception and modernity

Recognizing the historical significance of scientific work in the domain of perception during the mid-nineteenth century, Crary (1990: 3–4) is critical of the idea that it was in fact the French Impressionists (e.g. Edouard Manet) that single-handedly instituted a 'new model of visual representation'. Rather than being the source of such new ideas, the Impressionists were a product of a new dominant theory of vision jointly produced by a number of interrelated scientific, technological and artistic innovations and experiments in the first half of the century. Crary writes: 'What begins in the 1820s and the 1830s is a repositioning of the observer, outside of the fixed relations of interior/exterior presupposed by the camera obscura and into an undemarcated terrain on which the distinction between internal sensation and external signs is irrevocably blurred' (Crary, 1990: 24). The technological device of the camera obscura that enabled moving visual images and whose elementary function had been known for centuries, ceased to serve as a general model for vision in the nineteenth century; during the seventeenth and eighteenth centuries, the camera obscura 'was without question the most widely used model for explaining human vision, and for representing the relation of a perceiver and the position of a knowing subject to an external world' (Crary, 1990: 27). For Crary, Arthur Schopenhauer was among the first to conceive of perception not as a 'transcendental form of knowledge' but as a 'biological capacity' that is not uniform in all men and women but highly contingent and personal. In *The World as Will and Idea*, Schopenhauer (1995) rejects the idea of 'pure perception':

> What the eye, the ear, or the hands feel, is not perception; it is merely data. Only when understanding passes from the effects to the cause does the world lie before us as perception extends in space, varying in respect of form, persistent through all time in respect of matter . . .

perception is not merely of the senses, but is intellectual: that is, *pure knowledge through the understanding of the cause from the effect.* (Schopenhauer, 1995: 9, emphasis in the original)

Eleswhere, he continues:

The sight of beautiful objects, a beautiful view for example, is also a phenomenon of the brain. Its purity and perfection depends not merely on the object, but also on the quality and constitution of the brain, that is on its form and size, the fineness of texture, and the stimulation of its activity through the energy of the pulse of its brain arteries. (Schopenhauer, *The World as Will and Representation*, Vol. 2: 24, cited in Crary, 1990: 84)

Crary (1995: 46) argues that one of the 'most important developments' in the history of visuality was the emergence of 'models of subjective vision' in a range of disciplines. The dominant discourses and practices of vision were abandoned and new ideas were established within a few decades. The idea of 'subjective vision' – 'the notion that the quality of our sensations depends less on the nature of the stimulus and more on the makeup and functioning of our sensory apparatus' (Crary, 1995: 46) – produced a number of new research programmes but also gave rise to a number of procedures of normalization, of quantification, of discipline. As soon as vision was, as Crary (1995) says, 'determined to lie in the body', it also became subject to external techniques of manipulation and stimulation. The second half of the nineteenth century was also a historical threshold where the qualitative difference between the *biosphere* and the *mechanosphere* began to evaporate. As Leo Marx (1964) notices, in the nineteenth century, advances in the natural and engineering sciences brought new technological artefacts such as the train and the railway, thus gradually establishing what Marx calls 'the rhetoric of the technological sublime' (p. 195). Marx explains:

The idea that history is a record of more or less continuous progress had become popular during the eighteenth century, but chiefly among the educated. Associated with achievements of Newtonian mechanics, the idea remained abstract and relatively inaccessible. But with rapid industrialization, the notion of progress became palpable; 'improvements' were visible to everyone. During the nineteenth century . . . the awe and reverence once reserved for the Deity and later bestowed upon the visible landscape is directed towards technology, or, rather, the technological conquest of matter. (Marx, 1964: 197)

Technology was subsequently described in new terms, in a vocabulary that portrayed technology and techniques in terms of beauty, creation and other concepts rarely associated with artificial and technological artefacts but more often with nature (Nye, 1994; Kasson, 1976). The mechanosphere was thus perceived with less scepticism. In terms of human vision, it became increasingly instrumentalized and was regarded as a resource that could be fruitfully exploited. The nineteenth century was, in other words, the first century wherein human vision became a social factor to take into account: the spectacular and the visible became defining features of the forthcoming society that the Weimar theorists (i.e. Simmel, Benjamin and Kracauer) examined. Crary (1995) notes that the new theories of vision brought the concept of attention into discussion and rendered it socially significant:

> It was also in the late nineteenth century, within the human sciences and, particularly, the nascent field of scientific psychology, that the problem of *attention* became a fundamental issue. It was a problem whose centrality was directly related to the emergence of a social, urban, psychic, industrial field increasingly saturated with sensory input ... It is possible to see one crucial aspect of modernity as a continual crisis of attentiveness, to see the changing configurations of capitalism pushing attention and distraction to new limits and thresholds, with unending introduction of new products, new sources of stimulation, and streams of information, and then responding with new methods of managing and regulating perception. (Crary, 1995: 47)

What is of particular interest here is the reference to the *crisis* of attentiveness, the problematization of vision not only in terms of how to achieve attention but also in terms of the pathological effects that vision produced for the individual. In essence, modernity – or at least *urban modernity* (a concept that may appear as a pleonasm but that nevertheless makes some sense in this context) – may be conceived of as an ongoing and endemic crisis of attention or even visuality as such. As George Simmel points out in his classic essay on modern urban life, the perceiving subject quickly develops a '*blasé* attitude' to be capable of coping with the abundance of sense-impression in the metropolis. Simmel (1971) argues that the human psyche is incapable of handling too many 'swift' impressions:

> The psychological foundation, upon which the metropolitan individuality is erected, is the intensification of emotional life due to the swift and continuous shift of external and internal stimuli. Man is a creature whose existence is dependent on differences, i.e., his mind is stimulated by the difference between present impressions and those which have preceded. Lasting impressions, the slightness of their differences, the habituated regularity of their course and contrasts between them, consume, so to speak, less mental energy than the rapid telescoping of changing images, pronounced differences within what is grasped at a single glance, and the unexpectedness of violent stimuli. (Simmel, 1971: 325)

Life in the modern metropolis is characterized by ceaseless impressions and therefore what Simmel calls the 'metropolitan type' develops mechanisms for coping with a fleeting social reality:

> The metropolitan type – which naturally takes on a thousand individual modifications – creates a protective organ for itself against the profound disruption with which the fluctuations and discontinuities of the external milieu threatens it. Instead of reacting emotionally, the metropolitan type reacts primarily in a rational manner, thus creating a mental predominance through the intensification of consciousness, which in turn is caused by it. Thus the reaction of the metropolitan person to those events is moved to a sphere of mental activity which is least sensitive and which is furthest removed from the depths of the personality. (Simmel, 1971: 326)

The '*blasé* attitude' is therefore an emotional response '[i]n which the nerves reveal their final possibility of adjusting themselves to the content and the form of metropolitan life by renouncing the response to them' (Simmel, 1971: 330). Being *blasé* is then to disrupt one's 'instinctive' social capacities and to withdraw from the social and emotional realm. The look and facial gestures produced in such a condition are characteristic, described by Clark, (1984, cited in Crary, 1999: 99) in the following terms: 'The look which results is a special one: Public, outward ... impassive, not bored, not tired, not disdainful, not quite focussed on anything.' Being *blasé* is, in short, to turn one's face into a blank surface devoid of any social or emotional content, neither positive nor negative. The metropolitan type is thus a human being concerned not to become emotionally attached or to display private thoughts or beliefs in facial or bodily gestures.

Perception, attention and modern capitalist production

Crary insists on relating the new theories' vision to the operating mechanisms of capitalism as such:

> Part of the cultural logic of capitalism demands that we accept as *natural* the rapid switching of our attention from one thing to another. Capital, as accelerated exchange and circulation, necessarily produces this kind of human perceptual adaptability and becomes a regime of reciprocal attentiveness and distraction. (1995: 48)

Vision and perception are then not only a matter of being a subjective capacity to apprehend and relate to the external world but are also intimately bound up with the concept of modernity *per se*. Crary's (1990; 1995) contribution lies in his ability to point out how new formations of knowledge, addressing vision not as a transcendental category but as an embodied, personal and biologically constituted capacity, produces new modes of organization and a new structuring of society. What is at stake is not only the perceiving subject but also modernity itself. As a consequence, one needs to conceive of the amorphous concept of modernity in terms of its implication for perception, or, more broadly speaking, the experience of the perceiving subject. Gunning (1995) offers a useful definition, speaking of modernity as 'a change in experience':

> By 'modernity' I refer less to a demarcated historical period than to a change in experience. This new configuration of experience was shaped by a large number of factors, which were clearly dependent on the change in production marked by the Industrial Revolution. It was also, however, equally characterized by the transformation in daily life wrought by the growth of capitalism and advances in technology: the growth of urban traffic, the distribution of mass-produced goods, and successive new technologies of transportation and communication. While the nineteenth century witnessed the principal conjunction of these transformations in Europe and America, within a particular crisis coming towards the turn of the century, modernity has not yet exhausted its transformations and has a different pace in different areas of the world. (Gunning, 1995: 15)

Many of the changes sketched by Gunning (1995) are intimately bound up with organizational matters, for instance, the 'growth of capitalism' and 'the distribution of mass-produced' goods. Perception and organization are therefore co-evolutionary and recursive concepts; they mutually produce and reinforce one another. Gunning (1995: 15–16) emphasized the role played by the railway both to provide cheaper and safer 'networks of circulation', expanding industrial production geographically and enabling new opportunities for division of labour, and as what altered the perception of the new society capable of mastering time and collapsing geographical distances. In addition, the railway offered new perceptions through the new high-speed travel that shaped the human perception of time and space. Schivelbusch (1986: 62) argues that the railway experience brought a new form of experience of vision, a 'panoramic vision' that brought increasing demand for new forms of spectacularity: '[T]he railroad first and foremost, is the main cause for [the] panoramization of the world,' Schivelbusch writes (1986: 62). For instance, in Paris there was a number of 'dioramas' and 'panoramas' opening around 1840. The new quest for and preference for speed pervaded all spheres of social, economic and cultural life; at times, the emerging organizational life even served as the chimera of an animated machinery assemblage, capable of operating without any human intervention and obeying only its innate 'circulatory logic':

> Skill seemed to be absorbed by the circulatory logic of the factory itself, as each task took place within a chain of rationalized labor. This new arrangement of production seemed able to make anything out of anything, without the laborious effort of skilled handicraft. In such new system of labor, objects were transformed rapidly before one's eyes, and the stable identity of things became as uncertain as a panoply of magician's props. (Gunning, 1995: 17)

Upton Sinclair's classic *The Jungle* (published in 1906) gives an account of the new mechanized slaughter-houses in Chicago, portrayed as automatic killing machines where terrified hogs were transformed – as if by magic – into bacon and ham:

> It was all so very business-like that one watched it fascinated. It was pork-making by machinery, pork-making by applied mathematics ... Now and then visitors wept, to be sure; but this slaughtering-machine ran on, visitors or no visitors. It was like some horrible crime

committed in a dungeon, all unseen and unheard, buried out of sight and of memory. (Upton Sinclair, *The Jungle*, 1906: 38)

The increase in speed and the new technological breakthroughs brought opportunities for spectatorship and what the French situationist group leader Guy Debord (1977) would later call *la societé du spectacle*. The most significant changes took place in North America. For instance, Nye (2004), examining the electrification of the quickly expanding American metropolis, points out that 'as early as 1903 Chicago, New York, and Boston had five times as many electric lights per inhabitants as Paris, London, or Berlin, and by 1910 the electrical displays stunned foreign visitors' (Nye, 2004: 213). Visionaries and forerunners of the consumer society such as Gordon Selfridge exploited the demand for spectatorship and spectacle in the emerging *flâneur* culture (thoroughly discussed by Walter Benjamin, 1999) and turned shopping into a major experience when he brought together a range of services and opportunities for entertainment under the same roof in his new Selfridge's department store, opening in London's West End on 15 March 1909. Aristide Boucicaut opened the first Parisian department store, the Bon Marché, in 1852 (Schivelbusch, 1986: 188), and Selfridge's new creation can be seen as a culmination of the development over a number of decades. Previously, Selfridge had worked in Marshall Field's department store in Chicago wherein he introduced the first department store restaurant and 'the bargain basement', invited foreign royalty for personal visits and 'hired a well-known window-display artist to design spectacular shop windows' (Rappaport, 1995: 131–2). More than anything else, as a result of the contributions of Gordon Selfridge and his peers operating throughout European and North American cities, shopping became the defining mark of the perception-intensive modern era. Previously, shopping had been associated with women and in the Victorian era it was commonly dismissed as 'a wasteful, indulgent, immoral, and possibly disorderly female pleasure' (Rappaport, 1995: 131). Selfridge and other Edwardian entrepreneurs transformed the meaning of shopping and used publicity, particularly the print media, to 'turn disorder and immorality into legitimate pleasures'. Shopping was thus advanced as being pleasurable and respectable precisely because of its public setting. The Edwardian department store entrepreneurs presented shopping as a source of female self-fulfilment and independence; female customers were presented both as urban actors and bodies to be 'satisfied, indulged, excited, and repaired' (Rappaport, 1995: 131). Shopping, Gordon Selfridge repeatedly stated, 'promised women access to a sensual and social metropolitan culture'.

However, London's West End had been a place of commerce and enjoyment since at least the 1860s. Gordon Selfridge merely exploited a series of intersecting tendencies of a modern time with an insatiable demand for spectacle. However, even though some social groups could advance their positions and various social practices (most noticeably shopping *per se*) attained a new social meaning and status, modern times also brought new concerns and pathologies. Siegfried Kracauer, a sensitive observer and analyst of the emerging urban life, found the same failure of the modern man to accommodate all impressions as George Simmel noticed. The urban *flâneur* is ceaselessly being fed with new impressions and thus life becomes increasingly fluid and dissolving:

> The street in the extended sense of the word is not only the arena of fleeting impressions and chance encounters but a place where the flow of life is bound to assert itself ... an incessant flow of possibilities and near-tangible meanings appear. This flow casts its spell over the *flâneur* or even creates him. The *flâneur* is intoxicated with life in the street – life eternally dissolving the patterns which it is about to form. (Kracauer, cited in Vidler, 2000: 111)

Among the new bourgeoisie malaises emerging in these new urban modes of life were the psychosomatic illnesses of agoraphobia and claustrophobia, first identified and diagnosed at the end of the nineteenth century (Vidler, 2000: 25). The increased intensity of perception did not pass unmarked. Somewhat inconsistent with empirical observations – male patients predominated in the sample – these new disorders were regarded as being 'female' in character (Vidler, 2000: 36). Increased anxiety and/or physical symptoms when entering public spaces were regarded as an illness of the feeble and the weak.

Taken together, the nineteenth century brought, among other things (a range of new technologies, the consolidation and expansion of scientific disciplines such as chemistry and physics, the formulation of political ideologies), a new theory of vision and an emerging spectacular society consciously exploiting the attention and perception. The theory of vision underlined the subjective and embodied nature of perception, and the social practice derived from this new paradigm mobilized a range of resources using speed, light and sound to attract attention from the urban dweller. Above all, the historical development of the modern perceiving subject underlines the associations between perception and organization, vision and capitalism.

The concept of perception

Defining perception

The central concept of this book is perception, the human ability to perceive through the five senses: hearing, smell, touch, vision, taste. Although there is little reason to single out one of the senses as being more primordial, elementary or privileged over the others from an ontological or epistemological view, within an organization theory and management studies project it is the visual and auditory capacities that are primarily examined. There are of course domains where the other three senses are central but seeing and hearing remain the most important senses in organizational settings. One may claim that the Western culture is above anything else a culture of visuality, a 'scoptic regime'. Sight is the sense that has been examined as the most elementary human faculty. However, sight is not conceived of as being detached from mind and language but is rather – especially in Henri Bergson's thinking – what created the capacity for vision. Leppert writes:

> Sight is the principal means through which we learn to maneuver in time and space. Sight is a 'device' for recognition, prediction, and confirmation: This person is mother and not a stranger ... Her identity is 'seen' before her name is recognized and long before it can be spoken ... we also understand that seeing is simply not a matter of biology and physics, not a question of light waves' action on the retina. Seeing is very much about the mind and thought processes. (Leppert, 1996: 5)

Massumi (2002: 258) makes one important distinction when suggesting that perception commonly denotes 'object-oriented experience', while 'sensation' is the 'perception of perception' or 'self-referential experience'. Sensation can, with the vocabulary of Niklas Luhmann, be said to be a *second-order* construct, while perception is a *first-order* construct. Furthermore, Gibson (1950) distinguishes between, on the one hand, *literal perception*, denoting 'the world of colors, textures, objects, surfaces, edges, slopes, shapes and interspaces', and *schematic perception*, 'the world of objects, places, people, signals, and written symbols' (Gibson, 1950: 10). Before one can understand schematic perception one must understand literal perception, Gibson argues (1950: 11). The literal perception provides the 'fundamental repertory for all experience', that is, the 'elementary impressions' of surfaces and edges (Gibson, 1950: 8), and thus serves as the foundation for schematic perception.

In the following, perception is used to denote various forms of sense-impressions being registered by the human subject. Sense-impressions do not need to derive from so-called 'external' reality but are also what is embodied and somatic or of mental origin. Thus, perception is what is on the border between self and other, mind and body. Above all, perception is a means for relating to social reality, a sort of membrane between a range of categories making up the assemblage that constitutes the human subject and his or her relation to social reality.

The philosophical concept of perception

As has been suggested, the concepts of perception, vision and visuality have a long tradition and a central role in Western thinking. Aristotle addressed 'sense-perception' in chapters 5 through 12 in the second book (§§417–24) of his *De Anima (On the Soul)*. Later on, as Gombrich (1960: 15) notes, 'Ptolemy devoted much thought in his *Optics* (c. AD15) to the role of judgment in the process of vision' and the greatest Arab student of vision, Alhazen (c. AD1038), taught the medieval West to distinguish between sense, knowledge, and inference, 'all of which came into play in perception'. Later on John Locke denied, in polemics with the rationalists, that ideas are innate and suggested that all knowledge is based on sensual impressions. Moreover, George Berkeley (2004; 2007) addressed the relationship between knowledge and the senses in his *New Theory of Vision* (1709) and '[r]eached the conclusion that all our knowledge of space and solidity must be acquired through the sense of touch and movement' (Gombrich, 1960: 15). The same thoughts were given its most authoritative formulation in David Hume's empiricist philosophy, underlining the central role of impressions and perception and their function in the formation of ideas: 'The perceptions', Hume (1992: 1) writes, 'which enter with most force and violence, we may name impressions ... By *ideas* I mean the faint images of these in thinking and reasoning.' Hume continues to argue that the human mind is an inextricably bound up with such impressions: 'What we call a *mind*, is nothing but a heap or collection of different perceptions, united together by certain relations' (1992: 207). Hume is thus one of the major modern philosophers associating human reason and sense impression. For Deleuze (1991: ix), what makes Hume a key thinker in the Western tradition is the insistence on regarding ideas, the elementary forms of the human mind, as being related to sense-impressions and thereby claiming that ideas are 'cultural and *conventional* formations' rather than representing universal Platonic ideas. The mind is thus, Deleuze says, 'given

as a collection of ideas and not as a system' (1991: 22). As has been frequently noted, it was Hume's critical philosophy that made Immanuel
Kant re-evaluate his thinking and open up new philosophical territories.

'From Descartes to Berkeley to Diderot,' Crary argues, 'vision is conceived of in terms of analogies to the senses of touch' (1990: 59).
However, by the middle and end of the nineteenth century, new images
of vision and perception were articulated. The point of departure for the
review of the modern literature addressing perception is what William
James refers to as 'the intellectualist tradition of thinking' in the Western
episteme. This intellectualist credo, indebted to Socrates and Plato, connects things and their definitions, which in turn are related to the
essences of things (James, 1996: 218). Thus, proper definitions become
central to knowledge and understanding. In addition, it is a mode of
thinking that assumes that 'fixity' is of the essence of things. James
argues:

> The ruling tradition in philosophy has always been the platonic and
> Aristotelian belief in that fixity is a nobler and worthier thing than
> change. Reality must be one and unalterable. Concepts being them-
> selves fixities, agree best with this fixed nature of truth, so that for any
> knowledge of ours to be quite true it must be knowledge by universal
> concepts rather than by particular experiences, for these notoriously
> are mutable and corruptible. (James, 1996: 237)

The process of conceptualizing is then not a free play of creativity but is
instead a most stern philosophical engagement to sort out the order of
things and to locate them in a texture of relations: 'When we concep-
tualize, we cut and fix, and exclude everything but what we have fixed.
A concept means a *that-and-no-other*', James (1996: 253) argues. James
is critical of such an ontology and epistemology and says – drawing on
Bergson's process thinking – that this privileged position of fixity is problematic because it ignores that what exists is not things but rather 'things-
in-the-making' (James, 1996: 263). Things are thus only temporal and
transient states and our ignorance – a sort of 'trained ignorance', one may
say – undermines our ability to conceive of the true essence of things,
namely its becoming, its status of being 'in-the-making'. James (1912:
92) here speaks of 'pure experiences' as what 'seem perfectly fluent'. Later
on, the process philosopher Alfred North Whitehead would speak of the
similar concept of 'presentational immediacy': 'Presentational immediacy is our immediate perception of the contemporary external world,
appearing as an element constitutive of our own experience' (Whitehead,

1927: 21). However, intellectual effort makes such experience problematic and 'discovers incomprehensibilities in the flowing process'; it gives 'elements and parts' separate names – 'furnishes the material to our later reflection with its conceptual categories' (James, 1912: 93) – and thus once and for all disrupts the pure experience. Intellectualism arrests the pure experiences of 'the immediate flux of life'. Crary notices the central role of James and Bergson in terms of challenging the 'notion of a pure or simple sensation'; both contend that '[a]ny sensation, no matter how seemingly elemental, is always a compounding of memory, desire, will, anticipation, and immediate experience', Crary says (1999: 27).

William James (1950) used the expression 'stream of thought' in his *Principles of Psychology* (first published in 1890). Crary (1999) argues that James favoured the more 'act-oriented' concept of 'thought' instead of 'consciousness'. In addition, the image of the stream was invoked to '[d]escribe the fundamentally transitive nature of subjective experience – a perpetually changing but continuous flow of images, sensations, thought fragments, bodily awareness, memories, desires – which he sets against the older or even contemporary accounts for which consciousness has discrete contents and elements' (Crary, 1999: 60). For James (1950), attention is inseparable from the possibility of a 'cognitive and perceptual immediacy' wherein the self ceases to be separated from the world of objects. Attention is then the transient and temporal merging of perception and object: 'The stream of thought is like a river. On the whole easy simple flowing predominates in it, the drift of things is with the pull of gravity, and effortless attention is the rule,' James writes (1950: 451). The mind, the domain where streams of thought circulate and intersect, is here something similar to David Hume's 'bundle of impressions': 'Only those items which I *notice* shape my mind – without selective interest, experience is an utter chaos. Interest alone gives accent and emphasis, light and shade, background and foreground, in a word' (James, 1950: 402). Mind selects some objects of attention but also suppresses others through the 'inhibiting of attention'. Here, James compares the observer to an artist: 'Confronted with "the primordial chaos of sensations", we extricate our subjective worlds, selecting and rejecting, as a sculptor works on a block of stone,' Crary remarks (1999: 62). James's pragmatist thinking and its emphasis on selection and partial attentiveness – perhaps best captured by James's claim that 'my experience is what I agree to attend to' (James, 1950: 402) – are themes that were later further developed in the social sciences. For instance, in the phenomenological sociology of Alfred Schutz and the tradition of symbolic interactionism in sociology represented by Charles Horton

Cooley and George Herbert Mead, James's thought is present. In organization theory, Karl Weick's (1969) widely acclaimed concept of *enactment* is equally indebted to James's thinking. Some of the ideas originally formulated by James have been further developed in psychology. For instance, Jean Piaget, the great Swiss psychologist, connects perception and what he calls 'intelligence' (rather than 'mind' or 'consciousness') thus: 'Perception is the knowledge we have of objects or of their movements by direct and immediate contact, while intelligence is a form of knowledge obtaining when detours are involved and when spatio-temporal distances between subject and objects increase' (1950/2001: 59). Just as James emphasized the 'impurity' and multiple nature of perception and other psychic instances, Piaget (1950/2001: 7) speaks of the faculty of intelligence not as a distinct 'class of cognitive processes' but as a 'form of equilibrium' where various psychological structures integrate:

> [I]ntelligence itself does not consist of an isolated and sharply differentiated class of cognitive processes. It is not, properly speaking, one form of structuring among others; it is the form of equilibrium towards which all the structures arising out of perception, habit, and elementary sensori-motor mechanisms tend. It must be understood that if intelligence is not a faculty this denial involves a radical functional continuity between the higher forms of thought and the whole mass of lower types of cognitive and motor and adaptation; so intelligence can only be the form of equilibrium towards which these things tend. (Piaget, 1950/2001: 7)

Intelligence is not a 'thing'; it is a form of relay, to use Bergsonian vocabulary, connecting perception and memory. Another central figure in the field of psychology formulating theories sharing ideas with James's thinking is the Russian psychologist Lev Vygotsky, who examines the relationship between mind, perception and language. Vygotsky (1978: 26) claimed, on the basis of his laboratory research on juvenile children, that the unity of perception, speech and action constitute the human mind; '[C]hildren solve practical tasks with the help of their speech, as well as their eyes and hands', he contended. Just like James and Piaget, Vygotsky (1978) emphasizes the mind as something that is not to be reduced to one single structure but that is an assemblage of capabilities:

> [T]he mind is not a complex network of *general* capabilities such as observation, attention, memory, judgment, and so forth, but a set of specific capabilities, each of which is, to some extent, independent

of the others and is developed independently. Learning is more than the acquisition of the ability to think: it is the acquisition of many specialized abilities for thinking about a variety of things. Learning does not alter our overall ability to focus attention but rather develops various abilities to focus attention on a variety of things. (Vygotsky, 1978: 83)

The experimental psychology of Piaget and Vygostsky arguably adheres to the principles formulated by David Hume.

Bergson on perception and memory

Henri Bergson's foundational work in process thinking and in the philosophy of perception is another body of work developed in parallel with James's philosophy. If one may separate Bergson's rich work into categories and streams, one may speak of Bergson's process philosophy (most widely known through his influential *L'Evolution créatrice* [*Creative Evolution*], 1907) and his philosophy of the mind (formulated in *Matière et mémoire* [*Matter and Memory*], 1896 and the collection of essays published in *Mind-energy*, 1920). In the latter corpus, Bergson speaks of perception as what is foundational for human existence:

> Our perceptions and our sensations are at once what are clearest in us and most important for us; they note at each moment the changing relation of our body to other bodies; they determine or direct our conduct. Thence our tendency to see in the other psychical facts nothing but perceptions or sensations obscured or diminished. (Bergson, 1920/1975: 162)

Bergson's philosophy of mind connects perception, time (duration or *durée*, in Bergson's vocabulary) and memory, and suggests that we are in fact not starting with perception 'recollecting' previous impressions but, on the contrary, are starting with memory and moving to perception. Thus, we do not move from the present to the past, but from the past to the present in the act of connecting perception and memory in the instant of the look (Deleuze, 1966/1988: 63). Perception is then not an *impression*, a form of *recording*, but is a '[c]onstruction in which we partake through the active work of synthesis' (Lazzarato, 2007: 102). However, Bergson says that it is an 'illusion' that 'memory *succeeds* perception' (1920/1975: 160, emphasis in the original); instead, they develop in tandem, they are 'contemporaneous': '[T]*he formation of memory is never posterior to the formation of perception; it is contemporaneous with it.* Step by step, as perception is created, the memory of it is projected beside it, as the shadow falls beside the body' (Bergson, 1920/1975: 157, emphasis in the original). Bergson explains the relation between perception and sensation, on the one hand, and memory on the other:

> Sensation is warm, coloured, vibrant and almost living, but vague; memory is clear and distinct, but without substance and lifeless. Sensation longs for a form into which to solidify its fluidity; memory longs for matter to fill it, to ballast it, in short, to realize it. They are drawn towards each other; and the phantom memory, materializing itself in sensation which brings its flesh and blood, becomes a being which lives a life of its own, a dream. (Bergson, 1920/1975: 118)

Bergson's commentator Elizabeth Grosz (2005) explicates Bergson's idea of how perception, duration and memory coexist in simultaneity:

> Bergson defines perception and memory, our modes of access to the present and the past, in operational terms: the present is that which is acting, while the past is that which no longer acts ... Perception must be linked to nascent or dawning action, acting-in-potential, action that is on the verge of beginning or being undertaken. Perception, being linked fundamentally to action, is actual, and is directed to an impending or immediate future ... A present perception and a past recollection are not simply different in degree (one a faded, diminished, or muted version of the other) but different in kind. Perception is that which propels us towards the present, the real, to space, objects, matter, to the immediate or impending future; while memory is that which impels us towards consciousness, to the past, and duration. (Grosz, 2005: 96–7)

Expressed differently, 'perception can never be free of memory, and is thus never completely embedded in the present but always straddles elements with the past' (Grosz, 2005: 101–2). For Lazzarato too, perception is the continual passing from the past (the virtual) to the present (the actual) and *vice versa*. Therefore, the present is conceptualized in Bergson's writing as '[n]othing but the most contracted moment of our past' (Lazzarato, 2007: 104). Perception thus demands an 'intellectual effort' on part of the individual; it is an *act*, a form of accomplishment: '[P]erception depends on the power to act; not the reverse. Perception is the function of action and *the limits of perception are the limits of our action*,' Lazzarato (2007: 112) suggests. Consequently, attention is for Bergson,

Lazzarato argues, the force of the intellectual effort and serves, to use Spinoza's term, as the 'conatus' which 'actualize' virtual images into 'distinct, juxtaposed images' (Lazzarato, 2007: 11). In Bergson, perception is never 'given' as such but is always what is embodied and demands an effort. Hansen therefore suggests that Bergson remains first and foremost a theorist of 'embodied perception' (2004: 4), rendering perception not a pure act but as what is always temporal and residing in embodiment; 'Bergson correlates perception with the concrete life of the body,' Hansen (2004: 4) remarks.

When we perceive, we do not merely register movements and other physical entities and processes but actively relate to our own duration constituted as a multiplicity comprising the past, the present and anticipated future. Bergson even says that '[p]erception is less in the present than in the future' (1920/1975: 183); '[T]he past is not purely in itself, self-contained: it straddles both past and present, requires the past as its precondition, while being oriented towards the immediate future,' Grosz (2005: 102) summarizes. Thus, the past and the present coexist and are recreated simultaneously; every present, every moment of presence, a sense of a 'now', is split into an actual and a virtual component. What Bergson says is that perception is not a detached or autonomous human capacity that registers and pays attention to occurrences and things without what Gadamer (1960/1975) would call *prejudice*; instead, perception is always shaped by memory. Jorge Luis Borges (1999), discussing Bergson's thinking, captures this idea but also mentions embodied knowledge, what Pierre Bourdieu would later call *hexis*, schemes of action and behaviour inscribed into the body and repeated in specific situations:

> The very fact of perceiving, of paying attention, is selective; all attention, all focusing of our consciousness, involves a deliberate omission of what is not interesting. We see and hear through memories, fears, expectations. In bodily terms, unconsciousness is a necessary condition of physical acts. Our bodies know how to articulate this difficult paragraph, how to contend with stairways, knots, overpasses, cities, fast-running rivers, dogs, how to cross a street without being run down by traffic, how to procreate, how to breathe, how to sleep, and perhaps how to kill. (Borges, 1999: 61)

Perception is determined by memory, not the other way around. The duration of a human being means that perception and memory mutually constitute one another but with memory as the original faculty.

Therefore, perception has an elementary relation to the human mind as what is having an intimate relationship with cognition.

While Bergson's work on perception may give the impression of being separated from any social or cultural debates and controversies – Bergson's text is not polemical but argumentative and he does not define any specific target for his critique – it is in fact, Crary (1999) argues, a response to the common view of perception represented by, for instance, Hermann von Helmholtz's theories of vision: 'At the heart of Bergson's project is his attempt to establish a model of perception as opposed to various routinized and reified forms of perceptual experience within Western urban and scientific culture of the late nineteenth century' (Crary, 1999: 316). What is, again, at the centre of Bergson's concern, is the idea of 'pure' perception. Crary says that Bergson shares with the later Paul Cézanne the interest for perception as what is always 'mixed and composite' (1999: 316). More specifically, Bergson is concerned not primarily with perception *per se* but to theorize what happened 'in-between' the 'awareness of the stimulation' and 'reactions to it' (Crary, 1999: 317). In Crary's (1999) account, Bergson's philosophy of perception represents a culmination of a long tradition of thinking with ramifications for the arts, the sciences and capitalist institutions and practices; it is a work that bridges previous ideas of perception, assuming a certain degree of purity and embodiment, and the new theories and practices of perception emerging in the new 'scoptic regimes of modernity' brought by the cinema and, more recently, new media.

Perception in Merleau-Ponty and Lacan

Maurice Merleau-Ponty is another seminal thinker of the last century addressing perception as a major philosophical term. In Grosz's (2005: 118) account, Merleau-Ponty can be 'understood as a Bergsonian'. However, Merleau-Ponty is more commonly associated with the tradition of phenomenology founded by Edmund Husserl. Merleau-Ponty (1964a: 183) himself speaks of Bergson as a 'monumental thinker' but is critical of the Bergsonism movement that dominated French (and European) intellectual life in the first decades of the twentieth century. Merleau-Ponty's philosophy is a detailed engagement with the concept of perception. Merleau-Ponty (1964b: 25) speaks of the 'primacy of perception' as the moment when 'things, truths, values are constituted for us'. Merleau-Ponty defends his position:

It is not a question of reducing human knowledge to sensation, but of assisting at the birth of this knowledge, to make it as sensible as the sensible, to recover the consciousness of rationality. This experience of rationality is lost when we take it for granted as self-evident, but is, on the contrary, rediscovered when it is made to appear against the background of non-human nature. (Merleau-Ponty, 1964b: 25)

The primacy of perception means for Merleau-Ponty that the body 'gives significance' not only to 'natural objects' but also to 'cultural objects' such as words, that is, what belong to the domain of what is 'invisible' (Merleau-Ponty, 1968; 1974a; b). Merleau-Ponty (1962: 235) exemplifies: 'If a word is shown to a subject for too short a period of time for him to be able to read it, the word 'warm', for example, induces a kind of experience of warmth which surrounds him with something in the nature of a meaningful halo.' All experience is therefore embodied. Merleau-Ponty says that things are not material objects detached from humans but are instead 'clothed in human characteristics'. Merleau-Ponty (1948/2004) explains:

The things in the world are not simply neutral objects which stand before us for our contemplation. Each of them symbolizes or recalls a particular way of behaving, provoking in us reactions which are either favorable or unfavorable ... Our relationship with things is not a distant one: each speaks to our body and to the way we live. They are clothed in human characteristics (whether docile, soft, hostile or resistant) and conversely they dwell within us as emblems of forms of life we either love or hate. Humanity is invested in the things and these are invested in it. To use the language of psychoanalysis, things are complexes. This is what Cézanne meant when he spoke of the particular 'halo' of things which it is the task of painting to capture. (Merleau-Ponty, 1948/2004: 63–4)

'[V]ertiginous proximity prevents us from apprehending ourselves as a pure intellect separated from things and from defining things as pure objects lacking in all human attributes', Merleau-Ponty concludes (1948/2004: 66). Merleau-Ponty here introduces the concept of *the flesh* as an ontological category, an 'element' capable of bridging mind and matter, corporeality and cognition (1968: 139). The flesh is what is 'midway' between the 'spatio-temporal individual and the idea'; the flesh is what unifies and aligns perception and experience: 'The thickness of the body, far from rivaling that of the world, is ... the sole means I have to go unto the heart of the things, by making myself a world and by making them flesh,' Merleau-Ponty writes (1968: 135). He continues:

> When we speak of the flesh of the visible, we do not mean to do anthropology, to describe a world covered over with all our own projections, leaving aside what it can be under the human mask. Rather, we mean that carnal being, as a being of depth, of several leaves or several faces, a being in latency, and a presentation of certain absence, is a prototype for Being, of which our body, the sensible sentient, is a very remarkable variant, but whose constitutive paradox already lies in every visible. (Merleau-Ponty, 1968: 136)

In a most Bergsonian passage, Merleau-Ponty speaks of vision as what is already grounded in memory, in past embodied experiences:

> The light of a candle changes its appearance for a child when, after a burn, it stops attracting the child's hand and becomes literally repulsive. Vision is already inhabited by a meaning (*sens*) which gives it a function in the spectacle of the world and in our existence. (1962: 52)

Here, Merleau-Ponty defends an embodied and corporeal image of perception. This is what Jacques Lacan sees as the major contribution from Merleau-Ponty's oeuvre:

> *La Phénomenologie* [*The Phenomenology of Perception*] brings us back, then, to the regulation of form, which is governed not only by the subject's eye, but by his expectations, his movement, his grip, his muscular and visceral emotions – in short, his constitutive presence, directed in what is called his total intentionality. (1998: 71)

Lacan's theory of vision as always submitting to socially agreed descriptions is thus indebted to Merleau-Ponty. Bryson says that for Lacan, vision is 'socialized' and thus 'deviations' from socially legitimate constructions of visual reality are named as 'hallucination, misrecognition, or "visual disturbance" ' (1988: 91–2). Hence there is a difference between vision, as what Merleau-Ponty (1968: 38) calls 'brute perception', and 'visuality' as 'socially mediated vision', Bryson argues:

> Between the subject and the world is inserted the entire sum of discourses which make up visuality, that cultural construct, and make visuality different from vision, the notion of unmediated visual

experience. Between retina and world is inserted a screen of signs, a screen consisting of all multiple discourses on vision built into the social arena. (1988: 91–2)

This visuality, affected by the field of the Other, is named 'the gaze' by Lacan:

> The viewing subject does not stand at the center of a perceptual horizon, and cannot command the chains of signifiers passing across the visual domain. Vision unfolds to the side of, in tangent to, the field of the other. And to that form of seeing Lacan gives a name: seeing on the field of the other, seeing under the gaze. (Bryson, 1988: 94)

In Lacan's treatment of the term, visual perception becomes visuality under the gaze of the other; Lacan speaks about the 'split between the gaze and the eye' (1998: 78). There are no autonomous and primary positions of the viewer enabling 'pure vision' but vision is from the outset influenced by power and becomes visuality. Merleau-Ponty expresses his idea in terms of vision having its specific limitations: '[t]he privilege of vision is not to open *ex nihilo* upon a pure being *ad infinitum*; the vision too has a field, a range' (1968: 83). Vision is never pure but shaped and formed by what Merleau-Ponty (1968) calls the visible and the invisible. In, for instance, feminist theory and film studies, Lacan's concept of the gaze has served as an influential analytical model. For instance, in a seminal paper Laura Mulvey argues that 'cinema poses questions about the ways the unconscious (formed by the dominant order) structures ways of seeing and pleasures in looking' (1989: 15). For Mulvey, the gaze has been split into the binary couples male/active and female/passive. Consequently, 'the determining male gaze projects its fantasy onto the female figure, which is styled accordingly,' Mulvey claims (1989: 19). Cinema therefore is a visual medium already structured in accordance with predominant ideologies and beliefs. More recently, Beller (2006) uses Lacan's concept of the gaze to theorize what he calls the cinematic mode of production in the contemporary regime of capitalism. Here, the gaze is already vested with interest and bound up with predominant ideologies: according to Beller:

> *To look is to labor* … Like capital, the gaze is a structure of organization … that demands a certain kind of work from the body, from some bodies. Increasingly, part of the value of the commodity, be it

a painting or a Hollywood star, comes from the amount of (unpaid) visual attention it has absorbed. (2006: 181, emphasis in the original)

The concept of the gaze is useful when theorizing vision and attention as always entangled with the 'field of the other'.

In summary, the concept of perception and the variety of related terms (e.g. sensation, sense-impression, attention, consciousness, mind, intelligence) are central concepts in a number of disciplines and philosophical schools addressing the increasingly permeable and fluid relationship between the subject and the social world. Returning once again to Jonathan Crary's (1990; 1999) discussion of the new doctrines of perception and vision in the nineteenth century, one may notice that, while perception used to be comparatively unproblematic and uncontested as what is stable and predictable, perception gradually became more multiple and diverse in the course of the nineteenth and twentieth centuries. Crary (1999) concludes:

From the classical model of a mental stabilization of perception into a fixed mold, attention in the nineteenth century effectively became a continuum of variation, and it was repeatedly described as having a rhythmic or wavelike character. Though it appeared to hold the possibility of building up stable and orderly (though not necessarily truthful) cognitions, it also contained within itself incontrollable forces which would put that organized world into jeopardy. Within the general epistemological crisis of the late nineteenth century, attention became a makeshift and inadequate simulation of an Archimedean point of stability from which consciousness could know the world. Rather than perceptual fixity and the certainty of presence, it opened onto flux and absence within which subject and object had a scattered, provisional existence. (Crary, 1999: 64–5)

In these new modes of thinking, perception is a human, social, cultural and economic resource to be explored and exploited. It becomes one of the cornerstones of human organization.

Summary and conclusion

Perception and, even more specifically, vision, are elementary components in organizational activities. Yet, this epistemological category is barely explicitly discussed in the organization theory and management studies literature. Instead of thinking exclusively of organization as a building constituted by the bricks of fixed and lexically defined concepts, perception is what interpenetrates any organizational activity; organizing is, to use Merleau-Ponty's (1968) phrase, the integration and close proximity of the visible and the invisible. Even the very concept of *theory*, derived from Greek *theoria* – a term similar to the German term *Anschauung*, denoting both visual inspection and contemplation (as in the term *Weltanschauung*) – underlines the presence of perception in everyday life. As Jonathan Crary (1990; 1999) has shown, from the mid-nineteenth century radically new theories of perception were gradually established and perception became the object of study for a range of scientific disciplines. This was also the period wherein management thinking and organization theory was being first formulated and formed. Avoiding implying any linear causality between these two intellectual and practical interests, perception on the one hand, and managerial concerns on the other, one may at least suggest that these two tendencies in nineteenth-century thinking represent an intriguing coincidence, perhaps derived from the same human concern for concept, such as attention and predictability. Not only did manufacturing become subject to detailed analysis and monitoring; also in the liberal arts predictability, rational analysis and perception were invoked in a number of projects. In the following chapters of the book, three aspects of perception and organization will be examined: art, producing images that serve as organizational resources while itself being an activity subject to organizational activities and undertakings; music, operating on the level of organized and structured sounds, providing audible experiences that influence or, at times and during specific conditions, even shape human activity; finally, media, assemblages including technologies and regimes of representations and symbolism that are capable of *remediating* – to '*mise-en-media*' to allude to Pierre Duhem's (1996: 25) emphasis on how the mathematically minded scholar *mise-en-équation* his or her empirical material – images and sound but also texts into technological systems capable of producing, manipulating, storing and distributing information.

2
Art: Visual Perception and the Aesthetic

Introduction

In this chapter, the concept of art will be examined. Art has its own scientific disciplines, theoretical frameworks, and methodologies and attracts attention from all sorts of social science as being representative of certain social orders or concerns. This chapter does not in any way attempt to cover the domain of art theory or art history but aims to point out some of the central features of art and how it contributes to day-to-day organization. Thus the approach to the analysis can be seen as being eclectic and synchretic; philosophy of art (i.e. aesthetics), sociology of art and artists' own account of their work are discussed. The aim of the chapter is to show that art as social resource is a *multiplicity*; it can be examined from many perspectives and take on different meanings in various settings. The chapter is structured as follows: first, the concept of aesthetics is examined; then the concept of art *per se* is discussed. In the third section, art and perception is related and thereafter the literature on art and organization is reviewed. Finally, some concluding remarks are formulated.

Aesthetics

The concept of aesthetics is arguably as old as Aristotle's *Poetics* (Holquist, 2003: 368). However, it was not until the Romantic movement in Germany in the eighteenth century that the German philosopher Alexander Baumgarten and his more famous disciple Immanuel Kant instituted the discipline of aesthetics, 'the philosophy of art and beauty' (Shusterman, 2006: 237). Aesthetics is, since Baumgarten's work, part of continental philosophy but it still remains 'deeply ambiguous, complex and essentially contested' (Shusterman, 2006: 237). Shusterman (2006) suggests that this is the case because central terms such as 'art' and 'beauty' are themselves amorphous. For instance, the Greek concept for art is *techne* (τεχνη), a concept today widely associated with craft or skill. Similarly, in German, the concept of *Kunst* has its root in *können*, to know (Shusterman, 2006: 238). Moreover, the history of aesthetics is '[a]n especially complicated, heterogeneous, conflicted and disordered genealogy' (Shusterman, 2006: 237). Luhmann (2000b: 15) notices that the concept of aesthetics is 'founded upon the distinction' between *aistheta* and *noeta*, 'sensuous or rational cognition, or aesthetics or logic'. In the Western episteme, aesthetics is then what is supplementary or additional to rational cognition. However, Baumgarten's original formulation of an aesthetic programme was, Shusterman argues, much broader than today's use of the philosophical term. Here again the concept of perception is of central importance for the philosophical programme:

> Baumgarten's epistemological-scientific approach construed aesthetics as a general science of sensory-perception that was involved in discerning and producing beauty. Though beauty was important to the field, the emphasis of the aesthetic (as reflected in its epistemological root) was more on its mode of perception or consciousness, and the scope of aesthetics was much wider than art, including not only natural beauty but also daily practices, Baumgarten thus advocated improved aesthetics perception (achieved through various practical training) not simply for fine arts but as a way of improving our general, including practical, functioning. (Shusterman, 2006: 239)

Eagleton also remarks *apropos* Baumgarten that:

> the distinction which the term 'aesthetic' initially enforces in the mid-eighteenth century is not between 'art' and 'life', but between the material and the immaterial: between things and thoughts, sensations and ideas, that which is bound up with our creaturely life as opposed to that which conducts some shadowy existence in the recesses of the mind. (1990: 13)

Flusser (2002: 105) points out that the concept of aesthetics is derived from the Greek word *aisthesthai*, meaning 'perception'. For Baumgarten, there was not yet a clear separation between *aistheta* and *noeta*; aesthetics is a tool for improved 'practical functioning'. In addition to the concepts of aesthetics, art and beauty and its various linguistic derivations, in his *The Critique of Judgment* – for Shusterman (2006) the single most influential work on aesthetics – Kant speaks of the complicated concept of the *sublime* as an analytical category complementing the beautiful. Even though Kant's use of the term is paradigmatic, the sublime is a concept first used by the first-century Greek scholar Longinus, translated into French by Nicolas Boileau in 1674, and thereafter discussed by Edmund Burke in his influential book *A Philosophical Enquiry into Our Ideas of the Sublime and the Beautiful*, first published in 1757. For Burke, as for the romantic artists of the nineteenth century, the sublime is what invokes horror or a sense of danger or even horror in the beautiful. Coyne exemplifies:

> The sublime is an aesthetic category in tension with beauty. It implicated a sense of terror from a safe distance, as when standing on a precipice, sheltering from a violent thunderstorm, and beholding a raging cataract. The romantic artists sought to evoke the sublime in nature, raging rivers, spectacular mountain scenery, the struggle for survival within the animal kingdom, the lion attacking the horse. (Coyne, 1999: 189)

In Kant's *The Critique of Judgment*, the term is used somewhat differently. Here, the beautiful is an accomplished form, while the sublime is what actually transcends form: 'The beautiful in nature is a question of the form of the object . . . whereas the sublime is to be found in an object even devoid of form . . . a representation of limitlessness', says Kant (1952: 90). In *Observations on the Beautiful and the Sublime* (1763/1960), Kant develops a quite complex set of propositions regarding the nature of the sublime and the beautiful, including a theory of personalities derived from Galen's typology (Kant, 1763/1960, Section Two) and a theory of the differences between how men and women perceive and apprehend the beautiful (Kant, 1763/1960, Section Three). Similar to Burke, Kant emphasizes the element of horror in the sublime:

> The sight of a mountain whose snow-covered peak rises above the clouds, the description of a raging storm, or Milton's portrayal of the infernal kingdom, arouse enjoyment but with horror; on the other hand, the sight of flower-strewn meadows, valleys with winding brooks and covered with grazing flocks, the description of Elysium, or Homer's portrayal of the girdle of Venus also occasion a pleasant sensation but one that is joyous and smiling . . . In order that the former impression could occur to us in due strength, we must have a *feeling of the sublime*, and in order to enjoy the latter well, a *feeling of the beautiful*. (Kant, 1763/1960: 47, emphasis in the original)

Elsewhere, Kant (1952: 92) writes: '[T]he sublime, in the strict sense of the word, cannot be contained in any sensuous form, but rather concerns ideas of reason.' The sublime is thus what may serve as an intermediary category between *aistheta* and *noeta*.

The perhaps most widely cited text on aesthetics, critical of such binary separation between aesthetics and rational thinking, is Friedrich Schiller's *Letters on Aesthetic Education*, first published in 1795. The letters were originally written to help educate a Danish prince but they soon circulated in the Copenhagen court and were greatly appreciated by their readers. In Schiller's advocacy of 'aesthetic education', aesthetics is a pathway to reason. For Schiller, 'cultivation of the sensibility' is what enables man to apprehend the social and natural world:

> The more multiform the cultivation of the sensibility is, the more variable it is, and the greater the surface it offers to phenomena, the more world does Man *apprehend*, the more potentialities does he develop within himself; the greater the strength and depth that the personality achieves, and the more freedom the reason gains, the more does Man *comprehend*, the more form does he create outside himself. Thus his culture will consist of two things: first, providing the receptive faculty with the most multifarious contacts with the world, and as regarding feeling, pushing passivity to its fullest extent; secondly, securing for the determining faculty the fullest independence from the receptive, and as regards reason, pushing activity to its fullest extent. (Schiller, 1795/2004: 69)

Schiller then speaks of four 'different connections' in philosophy: the physical, the logical, the moral and the aesthetic connection. In addition, aesthetics is what is outside or cannot be explained with the first three. Being able to become a man of reason demands a movement from the brute physical conditions of man to an 'aesthetic condition' and further on to be capable of thinking logically and morally. Schiller thus places aesthetic cultivation at the centre of the development of man: 'In a word, there is no other way to make the sensuous man rational than by first making him aesthetic,' Schiller claims (1795/2004: 108). Schiller also argues that the 'transition' from the 'physical condition' to the 'aesthetic condition' is more complicated than the transition from aesthetic to logic and moral – 'from Beauty to truth and duty' (Schiller, 1795/2004: 80); aesthetics then represents the most decisive step towards the reasonable man. However, Schiller's work does not suggest that aesthetics on its own is the root of all things desirable. Instead, he warns against the 'dangerous tendency' to always pay heed to form and never to content: 'Precisely because taste pays heed only to form and never to content, it finally gives the soul a dangerous tendency to neglect all reality entirely and to sacrifice truth and morality to an attractive façade' (Schiller, 1795/2004: 57).

Schiller's work has been enormously influential in terms of defending the need for aesthetics in human life and for serving an intermediary role in-between moral and logic, reason and nature. Other philosophers of aesthetics do, however, call into question Schiller's 'transition theory'. The Italian Benedetto Croce distinguishes art and science: 'Poetry and classification, and worse still, poetry and mathematics, seem to go as little as fire and water. The *esprit mathématique* and the *esprit scientifique* are the most avowed enemies of the *esprit poétique*' (1913/1995: 17). In an argument reminiscent of Bergson's distinction between intuition and rationality, Croce says that art relies on intuition but that science is based on the ability to classify and separate into categories. Moreover, Croce (1995: 28) speaks of 'the aesthetics of content' (German, *Gehaltaesthetik*) and 'aesthetics of form' (*Formaesthetik*). For Croce, the two forms of aesthetics are brought together in the work of art:

> Content and form should be properly distinguished in art. However, neither one can separately qualify as artistic, precisely because their relation alone is artistic, that is, their unity, understood not as an abstract and lifeless unity, but that concrete and living one which constitutes the a priori synthesis. Art is a true aesthetic *a priori* of feeling and image within intuition. Of which it can be said anew that intense feeling without image is blind, and image without intense feeling is empty. (Croce, 1995: 31)

While Schiller conceived of aesthetics as a tool in the hands of social planners and authorities, Croce mystifies aesthetics as what is dependent on intuition. Similarly, Kant did not follow Schiller on his insistence on providing aesthetics with a social role but rather spoke of art as having a *Zweckmässigkeit ohne Zweck*, 'having a quality of being purposeful without having a purpose' (Holquist, 2003: 368). However, Croce's emphasis on intuition also makes any observer a co-producer of the work of art:

> Art is vision or intuition. The artist produces an image or picture. The person who enjoys art turns his eyes in the direction which the artist has pointed out to him, peers through the hole which has been opened for him, and reproduces in himself the artist's image. (Croce, 1995: 8)

As an individual discipline within philosophy, aesthetics remain conceptualized as what deals with the experience of the beautiful, the sublime,
and form and matter. Aesthetics is in many cases regarded as what is
additional or supplementary (in Derrida's sense of the term) to science,
technology and other human accomplishments, rather than being at the
centre of relations. For instance, in organization theory and management studies, the concept of 'aesthetic knowledge' has been proposed as
a term capturing what is embodied, residing in the five senses, or what
in general escapes the use of language (Marotto, Roos and Victor, 2007;
Mack, 2007; Piñeiro, 2007; Hancock, 2005; Linstead and Höpfl, 2000;
Strati, 1999). 'Aesthetic knowledge', Taylor and Hansen (2005: 1213)
argue, 'offers fresh insight and awareness and while it may not be possible to put into words, it enables us to see in a new way'. Taylor and
Hansen here contrast 'intellectual' and 'aesthetic knowledge' wherein
the former is 'driven by a desire for clarity, objective truth and usually
instrumental goals' and the latter is 'driven by the desire for the subjective, personal truth usually for its own sake' (2005: 1213). Ewenstein and
Whyte (2007b), studying architectural work, argue that aesthetic knowledge is 'embodied' and 'goes beyond words' and that aesthetic knowledge
is capable of opening up a 'conceptual space' where knowledge emerges
in the interaction between materials and actors. Aesthetic knowledge
may then be conceptualized as a form of *intuition*, a mode of thinking
that extends outside of the 'rational' domain of thinking (Khatri and Ng,
2000; Korthagen, 2005; Sinclair and Ashkanasy, 2005; Dane and Pratt,
2007). The use of such aesthetic knowledge is eloquently captured by
Guve (2007), speaking about the event when one is finally convinced
about something:

> Philosophers like Gilbert Ryle and Ludwig Wittgenstein claim that
> neither conviction nor doubt is matter of choice. Individuals cannot
> choose to be convinced if they are not. In this sense, judgment is a per-
> ception, something exercised in situations where the premises cannot
> tell a person what to do next, where a logical, deductive conclusion is
> simply not available. Further, when conviction does emerge, it is not
> concerned with parts but with the whole. When the sun eventually
> rises, it shines over the entire field. (Guve, 2007: 128)

Intuitive thinking does not emphasize the parts but the whole; it is a form
of synthesis, a bringing together of heterogeneous components such as
information, emotionality and ambition in the process of selection and
choice. Aesthetic knowledge is then what is capable of contributing a
complementary form of thinking. Work in organizations is not only

determined by what Bruner (1986) calls 'logico-scientific knowledge' but is also strongly influenced by aesthetic knowledge.

The concept of art

Instead of providing some lexical definition of art, the concept will here be approached from different angles in order to point at the complications derived from aiming to pin down one single and universally valid definition of art. One of the first things to notice is that writings on art and aesthetics are rarely formulating 'theories' in the conventional sense of the term. Instead, aesthetic theory is a specific genre of essay wherein the concept of art is continually being rephrased and examined from new perspectives. The second thing to notice is that the function of art and its social position are envisaged very differently by various authors. For instance, in Deleuze's (2004: 134) view of art, art is in essence joy and creation: '[T]he essence of art is a kind of joy, and this is the very point of art. There can be no tragic work because there is a necessary joy in creation: art is necessarily a liberation that explodes everything, first and foremost the tragic.' Adorno, on the other hand, the foremost representative of critical theory, conceives of art as what 'estranges' (to use Shklovsky's [1990] term) reality: 'Among artists of the highest rank, such as Beethoven and Rembrandt, the sharpest sense of reality was joined with estrangement from reality' (Adorno, 1997: 9). A radical position is formulated by the literature theorist Shklovsky, who stresses the process of creativity at the expense of the final product, the artefact of art: 'Art is a means of experiencing the process of creativity. The artefact itself is quite unimportant' (1990: xix). Similarly, for John Dewey, art is constituted in the experience wherein matter and meanings become aesthetic:

> Art is a quality that permeates an experience; it is not, save by figure of speech, the experience itself. Esthetic [sic] experience is always more than esthetic. In it a body of matter and meanings, not in themselves esthetic, become esthetic as they enter into an ordered rhythmic movement toward 'consummation'. (1934: 329)

That is, art is never solely aesthetic but is instead constituted at the nexus of various resources and human experiences. 'Where object and subject touch each other, there is life,' Goethe said in a passage (cited in Kramer, 1990: 26) that shares with Dewey the emphasis on the encounter between the work of art and the spectator. One of the problems with art, in Dewey's (1934) view, is that it originates from certain human conditions and experiences but as soon as a work of art is canonized it loses its connection with this domain and time. For instance, we learn from history that the initial reception of a work of art or a broader movement (e.g. Impressionist painting) is not always affirmative. Dewey offers some examples of how the Impressionists were reviewed by an American critic in the Armory exhibition in 1913: Cézanne was portrayed as 'a second-rate Impressionist who had now and then fair luck in painting a moderately good painting'; van Gogh was 'a moderately competent Impressionist who was heavy-handed, and who had little idea of beauty and spoiled a lot of canvas with crude and unimportant pictures'; Matisse 'relinquished all respect for technique, all feeling for his medium; content to daub his canvas with linear and tonal coarseness. Their negation of all that true art implies is significant of smug complacency … They are not true art but feeble impertinences' (all cited in Dewey, 1934: 306. See also Bourdieu, 1993: 247–9, on the reception of Manet in French cultural life). It is easy to poke fun at past accounts that, over the course of time, have 'proven' to be mistaken, but what is noteworthy with these accounts is that it is not straightforward to evaluate artistic works. What Dewey shows is that art cannot be examined and understood simply on basis of common-sense categories and personal preferences but that there is a need for an elaborate vocabulary and the ability to locate art in its historical and cultural context.

One such more qualified attempt at understanding painting is Merleau-Ponty's (1993a; 1993b) analysis of Cézanne's work, capturing the creative painter's ability to transcend mere representation and to paint 'autofiguratively':

> The painter's vision, is not a view upon the *outside*, a merely 'physical-optical' relation with the world. The world no longer stands before him through representation; rather it is the painter to whom the things of the world gives birth by a sort of concentration or coming-to-itself of the visible. Ultimately the painting relates to nothing at all among experienced things unless it is first of all 'autofigurative'. (Merleau-Ponty, 1993b: 141)

For Cézanne, the painter's work is always to bridge the inner and the outer realities; for instance, colour is the 'place where our brain and the universe meet', Paul Cézanne says (cited by Merleau-Ponty, 1993b: 141). Merleau-Ponty (1993a) points at the problems with moving from mere figurative paintings to the realm of the autofigurative in Cézanne's work:

> His painting was paradoxical: he was pursuing reality without giving up the sensuous surface, with no other guide than the immediate

impression of nature, without following the contours, with no outline
to enclose the color, with no perspectival or pictorial arrangements.
This is what Bernard called Cézanne's suicide: aiming for reality while
denying himself the means to attain it. (Merleau-Ponty, 1993a: 63)

Cézanne's work is then emerging as an attempt at moving beyond
the ready-made modes of artistic expression, aiming to find new ways
of portraying the world. Deleuze (2006: 183) underlines the need for
undermining predominant clichés in any artistic work:

A canvas is not a blank surface. It is already heavy with clichés, even
if we do not see them. The painter's work consists in destroying them:
the painter must go through a moment when he or she no longer sees
anything thanks to a collapse of visual coordinates.

Creativity is such a destruction of what is ready-made and already
expressed elsewhere. Osbourne (2003) emphasizes Cézanne's inventiveness in continuously repeating the same procedures:

In Cézanne we have the idea of inventiveness deployed without need
for the concept – as opposed to the word, which does of course appear
on occasion – of creativity. Inventiveness comes through work. None
of this has anything to do with psychological powers of creativity.
Plenty of people have those. But not everyone is Cézanne. Work
involves repetition. Not repetition of the same activity, repetition in
the name not just of seeking an answer to something but of locating,
deepening, embellishing a *problem*: in painting, Chardin's repeated
focusing on a few grapes, Giogio Morandi's endless little bottles
arranged and re-arranged on a shelf, Cézanne's own obsessive pre-
occupation with the capture of nature – and particularly great lumps
of it, repeatedly, such as Mont Saint-Victoirie. (Osbourne, 2003: 520)

'What we call his work was, for him, only an attempt, an approach to
painting,' Merleau-Ponty (1993a: 59) says of Cézanne. Similarly to Viktor
Shklovsky's argument that the creative process *per se* is of interest while
the artefacts produced are of less importance, Cézanne thought of his
work as being a series of engagements to accomplish what Merleau-Ponty
calls autofigurative painting; the artefacts are mere by-products from
this endeavour. The ability to endure long-term engagement is based
on the artist's craftsmanship and his or her love of the work, Dewey
says: 'Craftsmanship in the final sense must be 'loving'; it must care
deeply for the subject matter upon which skill is exercised' (193/1987:
54). Without care for art, there are few opportunities to overcoming the

clichés of art. Still, and somewhat paradoxically, it is not the artefacts (e.g. paintings) *per se* that are of interest to the artist, Merleau-Ponty (1974a) argues; the work as such and the sense of progression towards a more complete and 'authentic' or 'true' form of painting is what is rewarding for the painter (Derrida, 1987): 'The painter works and leaves his wake: and except when he amuses himself with earlier works by discovering what he has become, he does not like very much to look at his work' (Merleau-Ponty, 1974a: 49).

The literature on art and aesthetics does not provide any conclusive model or definition of art; art is what is capable of defamiliarizing the real or is based on the joy of creation; art may be, as in the case of Cézanne, the ability to continuously repeat a specific procedure in order to move beyond the clichés besieging the painter's canvas. Art is a concept that takes the form of a multiplicity, a manifold composed of many parts and many components. Art is what derives from certain times and certain ideas and beliefs, yet is capable of transcending these connections and embodying insights and ideas that are partially independent from local conditions. Similarly, art is complicated to evaluate in absolute terms because works of art are opening up new terrains and territories in their course of action. For the impatient theorist, art may then appear as a weak and feeble construct because it is incapable of being forged within stable categories and remaining confined by lexical definitions. If nothing else such impatience suggests an inability to elaborate with concepts whose usefulness derives from the connectivity rather than their interior stability.

The sociology of art and Luhmann's social systems view of art

The field of art has been a source of interest for sociologists. While art theorists and writers on aesthetics are more concerned with defining the nature of art or establishing taxonomies or standards for how to judge and value art, sociologists tend to be more interested in artists' work in terms of being a professional or semi-professional work located in a system of relations (Becker, 1982), constituting a social system (Luhmann, 2000), a field (Bourdieu, 1993), or, more generally, being a specific form of production (Peterson and Anand, 2004). Zolberg (1990) dedicates considerable effort to define a 'sociology of art' *vis-à-vis* other disciplines. For Zolberg (1990) art is a 'social process' and needs to be examined as such. Thus, in the sociology of art there is little interest for romantic ideas conceiving of art as the product of talent or even genius; instead, it is the mechanisms and structures underlying such ideas and other ideas regarding the nature and qualities of works of art that are carefully examined and revealed by sociologists. Howard S. Becker's much-cited book *Art Worlds* (1982) is one study of this category. Becker, locating himself in the 'Chicago tradition' of sociology and symbolic interactionism represented by, for instance, Herbert Blumer (1969) and Everett C. Hughes (1958), is concerned with being able to report detailed empirical data on the subject matter. *Art Worlds* strongly emphasizes the collective and collaborative characteristics of art. Many groups of artists, and especially composers, choreographers and film directors rely on the collaboration of other groups of specialists; composers on musicians and music directors, choreographers on dancers, and film directors on actors, photographers, and a great variety of experts being responsible for specific activities during the work. Becker's (1982) study is empirically grounded, filled with anecdotes and notes on personal experiences (including his own work as a professional piano player and stories from his wife's ceramics classes), but is nevertheless fairly untheoretical; Becker does not aim to formulate a theory of 'art worlds' but rather seeks to delineate the various actors, positions and relations in various art worlds. For instance, his distinction between 'integrated professionals', 'mavericks, 'folk artists' and 'naïve artists' (Becker, 1982: 226–71) is a well-known typology capturing the whole range of artistic work from the widely acclaimed art celebrities to the idiosyncratic and vernacular works of local artists decorating their gardens or erecting fascinating sculptures (e.g. Simon Rodia's *The Watts Towers* in Los Angeles). In Becker's (1982) account, art worlds are assemblages of interrelated and mutually constitutive 'artistic ecologies' coexisting side-by-side. If there is one single lesson Becker's (1982) work emphasizes, it is about the collaborative and distributed qualities of art work; no artist is an island and it is always socially embedded evaluations of art, articulated by professional critics and the broader public (two categories of actors in art worlds often conceived of as representing antagonist positions, pursuing divergent views of art), that distinguish the talent from the mediocre or dilettante artist. Art worlds are thus, if nothing else, collective accomplishments.

Bourdieu (1993) examines what he calls *the field of cultural production* from the formal sociological framework that he has outlined in a number of publications (Bourdieu, 1990; 1977; Bourdieu and Wacquant, 1992) and applied in the analysis of social processes such as taste and consumption (Bourdieu, 1984), the use of language (Bourdieu, 1991), or to examine various social fields such as the sciences (Bourdieu, 2004) or the economy at large (Bourdieu, 2005). In this perspective, a field is a delimited domain of practice and expertise, constituted by social actors and their relations. All fields are characterized by the struggle over symbolic and economic capital, that is, recognition, reputation and other forms of intangible resources, and financial and other material resources safeguarding a position in the field. All fields are thus fields of forces; of coalitions and collaborations; of antagonism and conflict; of exclusions and inclusions. A field is a dynamic and continuously changing social domain embedded in social practice and verbal and written communication. The field of cultural production demonstrates certain idiosyncrasies but also generic social traits. In comparison to Becker's (1982) empiricist account of art worlds, Bourdieu's concept of field is a theoretical model underscoring the political and conflictual nature of all fields. While Becker (1982) stresses the collaborative qualities of art, the world of art is for Bourdieu primarily characterized by the struggle for recognition, and, at the bottom line, survival as an artist (see Bourdieu and Haake, 1995). While Becker (1982) is explicitly empirical in his account of art worlds, Bourdieu tends to regard artwork as what emerges in a general form of social production, not essentially differing from, say, scientific work or consumption of commodities or services. In order to capture the more specific qualities of art as a social process or entity, we turn to Niklas Luhmann's formal systems theory of art, representing a view of art that examines the idiosyncrasies of art without succumbing to the 'exotic' view of artwork at times observable in the arts management literature, assuming that art is what is fundamentally separated from other forms of social processes and entities.

Luhmann's work differs from Becker's (1982) and Bourdieu's (1993) studies, for instance, since it examines art as a social component *a priori* and not as an empirical or social fact. As a starting point for his comprehensive and complicated analysis of art, Luhmann says that social theory still reproduces a hierarchical image of psychological faculties wherein perception is still located in 'lower positions' in comparison to 'higher, reflective functions of reason and understanding' (Luhmann, 2000b: 5). Luhmann, conceiving of social systems as being constituted by communication and – this is strongly repeated throughout his work – nothing else, says that 'all communication . . . depends on perception' (Luhmann, 2000b: 6). Luhmann proceeds:

Today we know that the external world is the brain's own construction, treated by consciousness as if it were a reality 'out there'. The extent to which perception is prestructured language is equally well known. The perceived world is nothing but the sum total of the 'eigenvalues' of neurophysiological operations. (Luhmann, 2000b: 6)

The concept of perception is therefore central to any system based on communication. Contrary to other theories of communication (notably Habermas's concept of communicative action), Luhmann's view of communication does not exclude misunderstandings and conflict, vagueness, ambiguity and tropes such as irony (Luhmann, 2000b: 11–12); communication *per se* can never promise anything but to produce further communication: Luhmann argues:

> [V]erbal communication operates in a very slow-moving and time-consuming manner. Whatever it communicates must be converted into a temporal sequence of information that amounts to a series of alternating system states. At any time, verbal communication may be arrested or reflexively turned back upon itself. (2000b: 16)

Similar to communication, '[p]erception is intrinsically restless' (Luhmann, 2000: 13); it never ceases. Here art serves the function of a means of communication based on perception: 'Art renders accessible what is invisible without it,' Luhmann notes (2000b: 17). Art thus communicates what words cannot fully capture or what words capture less effectively: 'Art functions as communication although – or precisely because – it cannot be adequately rendered through words (let along through concepts),' Luhmann says (2000b: 19). Art, engaging the observer's perception, thus has a unique ability to move beyond simple evaluative terms (e.g. 'yes'/'no', 'good'/'bad') because it functions outside of language. However, 'in avoiding and circumventing language', art nonetheless establishes a 'structural coupling' between systems of consciousness and communication, that is, the *psychic system* (human beings) and the *social system* (society) (Luhmann, 2000b: 20). Luhman further explicates his position:

> Art makes perception available for communication, and it does so outside the standardized forms of a language (that, for the most part, is perceptible). Art cannot overcome the separation between psychic and social systems. Both types of systems remain operatively inaccessible to each other. *And this accounts for the significance of art.* Art integrates perception and communication without merging or confusing their respective operations. Integration means nothing more than that disparate systems operate simultaneously (are synchronized) and constrain one another's system. (Luhmann, 2000b: 40)

The value of art, as a mechanism in Luhmann's social systems theory, is its capacity of bridging 'psychic systems' and 'the social system' while still keeping them apart. At the same time, art is merging perception and communication in one single artefact or event. However, for Luhmann art does not have a stable innate essence but attains its meaning and operational function on the level of 'elemental events':

> The art system has no reality except at the level of elemental events. It rests, one might say, on the ongoing dissolution of its elemental events, on the transitory nature of its communication, on an all-pervasive entropy against which anything that persists must organize itself. (Luhmann, 2000b: 49)

Art is then, similar to the production of new information in media (Luhmann, 2000a), made legitimate through its ability to produce novel ideas and new artefacts and events. For Luhmann, art is by definition what is new: '[A]rt – once it is differentiated as an autopoietic system – must always present something new, something artistically new; otherwise its communication breaks down or turns into generalized social communication about artistic quality, prices, the private life of artists, their successes or failures' (Luhmann, 2000b: 50). Such a view may explain what is, at times, even regarded as a frivolity outside of artistic circles, the ceaseless search for new means of expressions in artistic communities; it is of the essence of art to enable means of communication that are not yet signified, not yet taking part in the symbolic register. A failure to produce novelty implies that art ceases to function as art in the social system.

Luhmann also introduces the important distinction between first- and second-order observations in his analysis. Using an illustration from economic theory, Luhmann speaks of value and price of a commodity as being representative of first- and second-order constructs. Value is defined in terms of its use-value and price in terms of its exchange value; the two instances are not of necessity related but market prices may fluctuate notwithstanding the value of an entity. Still, the concept of price enables second-order observations so vital to the administration and monitoring of the economy:

> Without market-dependent prices, there can be no second-order observations and thus (as socialist state planning learned the hard way) no specific economic rationality. That is why economic theory must distinguish values and prices, depending on whether it observes an observer of the first or of the second order. (Luhmann, 2000b: 64)

The consumption of art, music or literature, that is, operating on the level of first-order observations, does not demand that one is capable of formulating second-order accounts (that is, judgments) of the piece of art. 'The naked eye does not recognize artistic quality,' Luhmann

(2000b: 80) flatly states (a point also emphasized by Bourdieu, 1993). This position does not of necessity imply an elitist position but simply suggests that to be able to pass judgements one needs to take part in second-order communication. Mingling private impressions and public opinions effectively is a mark of the skilful reviewer's integration of first- and second-order observations. In more general terms, Luhmann argues that the whole literature on social constructivism and the sociological literature known under the label of symbolic interactionism is based on the idea of second-order observations of the self, that is, self-observations:

> Individuals are self-observers. They become individuals by observing their own observations. Today, they are no longer defined by birth, by social origin, or by characteristics that distinguish them from other individuals. Whether baptized or not, they are no longer 'souls' in the sense of indivisible substances that guarantee an eternal life. One might argue with Simmel, Mead, or Sartre that they acquire their identity through the gaze of others, but only on condition that they observe that they are being observed. (Luhmann, 2000b: 93)

In Luhmann's view of art, art attains its social value or its social function through its ability to enhance and speed up communication of what is poorly communicated through other means. Art is inextricably entangled with perception and perception is a human faculty that enables *instantaneous* recognition:

> In a manner that is matched neither by thoughts nor by communication, perception presents *astonishment and recognition* in a single instant. Art uses, enhances, and in a sense exploits the possibilities of perception in such a way that it can present the *unity of this distinction*. (Luhmann, 2000b: 141, emphasis in the original)

Art is then not serving any specific function, as at times is articulated in common-sense thinking and in the critical theory framework, as what is capable of criticizing society from some omniscient point of view, unaffected by predominant social views of society: 'Contrary to widely held notions, the function of art is not (or no longer) to represent or idealize the world, nor does it consist in a "critique" of society' (Luhmann, 2000b: 148–9). Luhmann's view of art is then not even remotely influenced by romantic images of art and artists but integrates art as a social mechanism operating within the system of generalized communication. In Luhmann's view, art has 'no ambition' to 'redeem society' by exercising 'aesthetic control'; art is instead 'merely one of society's functional systems, and even though it may harbor universalistic ambitions, it cannot seriously wish to replace all the other systems or force these systems under its authority' (Luhmann, 2000b: 149).

In summary, Luhmann's sociology is a systems theory view of society postulating that communication is what constitutes and reproduces society. Society is constituted in a process of *autopoesis*, the continuous self-formation in an enclosed system separated from, yet responding to the environment. Art serves as a means for communicating what is poorly communicated through other means; art is what is embedded in perception and perception is a capacity of psychic systems (i.e. human beings) that provides instant impressions capable of speeding up communication. Art is therefore not social critique but is merely a mechanism of communication playing a specific role in the autopoietic constitution of society. However, just because art is conceived of in functionalist terms, it does not mean that works of art *per se* are always of necessity serving their function effectively. For instance, later on in the chapter the concept of kitsch will be examined as 'corrupt art', and that, in Luhmann's vocabulary, is what makes the relationship between first- and second-order observations complicated.

The politics of art: art and agency

While the classic view of aesthetics underlined beauty and the sublime as timeless experiences detached from their context, the political uses of aesthetics have been recognized from the outset. For instance, among the representatives of the Enlightenment movement such as the French encyclopaedia editors, art was regarded as a problem because it was seen as being 'necessarily political' (Goody, 1997). In his article in the *Encyclopédie*, Diderot declared that 'the governors of man have always made use of painting and sculpture in order to inspire in their subjects the religious and political sentiments they desire them to hold' (Goody, 1997: 120). With the French revolution, art of the *ancien régime* was held to 'carry the wrong message' but the *Commission de monuments* agreed to preserve the best. However, by 1790, a group of artists requested the king to 'order the destruction of all monuments created during the feudal regime'. After the collapse of the monarchy in 1792, a period of iconoclasm lasting for three years led to the smashing of statues and the burning of pictures (Goody, 1997: 120–1). Art was playing a central symbolic role in the political turmoil following the French revolution.

While classic aesthetic theory largely dismissed politics as what is excluded from the domain of aesthetics, more recent thinkers such as

Theodore Adorno (1997) have strongly underlined the political content of art. More recently, Bourdieu (1993) emphasizes that politics is always an indispensable component of any artistic field. Bourdieu shows how the dogmatic view of art dominating in the French Academy of Arts in the nineteenth century inhibited an understanding of, for instance, Edouard Manet's work. In the academy, dominated by a certain type of individuals that Bourdieu (1993: 243) names 'homo academicus', a scholastic and authoritarian mode of thinking prevailed and neophytes were always expected to pay careful attention to past accomplishments, learn to reproduce their techniques and themes, and to subscribe to the ideologies inherent to these works. For these guardians of the tradition of art, Manet's work could not be tolerated. Bourdieu provides a series of examples of how Manet was continuously criticized for being ignorant of the canon:

> Convinced that Manet is totally ignorant of the art of painting, critics take pleasure in highlighting his defects, speaking for instance of an 'almost childish ignorance of the fundaments of drawing'; they perceive this style of painting, which banishes middle-range values, as being 'flat' (which led to *Balcon*'s [Manet's painting *Le Balcon*, 1868] creator to be compared to a house painter) and most of all they tirelessly lament this lack of finish. "Manet believes he is making paintings, but in reality he only brushes in sketches," says Albert Wolff in 1869. (Bourdieu, 1993: 247)

Not only was Manet's technique subject to criticism; also the alleged lack of underlying 'morals' in the paintings was addressed. In academic art, the painter was expected to express, in Bourdieu's formulation, 'if not the message then at least a feeling, preferably of a higher nature, and that aesthetic propriety comes from a sort of moral propriety' (1993: 249). Rather than being animated by such legitimate and high-standing 'feelings', Manet's subjects were treated in a 'cold', objective manner, very much devoid of the interiority sought for in academic art (see for instance Crary's, 1999, discussion of Manet's *In the Conservatory*, 1879, emphasizing the emotional condition of being *blasé*). However, as is well known, the *Salon des refusés* became a landmark in the history of modern art. In addition, academic art is no longer endowed with the authority it once had. In Bourdieu's view, Manet and other modernist painters instituted an entirely new field of art and such an accomplishment of necessity produces what Émile Durkheim called *anomie*, a sense of 'normlessness'. Manet and others (e.g. Gustave Courbet) overturned the predominant order of things and replaced an established 'political economy of authority' with a 'polytheist' *Weltanschauung*:

> The constitution of a field is, in the true sense of the word, an *institutionalization of anomie*. This is a truly far-reaching revolution which, at least in the realm of the new art in the making, abolishes all references to an ultimate authority capable of acting as a court of appeal: the monotheism of the central *nomothete* gives way to a plurality of competing cults with multiple uncertain gods. (Bourdieu, 1993: 252–3)

More recently, Ziarek (2004: 2) presented an affirmative view of art as what is capable of serving as a 'transformative force' similar to that of Edouard Manet's art. Drawing on a poststructuralist theoretical framework, Ziarek speaks of art as a 'forcework' capable of bringing together various social forces:

> I approach art as a force field, where forces drawn together from historical and social reality come to be formed into an alternative relationality, I call this transformative even 'forcework' and understand it as a specifically artistic redisposition of forces, in which relations are freed from power structures and the unrelenting, intensifying manipulative drive characteristic of modernity. (2004: 7)

Ziarek (2004) is here defending what he calls a 'postaesthetic understanding of art' wherein art is an 'event' rather than an 'artefact':

> A forcework, art can no longer be conceived as an object but instead should be understood as an event, that is a dynamic, 'force-ful' redisposition of relations inscribed in it through the sociocultural determinations of artistic production. The emphasis here on the 'event' of art does not cancel the inevitable, and necessary, materiality and objectification of art work but points to their double character as both 'act' and shaped product. (Ziarek, 2004: 8)

While there is a significant degree of pessimism on the function of art in the literature, Ziarek (2004) sees art as what is capable of 'contesting power' and 'redefin[ing] freedom'. In a technological society, where everyday life is pervaded by technoscientific entities, procedures and practices, coding and structuring human action, freedom is not given by legal declarations and political decisions but is produced through technological means (see Virilio, 2003). For Ziarek (2004: 16–17), art is what calls our attention to the 'restricted, technicist view of being, experience, and action':

> The work of art, understood as a force field, immediately reveals a different internal momentum and a new set of relationships to society. For one thing, the tensions and constellations of forces render the artwork dynamic, disclosing it as an event, a temporalizing occurrence and a transformative rupture, whose features become recognizable in the notion of an aesthetic object. The idea of art as an object, constitutive of aesthetic reflection and pivotal to the logic of commodification, distorts the most significant aspects of artworks, concealing the very force that makes art artistically and socially significant. As a field of forces, the artwork remains irreducible to its socially dictated functions – discrete objects of aesthetic experience, and commodity – no matter how strenuously these roles are enforced by cultural commerce. At the same time, art's relation to society acquires a transformative force: art does not just reflect and represent society, bearing the power inscriptions of the existing order of things, or at best try to resist and subvert social forms of power. Rather, the artwork has to be thought of as force whose artistic momentum is performative in just this sense: that it redisposes the social relations beyond the power impetus constitutive of them. (Ziarek, 2004: 19–20)

Speaking in Ziarek's (2004) Deleuzian vocabulary, shared with technology theorists such as Wise (1997) and De Landa (1991), art is de-territorialized as a field of forces rather than a delimited, unified and coherent object or ensemble of objects. Art is inherently transformative and political and is capable of shedding light in the human condition in a society increasingly being structured by technological means. Ziarek (2004) also emphasizes the liberating function of art without reducing it to morals or strictly educational objectives; art is what is capable of making us conceive of contemporary society by new means. Thus, for Ziarek (2004) there are clear opportunities for agency in the field of art and art is therefore a resource in the hands of artists and the wider social community. Art is then not only a social system but a set of relations, an assemblage, bringing together heterogeneous entities and processes.

While art theorists such as Ziarek and, previously, Adorno emphasize the political nature of art, the concept of kitsch is exactly that of forms of art (or attempts at producing art) that explicitly abandon all such political and transformative objectives. Instead, kitsch is art devoid of any wider social function than to please and satisfy the audience. Still, kitsch is what is inextricably entangled with art, what serves, in the vocabulary we will use, the *abject* of art. That is, what cannot be accommodated by art but that still cannot be fully excluded.

The problem of kitsch

Art is, in its common-sense conceptualization, what demands a certain authenticity to qualify as art; art cannot be mass produced. The authenticity, or what Walter Benjamin (1973) calls the *aura*, of art is threatened by art being mixed up with non-art elements. Art thus demands a specific degree of purity to subsist *qua* form of art. In the early twentieth century, German-speaking scholars formulated and developed the concept of *kitsch* to denote the situation wherein art is being gradually affected by other social resources. The Austrian author Hermann Broch formulated his view of kitsch in a seminal work first published in 1933. For Broch, kitsch is an elusive concept, one that is complicated to define in absolute terms since kitsch varies and emerges in many forms in different communities. For Broch 'kitsch is certainly not "bad art"' – it is rather what 'forms its own closed system, which is lodged like a foreign body in the overall system of art, or which, if you prefer, appears alongside it' (Broch, 1968: 62). Kitsch is thus what is supplementary to art. What is of specific interest for Broch is the insistence on 'the beautiful' in kitsch; this 'beautiful' is a form of 'evil': 'The kitsch system requires its followers to "work beautifully", while the art system issues the ethical order: "work well". Kitsch is the element of evil in the value system of art' (Broch, 1968: 63). Broch further explicates this point:

> The essence of kitsch is the confusion of the ethical category with the aesthetic category; a 'beautiful' work, not a 'good' one, is the aim; the important thing is an effect of beauty. Despite its often naturalistic character, despite its frequent use of realist terminology, the kitsch novel depicts the world not as 'it really is' but 'as people want it to be' or 'as people fear it is'. (Broch, 1968: 71)

In addition, kitsch is what aims to be beautiful without being willing to create the new, that is, to invest the effort and time to develop creative ideas: 'As a system of imitation kitsch is in fact obliged to copy art in all its specific features. It is impossible, however, to imitate methodically the creative act from which the work of art is born; only the most simple shapes can be imitated' (Broch, 1968: 73–5). The Czech author Milan Kundera argues that Broch's notion of kitsch is a product of the encounter with German sentimental romanticism and the modernist stream of thought in the first decades of the twentieth century. For Kundera, kitsch is then a typical German construct: 'Because in Germany and central Europe the nineteenth century was far more romantic (and far less realistic) than elsewhere, it was there that kitsch flowered to excess, it is there that the word "kitsch" was born, there that it is still in common use (Kundera, 1988: 135). Writers like Hermann Broch and Ludwig Giesz even conceived of archetypical *Kitschmensch*, 'a man of bad taste' (Dorfles, 1968: 15), populating the emerging modern society.

Since Broch's (1968) original work, the concept of kitsch has been further examined. Dorfles (1968: 11–12) says that kitsch is a concept bound up with contemporary taste and thus cannot be used in historical perspectives: '[W]e should not talk about kitsch outside of our own age; or at least no earlier than the Baroque period.' For Dorfles, kitsch means that 'fashion prevails over art' (1968: 17); fashion is here representing ephemeral and commercial values and ideologies devoid of claims to authenticity or originality. More specifically, kitsch represents the movement from one domain to another: kitsch '[o]ccurs each time a single element or a whole work of art is "transferred" from its real status and used for a different purpose from the one for which it was created' (Dorfles, 1968: 17). Such transformations includes the image of *Mona Lisa* on cigarette packages or mass-produced garden gnomes – 'the archetypical image conjured by the word "kitsch" ' (Dorfles, 1968: 14) – decorating suburban gardens. There are thus two major qualities of kitsch: first, its commercial orientation and its willingness to 'please the greatest number at any cost':

> To please, one must confirm what everyone wants to hear, put oneself in the service of received ideas. Kitsch is the translation of the stupidity of received ideas into the very language of beauty and feeling. It moves us to tears of compassion for ourselves, for the banality of what we think and feel. (Kundera, 1988: 163)

Second, kitsch denotes the transfer of elements or whole works of art to new settings and domains. Thus, kitsch operates as a form of synecdoche, where isolated components of works of art are mingling with commercial and sentimental interests. *Mona Lisa*, appearing on a packet of cigarettes, is brought out of the Louvre and located in the centre of commercial culture on the shelves of the tobacconist or in the supermarket. Naturally, a critical theorist like Theodore Adorno has something to say about kitsch. For Adorno (1997: 36), 'kitsch is an idiosyncratic concept that is as binding as it is elusive to definition'. For instance, such elusive qualities imply that kitsch is neither rejecting nor wholly exploiting art but instead serves as something inbetween art and non-art:

> Kitsch is not, as those believers in erudite culture would like to imagine, the mere refuse of art, originating in disloyal accommodation to the enemy; rather, it lurks in art, awaiting ever recurring opportunities to spring forth. Although kitsch escapes, implike, from even a historical definition, one of its most tenacious characteristics is the prevarication of feelings, fictional feelings in which no one is actually participating, and thus the neutralization of these feelings ... It is in vain to try to draw the boundaries abstractly between aesthetic fiction and kitsch's emotional plunder. (Adorno, 1997: 239)

Kitsch is thus not relating to art as science relates to its anomalies produced, that is, as some kind of primary by-product causing great concern for the researchers within a discipline, but is instead living a life of its own in parallel with art and obeying its own principles and own ideologies:

> Kitsch is art that cannot be and does not want to be taken seriously and yet through its appearance postulates aesthetic consciousness. But, however illuminating this may be, it is not adequate, and this applies not only to that broad range of base and unsentimental kitsch. (Adorno, 1997: 315)

While art is, as we have seen, for Adorno that which is capable of de-familiarizing the functioning of society, kitsch is, on the contrary, as Broch, Dorfles and Kundera emphasize, what seeks to accomplish 'sensual satisfaction': 'Sensual satisfaction, punished at various times by an ascetic authoritarianism, has historically become directly antagonistic to art: mellifluous sounds, harmonious colors, and suaveness have become kitsch and trademarks of the culture industry' (Adorno, 1997: 276). Speaking in terms of Luhmann's systems theory view of art as a specific form of communication embedded in perception, one may say that kitsch is what functions properly on the level of first-order observation but is what is rejected as being an overtly sentimental and impure attempt at mimicking art with the intention of pleasing the largest number of individuals in second-order observations. Such a framework may handle the 'problem' of kitsch as being inauthentic art obeying its own principles and objectives. However, although aesthetic theory may pay attention to kitsch as navigating the domain between art and non-art, in practice kitsch is only marginally influencing the commercial 'art world'. Since all authority is based on an affiliation with institutions, the problem of kitsch is eliminated by making kitsch what lacks such affiliations. For instance, artists trained in prestigious art schools cannot by definition produce kitsch. Nevertheless, kitsch remains an interesting concept within the domain of aesthetic theory.

Kitsch, the parasite logic and the abject

In the discourse on kitsch, kitsch is treated as what is mingling and co-aligning with other forms of more 'pure' or determinate forms of aesthetics. Thus we treat kitsch as what is continuously shifting positions, between authentic artistic work and mere copies, between realistic accounts of society and human relations and fantasies and folktales portraying social reality in rosy terms; kitsch is what is indeterminate and fluid (Linstead and Brewis, 2004), what is moving inbetween fixed or predefined positions. That is the problem of kitsch that various writers have struggled with: its ability to move back and forth, to be located in a domain characterized by innate instability and continuous movement at one spot. Kitsch *becomes* kitsch because it mixes two pure aesthetic forms into a *mélange*, a mixture comprising both. Kitsch is then a form of *teratology*, a monstrous assemblage. This epistemological oscillation may be examined through discussing Michel Serres's (1982) notion of the *parasite* as the entity that is capable of maintaining an indeterminate position. Serres (1982), exemplifies this by narrating a fable by La Fontaine about the country rat that visits his cousin the town rat, who in turn is living with the local tax collector (see Brown, 2002, 2004). The two cousins are having dinner together to celebrate their reunion. However, during their meal, the two rats are interrupted by a noise outside the door and the cousins flee. When the town rat suggests that they should return to the meal, the country rat refuses because he cannot stand the fear of being scared anew. He would rather return to the safe countryside where one does not become brutally interrupted during meals. The fable points at a series of parasite relations: the country rat who takes advantage of his cousin, the town rat who lives off the tax collector, and the tax collector who in turn, in one way or another, benefits from the work of others. The noise outside the door is what interrupts the whole series of parasitic relations but is simultaneously what is in its essence parasitical in terms of being 'unorganized' and not determinate. For Serres, human lives – and, for Brown (2004: 395) *organizational* lives – are always dependent upon the activities of parasites, in communication, in relations. Parasites are 'taking without giving'. This Serres calls 'abuse value' (Brown, 2004: 391). Still, parasites mediate relations through their ability to operate inbetween the host and the guest as *the third party*. 'Abuse value' is a form of evil, Serres argues, but it is still indispensable for social relations.

Social relations are bound up with the parasite logic but are generally not recognized as such.

For Serres (1982), the parasite is a metaphor for what he calls the *quasi-object*, the object that is capable of being both a subject and an object and therefore forges relations between actors (see Massumi, 2002: 71ff; Letiche, 2004; Carr and Downs, 2004; Assad, 1999). Money, for instance, in the form of coins and notes or in the form of credit card payments, serves its function to mediate relations without being part of the relation itself, but rather operates between individuals in the form of a token. Yet money is not solely an object but plays a rather active part in the constitution of relationships (see e.g. Le Goff, 1988). Serres (1982: 233) writes: 'The quasi-object itself is a subject. The subject can be a quasi-object.' For instance, a football is a quasi-object in terms of being both an object used when playing but also a subject in terms of being exactly that agent that is enabling for others to join the game as football players. Serres explains:

> Look at the children out there, playing ball. The clumsy are playing with the ball as if it was an object, while the more skilful ones handle it as if it were playing with them: they move and change position according to how the ball moves and bounces. As we see it, the ball is being manipulated by human subjects; this is a mistake – the ball is creating the relationships between them. It is in following its trajectory that their team is created, knows itself and reproduces itself. Yes, the ball is active. It is the ball that is playing. (Serres, 1995a: 47–8)

'[T]he thing is nothing else but a centre of relations, crossroads or passages,' Serres (1982: 39) says. The ball is here serving as a quasi-object:

> This quasi-object is not an object, but it is one nevertheless, since it is not a subject, since it is in the world; it is also a quasi-subject, since it marks or designates a subject who, without it, would not be a subject ... This quasi-object, when being passed, makes the collective, if it stops, it makes the individual. (Serres, 1982: 225)

Serres's notion of the quasi-object has been of central importance for the development of the actor-network theory advocated by sociologists such as Bruno Latour, Michel Callon and John Law (see Latour, 1988) in terms of bringing the object – the actant or non-human – into fruitful relations with humans – scientists, engineers, or anyone.

The parasite is then a quasi-object, the thing or individual who is capable of migrating between different positions and roles. The parasite is by definition neither the host nor the guest but he or she who sneaks in to take the benefit of available resources, to exploit the 'abuse value'. As Clegg, Kornberger and Rhodes (2004: 38) argue, the parasite is therefore bringing noise into the system, for instance, an organization; the parasite 'disturbs and disrupts', emerging in the site 'inbetween' where order becomes 'blurred into disorder' and where noise produces new order. Speaking in terms of kitsch, the parasite logic of being neither the host nor the guest applies. Kitsch is not constituting an aesthetic form in its own right but is rather by definition what is failing to maintain its own aesthetic form, that does not, to quote Spinoza (1994: 75), have a *conatus*, an innate force consolidating into one single, unified form. Kitsch is instead continually moving between the two positions either drawing on certain stylemes or refusing to follow such stylemes.

A concept that effectively makes sense out of what Brown (2002; 2004), drawing on Michel Serres, calls the parasite logic is Julia Kristeva's (1982) concept of *the abject*. The abject is a complicated concept, anchored in Kristeva's psychoanalytic thinking, representing what is part of the individual's I, yet being in opposition to it. Kristeva (1982: 1) writes: 'The abject is not an object [sic] facing me, which I name or imagine ... The abject has only one quality of object – that of being opposed to *I*.' The abject is the part of our psyche that we would like to exclude, that we are ashamed of, that we seek to conceal but that nevertheless in its repressed absence defines who we are. Westwood (2007) – examining stand-up comedy, of all conceivable human activities – speaks of the abject in the following terms:

> [T]hose aspects of the self that are antithetical or challenging to one's preferred, presented and valued sense of self-identity, but which cannot be fully repressed or masked ... The abject is something that is both repellent to and repelled by the person, but which, in the end, cannot be dispatched and has to be incorporated and somehow responded to ... The abject is a kind of in-between category; neither one nor the other, neither filth nor purity, neither fully repressed nor fully integrated. It is material that is not fully rejected but nor is it openly accepted either. It is a liminal space that irritates the system. (Westwood, 2007: 291)

The 'inbetween' nature of the abject, the status of 'neither one nor the other, neither filth nor purity, neither fully repressed nor fully integrated' is compatible with the parasite logic. Kitsch is here what cannot be effectively accommodated by the category of art, yet it cannot be fully excluded because art feeds on what is non-art and kitsch. The parasite logic of kitsch is the mechanism producing an integrated and legitimate position of art as what is pure and uncompromised. Similar to human beings, capable of constituting themselves as ethical subjects through repressing the abject, art is situated in the social fabric as a legitimate resource through repressing what is non-art, that is, kitsch.

Art and perception

Even though some artists have sought to 'resist interpretations' (Sontag, 1966) – for instance, Andy Warhol (cited in Virilio, 2002: 47) claimed famously that: 'If you want to know Andy Warhol, just look at the surfaces of my paintings . . . there's nothing behind it' – sociologists stress the capacity to apprehend and decode works of art as a central component of individual and collective cultural capital. For instance, as Luhmann (2000a) points out, the untrained and uneducated eye is of necessity not capable of formulating credible second-order observations. Like few other human accomplishments, art history and art theory evolves as a coding and interpretation of symbols carefully placed onto the canvas. Therefore seeing is not detached from cognition and culture but is, on the contrary, what is constituted through training and education. John Berger (1972) suggests that there are 'ways of seeing' art that in their own particular way open up for specific interpretations. For Bourdieu (1993), perception is what is always laden with preconceived ideas of what counts as art and capacities for decoding and deciphering art:

> There is no perception which does not involve an unconscious code and it is essential to dismiss the myth of the fresh eye, considered a virtue attributed to naïveté and innocence. One of the reasons why the less educated beholders in our societies are so strongly inclined to demand a realistic representation is that, being devoid of specific categories of perception, they cannot apply any other code to works of scholarly culture than that which enables them to apprehend as meaningful objects of their everyday environment. (Bourdieu, 1993: 217)

Bourdieu (1993: 217) continues: 'The disorientation and cultural blindness of the less-educated beholders are an objective reminder of the objective truth that art perception is a mediate deciphering operation.' Bourdieu (1993: 219) thus agrees with what Nietzsche called 'the dogma of the immaculate perception'. There is no 'fresh eye' but only unevenly distributed capacities for decoding art; 'Any deciphering operation requires a more or less complex code which has been more or less completely mastered,' Bourdieu (1993: 218) contends. Zembylas (2004: 112) here correctly points out that such decoding is not so much a *subjective* procedure but an *intersubjective* process wherein emotionality and language play a central role: 'The results of perception and understanding are often articulated emotionally because the articulation in language of the tacit and semi-subconscious thoughts that constitute the ascribing of meaning and value is only possible to a certain degree,' Zembylas (2004: 112) says.

In this section, addressing the intersection between perception and art, we will separate classic painting and the more modern forms of art such as photography and cinema. Even if these various art forms share basic characteristics, they are the effects of different technologies and practices and they therefore need to be examined as forms of art that enable different ways of seeing.

Painting

Richard Leppert (1996) investigates the history of painting as the use of a rich variety of codes and symbolic systems to portray social reality. Consistent with Luhmann's emphasis on art as a specific form of generalized communication, Leppert (1996: 7) says that images are capable of saying more than words can: '[E]ach image embodies historically, socially, and culturally specific competing, and contradictory, ways of seeing. Precisely on that account, the "contents" of images are not simple substitutes for words, because they call upon so much more than words' (Leppert, 1996: 7). However, being capable of decoding the messages and intentions with paintings demands a familiarity with the thinking and customs of the times and societies portrayed. Without the ability to examine a painting as a socially embedded and historical artefact, a painting tends to naturalize certain ways of seeing. Leppert explains:

> The conventions of painting – manifested in formal organization, the handling of color, light, space, and figural pose, and so on – sometimes have provided the opportunity to 'naturalize' certain ways of seeing, as though what is represented is just the way things and people really *are* or ideally ought to be. For example, the conventions of European portraiture – by definition involving representations of the upper classes – required that the elite virtually never be shown to smile so as to expose their teeth (and usually not to smile at all), but it was quite the opposite for images of the poor, who commonly grin broadly. (Leppert, 1996: 9)

The custom of the upper classes to not expose their teeth is a social fact that may be explained from many perspectives; in terms of the symbolism of smiling and showing emotions, in terms of the economic privileges of certain economic strata of society, in terms of the limited access to modern oral health care and dentists, etc. Smiling is, notwithstanding such potential explanations, a factor to take into account when observing and interpreting a painting from previous historical periods. For instance, Leppert examines Philippe de Champaigne's portraits of Cardinal Richelieu as an example of how the trained eye may see specific codes in a portrait. In a series of portraits, Richelieu is *standing* before the artists. What is remarkable about this pose is that church figures were conventionally painted while seated and it was the prerogatives of kings to stand for their portraits (Leppert, 1996: 158). During the period, Richelieu obviously thought of his political influence and position in France as being comparative with that of a legitimate king. The unwillingness to comply with the tradition is then indicative of the *Realpolitik* in France in the age of Richelieu. In Leppert's account, representation, and above all official representation, is unobtrusively political: '[F]rom the dawn of Western civilization, representation was correctly understood to have an enormous potential to shape the polis; representation at its core was political' (Leppert, 1996: 20).

Another regime of symbolism examined by Leppert is the genre of *Vanitas* still life paintings wherein an assemblage of artefacts is portrayed and where text or symbols underline the vanity of humans to believe they can escape their ultimate fate – death. Inscriptions such as *Mors omnia vincit*, 'Death triumphs over everything', and *Memento mori*, 'Remember death', in these genre paintings were commonly accompanied by a rich variety of symbols denoting death, for instance watches and clocks (Leppert, 1996: 57ff). Another aspect of painting open for interpretation is how social classes are portrayed during different times. Leppert (1996) argues that the lower stratum was painted with brute bodies bereft of any deeper interior refinement, while higher classes revealed some of their higher innate qualities:

In most of Western painting, common men's bodies, as repositories of often raw sensing, define the totality of their being. Their bodies are treated as surface entities deprived of depth; viewers could easily see what little there was to be seen. By contrast, the bodies of the social elite signified principally as vessels less of sensing than of 'soul'. Their bodies possessed surface and depth. Soul, the interiority that produces identity, was made evident but inaccessible. (Leppert, 1996: 184)

The sharp contrast between the classes and social strata in historical societies is then observable on the canvases of the world's fine art museums.
Lower classes denote bodies and primary human demands and folksy
activities, while the higher classes are characterized by their intellectual capacities and refinement. At times the decoding of paintings calls
for even more advanced theoretical frameworks than the reference to
the conventional Western mind–body duality. Leppert (1996) examines
some of the eighteenth- and nineteenth-century paintings of colonial
life or everyday life in exotic places like the Orient, the Far East, China,
or Southeast Asia. In the French Academy of Fine Arts, a doctrine of the
significance of line and colour, useful when interpreting paintings from
the period, was formulated: line (drawing) was commonly characterized
as 'a vehicle of the mind', appealing to 'reason and rationality' (Leppert,
1996: 201). By contrast, colour was judged to be a 'vehicle of the emotions', hence it was 'anti-reason'. As being a pictorial vehicle of affect,
colour was 'feminine, soft and irresponsible'; while line appealed to the
mind, colour appealed to the 'hierarchically lower body'. This is a decep-
tively simply doctrine: lines signify reason and (Western) masculinity;
colours signify emotions and (non-Western) anti-reason embodied in
femininity.* Leppert examines Jean-Léon Gérôme's *The Carpet Merchant*
(c. 1887), showing an open space wherein an oriental carpet merchant
is showing his carpets for sale. In the painting, there is an impressive
range of colours but rather than being a celebration of one of the world's
finest handicrafts and a great source of pride in the Orient, Leppert (1996:
201) argues that Gérôme, in fact, 'feminizes his conception of the Orient'. Too much colouring represents what is in opposition to Western
reason and therefore the carpet merchant, a representative of the Orient, is envisaged as an effeminate figure. Similarly, Gérôme's *The Slave*

---

* One of Paul Cézanne's contributions to modern art was to undermine and render such doctrines irrelevant in what Bourdieu (1993: 234) calls 'scholastic art',
art guarded by teachers endowed with 'statutory authority' granted by institutions such as the French Academy of Fine Arts. Merleau-Ponty (2004: 51) writes:
'Classical doctrine distinguishes between outline and colour: the artist draws
the spatial pattern of the object before filling it with colours. Cézanne, by contrast, remarked that "as soon as you paint you draw", by which he meant that
neither in the world as we perceive it nor in the picture which is an expression
of that world can we distinguish absolutely between, on the one hand, the outline or shape of the object and, on the other hand, the point where colours
end or fade, that play of colour which must necessarily encompass all that there
is: the object's shape, its particular colour, its physiognomy and its relations to
neighbouring objects.'

Market (c. 1867) is a painting rich with xenophobic codes. A male figure, dressed in oriental clothing, is inspecting the teeth of a nude woman with his hands. The inspection of teeth is, Leppert points out, strongly associated with horse-trading in Europe, and therefore this procedure is portrayed to underline the alleged barbarism of the Orient. Gérôme has even painted the hand of the inspecting man disproportionately large to further underline the immorality of the act. In addition, while the male figures are dark-skinned with a stereotypical oriental look, the woman has fair skin and looks more European. It is also important to know that, during the nineteenth century, there was a doctrine suggesting that physiognomy and personal character were related, that is, a close inspection of someone's face, figure and posture could reveal, it was suggested, quite a bit about a person's character. For instance, Samuel R. Wells's *New Physiognomy or, Signs of Character* published in the mid-nineteenth century is representative of this genre of books. For painting, this suggested that there was a close connection between physiognomy and character that could be exploited. Even though Gérôme's paintings are produced during the period when about 10 million people were killed and died under the regime of Leopold II in Belgian Congo and hundred of thousands of humans were killed in other European colonies in Africa, Gérôme is concerned to portray oriental life as remaining archaic and still engaging in a trade that many Europeans strongly denunciated. If nothing else, Gérôme's paintings – very popular during his lifetime but thereafter less admired – are a form of political symbolism, an attempt at making the oriental Other suspicious and potentially dangerous for European values and freedom.

In summary, Leppert offers a great many inroads to the codification of art; art is, as Bataille (1985) said of literature, never innocent. Instead, it captures the thinking of a particular time and draws together various ideologies and beliefs in one single image. Indeed, it can communicate a great many things where words fall short. One excellent example of the ability to see or to communicate what otherwise is complicated to articulate, is Simmel's treatment of the work of Rembrandt van Rijn. The starting point for Simmel's analysis is that the experience of art is not what is objectively true: '[The] primary experience of a work of art, from which these philosophical extensions are nourished, is not to be determined with objective clarity' (Simmel, 2005: 3). Instead, each observer sees, as Berger (1972) emphasizes, different things in a painting. What Simmel appreciates in Rembrandt is his ability to portray life in its 'unity and totality, rather than in its individual content'. Since life takes the form of process, it is complicated to see beyond the individual moments that tend to be captured by family photo albums: birthdays, weddings, Christmas celebrations and occasional holidays. Life then emerges as discrete moments with few connecting points. Simmel writes:

> *Life* ... is an absolute continuity in which there is no assembly of fragments or parts. Life, moreover, is a unity, but one that at any moment expresses itself as a whole in distinct forms. This cannot be deduced further because life, which we attempt to formulate here in some way, is a basic fact that cannot be constructed. Each moment of life is the whole life whose steady stream – which is exactly its unique form – has its reality only at the crest of the wave in which it respectively rises. Each present moment is determined by the entire prior course of life, is the culmination of all preceding moments; and already, for this reason, every moment of life is the form in which the whole life of the subject is real. (Simmel, 2005: 6)

Simmel says that Renaissance art is what is envisaging the individual as a 'self-contained' and 'timeless' essence; then the 'factors of *becoming*' such as 'fate and inner development' are excluded (Simmel, 2005: 9): 'The classical portrait captures us in the moment of its present, but this is not a point in a series of comings and goings, but designates a timeless idea beyond such series: the trans-historical form of the spiritual-physical existence.' Simmel continues: 'The portraits from Florence or Venice certainly do not lack life and soul. There is a general design however, that tears the elements away from the immediacy of their experience and thereby from the order of their succession' (2005: 10). Contrary to this 'atemporal' genre of painting, not fully representing a person but the image of an essence of a person, Rembrandt is masterfully showing the 'course of life' before our eyes:

> In the physiognomies of Rembrandt's portraits we feel very clearly that the course of a life, heaping fate on fate, creates this present image. It elevates us, as it were, to a certain height from which we can view the ascending path toward that point, even though none of the content of its past could be naturalistically stated in the way that portraits with a psychological slant might seek to suggest ... Miraculously, Rembrandt transposes into the fixed uniqueness of the gaze of all the movements of the life that led up to it: the formal rhythm, mood, and coloring of fate, as it were, of the vital process. (Simmel, 2005: 9–10)

In a passage strongly reminiscent of Bergson's concept of *durée*, Simmel says that when we perceive life, we constantly 'perceive a becoming' because 'otherwise it could not be life' (2005: 35). Seeing life is then to perceive movement. For Simmel, this means that paintings much more adequately portray human life than photographs:

> The artist brings movement to its climax ... by knowing how to bind movement into a factually static painting. And only when we make it clear to ourselves that we, too, *vis-à-vis* reality do not 'see' things the way they are captured in the photographic moment, but rather movement as continuity made possible, as suggested, by the fact that our subjective life is itself a lived continuity and not a composition made up of individual moments that were neither a process nor an activity, so then we realize that the work of art offers much more 'truth' than does the photographic snapshot. (Simmel, 2005: 39)

Rembrandt's work is the richest and most moving, Simmel says, when he portrays old people, because 'in them we can see a maximum of lived life' (2005: 11). Rembrandt's ability, in one single image, to bring together the entire *durée* of an individual is a remarkable accomplishment for Simmel. The course of life rarely reveals itself for us in such a manner. Simmel argues that Rembrandt shares this specific ability to see the subjective experiences of a life passing, a quality that other great writers, artists and composers may not share, notwithstanding skills and vision:

> Neither Rembrandt nor Shakespeare confronts the totality of the world with the eternity of its laws and fates, as do Dante and Goethe in an immediate way, and Michelangelo and Beethoven in the reflexes of their subjectivity. Life, in the specific form of its subjective realization of fate, insofar as it can be found within this realization as its basic destiny, is the task which Rembrandt's and Shakespeare's representation brings to a conclusion. (Simmel, 2005: 108)

Simmel finally addresses the question of what one actually sees in a piece of art. Simmel says that to examine a work of art one must accept opposing qualities of art:

> On the one hand, it must leave the work of art as self-sufficient, requiring no borrowed supplement; on the other hand, render intelligible how it came to pass that what we are claiming 'seeing' in a work of art is derived from experience that has taken the sphere of reality as distinct from the artistic realm. (Simmel, 2005: 144–5)

Works are then both self-enclosed *qua* art but also open to interpretations that derive from individual experiences. To fully comprehend a work of art, one must also live, Simmel seems to suggest. In summary, Simmel put forth Rembrandt as an artist capable of arresting the flow of time and the accumulation of experiences without freezing them in a single moment removed from the totality of previous experiences. In Bergsonian vocabulary, one may say that Rembrandt's art brings together the virtual and actual components of a life; that which *has passed* but is still real for the individual, and that which *is*, or will *become*. For Simmel, the remarkable accomplishment of Rembrandt is his capacity to make the virtual and the actual coexist on the canvas. Therefore, his art is more 'true' to human existence than the photograph.

Simmel's critique of the photograph has been, as we will see, formulated in similar terms by other commentators. For instance, the Irish-British artist Francis Bacon (1909–1992) expresses his disregard for the photograph: 'A photograph, basically, is a means of illustrating something and illustration doesn't interest me' (cited in Archimbaud, 1993: 12). Bacon is consequently critical of art that is 'decorative' and figurative: '[D]ecorating is the opposite of painting, its antithesis. I also loathe painting that tends towards decoration' (cited in Archimbaud, 1993: 23). Elsewhere he repeats this position: 'Painting has nothing to do with illustration, it is in a way quite the opposite' (Archimbaud, 1993: 104). On the other hand, Bacon is sceptical of 'abstract art', which he conceives of as being unable to 'report anything': 'I believe that art is recording; I think it's reporting. And I think that in abstract art, as there's no report, there's nothing other than the aesthetic of the painter and his few sensations. There's never any tension in it' (Sylvester, 1980: 60). In another publication, Bacon dismisses abstract art for being decorative: '[T]he human figure with its constant changes is very important. It seems to me that abstraction basically reduces painting to something purely decorative' (cited in Archimbaud, 1993: 145). Bacon's contribution to art is, Deleuze argues in his *Francis Bacon: The Logic of Sensation* (2003), that he is capable in following Paul Cézanne in attempting to paint what Cézanne called *the sensation*, that is, what is neither figurative, nor abstract but in a position inbetween – 'an event'. Since painting, for Deleuze (2003: 10), is always 'besieged by photographs' it needs to radically break free of the idea of figuration. For instance, Bacon testifies that he is obsessed with Vélasquez's portrait of Pope Innocent X, a portrait that qualifies as neither figurative nor abstract but being capable of capturing the qualities of the religious leader. Bacons says: '[I] think it is one of the greatest portraits that has ever been made, and I became obsessed by it. I buy book after book with this illustration in it of the Vélasquez *Pope*, because it haunts me, and it opens up all sorts of feelings and areas of – I was going to say – imagination, even, in me' (cited in Sylvester, 1980: 24).

Bacon's own paraphrases of Vélasquez's work are excellent examples of what Deleuze calls 'the sensation'; it portrays innate forces and movements and brings them to the surface of the canvas. In Brighton's (2000: 139) formulation: 'Bacon escaped a way of painting that had its roots in delineation of the inert human body. He worked by synthesis of images, memory and observation rather than the linear analysis of appearance.' Speaking of one of his other paintings, *Figure at a Washbasin* (1976), Bacon argues that what he attempted was to portray not horror but the scream *per se*, the very sensation:

> You could say that a scream is a horrific image; in fact, I wanted to paint the scream more than the horror. I think if I had really thought about what causes somebody to scream it would have made the scream that I tried to paint more successful. Because I should in a sense have been more conscious of the horror that produced the scream. In fact they were too abstract. (Cited in Sylvester, 1980: 48)

The sensation is thus what escapes figuration but still reports a sensation. For Bacon, it is important that the painting is capable of producing this sense of being affected. He says: '[I]t isn't so much the image which matters, but what it can do with you, and what effects some images have on other images' (Archimbaud, 1993: 145). As a consequence, the use of colour becomes central to producing desired effects and Bacon discussed how choices of colour are central to his work: 'It's a very, very close and difficult thing to know why some paint comes across directly onto the nervous system and other paint tells you the story in a long diatribe through the brain' (cited in Sylvester, 1980: 18). One of the principal skills (or even virtues) of the artist is then to follow their 'instinct', to be able to be critical of their own work:

> In working you are really following this kind of cloud of sensation in yourself, but you don't know what it really is. And it's called instinct. And one's instinct, whether right or wrong, fixes on certain things that have happened in that activity of applying paint to the canvas. I think an awful lot of creation is made out of, also, the self-criticism of an artist, and very often I think probably what makes an artist seem better than another is that his critical sense is more acute. It may not be that he is more gifted in any way but just that he has a better critical sense. (Bacon, cited in Sylvester, 1980: 149)

As a consequence, Bacon believes not so much in formal education and training programmes as in working. More specifically, artistic work is a matter of perception, of vision: 'One learns by looking. That's what you must do, look,' Bacon says (Archimbaud, 1993: 153).

In summary, Bacon's work is, Deleuze (2003) argues, capable of transcending the photographic image already projected on the empty canvas; rather than representing abstract or figurative, Bacon operates *in medias res*, inbetween, on the level of intensities, forces, events and movements. Accomplishing these artistic effects demands from the artist a vision and the ability to choose colours to produce these sensations. Just as Rembrandt, in Simmel's (2005) view, transcends the photographic doctrine of 'natural' or 'ambiguous' representation and embodies lived experience – *durée* for Bergson – in his portraits, so does Bacon break with the duality of figuration/abstraction through his concern for the object's innate qualities. As we will see next, the criticism of the photograph articulated by Simmel, Deleuze, Bacon and many others, is also a predominant idea in the writing on photographs.

Photography

The photograph was one of the major technological innovations in the domain of media in the nineteenth century. Early technologies such as the Daguerreotype enabled for the first time an immediate and instant representation of reality. Scholars have paid much attention to the functioning of the photograph and its social implications. Gunning (1995: 19) speaks of the photograph as a particularly 'modern means of representation', standing at the 'intersection of a number of aspects of modernity'. Early accounts of the photograph, like those of the Weimar theorist of urban life Siegfried Kracauer (1995), formulated a critique of the photograph as in fact being incapable of capturing reality. In Kracauer's view, it is the incompatibility between memory and photograph that is problematic: '*Memory* encompasses neither the entire spatial appearance of a state of affairs nor its entire temporal course. Compared to photography, memory's records are full of gaps' (Kracauer, 1995: 50, emphasis in the original):

> Photography grasps what is given at a spatial (or temporal) continuum; memory images retain what is given only insofar as it has significance. Since what is significant is not reducible to either merely spatial or merely temporal terms, memory images are at odds with photographic representation. From the latter's perspective, memory images appear to be fragments – but only because photography does not encompass the meaning to which they refer and in relation to which they cease to be fragments. Similarly, from the perspective

of memory, photography appears as a jumble that consists partly of garbage. (Kracauer, 1995: 50–1)

In Kracauer's view, the photograph captures everything while memory recalls what is significant. Thus, the photograph is always providing more than needed and is therefore incompatible with memory. Kracauer also formulates a social critique of the use of photography to depict social life without accompanying explanations that would enable a broader understanding of social life:

Never before has a period known so little about itself. In the hands of the ruling society, the invention of illustrated magazines is one of the most powerful means of organizing a strike against understanding. Even the colorful arrangement of the images provides a not insignificant means for successfully implementing such a strike. The *continuity* of these images systematically excludes their contextual framework available to consciousness. The 'image-idea' drives away the idea. The blizzard of photographs betrays an indifference towards what the things mean. (Kracauer, 1995: 58)

For Kracauer, the photograph is not a blessing but is instead what is potentially deceiving and what is hindering rather than enabling social conversations. Such critiques have been rephrased by later commentators. Vilém Flusser (1983/2000) formulates what he calls 'a philosophy of photography' sharing many themes with Kracauer (1995). In Flusser's historiography, human history begins with images, paintings or symbols carved into wood or stone. This social practice led to what Flusser calls 'idolatry', the 'the faithfulness of images', manifested in the belief that images represent reality. With the invention of writing, 'a new ability was born called conceptual thinking, which consisted of abstracting lines from surfaces, i.e., producing and decoding them' (Flusser, 1983/2000: 11). Writing enabled an abstract understanding of images, but it also produced what Flusser called 'textolatry', a 'faithfulness to texts' similar to the idolatry preceding the textolatry. Photography, Flusser (1983/2000) argues, represents a third level of abstraction operating on the level of rendering texts more abstract. Beginning in the mid-nineteenth century, the invention of photography is for Flusser '[a] historical event as equally decisive as the invention of writing'. He continues: 'With writing, history in the narrower sense begins a struggle against idolatry. With photography, "post-history" begins as a struggle against textolatry' (1983/2000: 18). For Flusser, the camera is a tool, an 'extension of human organs' capable of producing images. In addition, the camera is an apparatus programmed – a central term in Flusser's thinking – to provide a certain number of opportunities:

> Photographs are intentionally produced, negatively entropic clusters. Negative entropy can be called 'information'. From the perspective of formal consciousness, photographs are information intentionally produced from a swarm of isolated possibilities. Thus, photographs differ in principle from prehistoric images. Prehistoric images are worldviews (copies of the environment). Photographs are computer possibilities (models, projections onto the environment). (Flusser, 1983/2002: 129)

'In the world of apparatus', Flusser says, 'all "waves" are made up of grains, and all "processes"' are made up of punctuated situations' (1983/2000: 67). For Flusser, the camera is thus not so much a 'tool' as a 'plaything'. Therefore a photographer is 'not a worker but a player: not *Homo faber* but *Homo ludens*', Flusser (1983/2000: 26) says. Flusser thus defines a photograph as '[a]n image created and distributed by photographic apparatus according to program, an image whose ostensible function is to inform' (1983/2000: 76). This is not a common-sense definition but includes a series of concepts – 'apparatus', 'programme', 'images', 'inform'/'information' – denoting specific qualities or processes in Flusser's media and communication theory. For Flusser, the photograph is by no means an uncomplicated representation of the world; instead, it is an image on a high level of abstraction that needs to be decoded and explained itself. Flusser (1983/2002) also emphasizes the difference between former images and photography in terms of what he calls 'imagination' (abstraction) and 'visualization' (actualization of possibilities provided by the apparatus):

> They [photographs] are not actually surfaces (like the prehistoric and historical surfaces), but are rather mosaics. Thus, to be more exact in speaking about photographs, we should not say imagination, but visualization. For imagination is the ability to step back from the environment and create an image of it. In comparison, visualization refers to the ability to turn a swarm of possibilities into an image. Imagination is the consequence of an abstraction from the environment. Visualization is the power to concretise an image from possibilities. (Flusser, 1983/2002: 129)

Contrary to common belief, the photograph is not capable of explaining anything; on the contrary, it is what needs to be explained itself. Flusser exemplifies with reference to an illustrated newspaper article where the

photograph is playing the role of denoting the text: 'It is not the article that explains the photograph, but the photograph that illustrates
the article. This reversal of the text–photo relationship is typically postindustrial and renders any historical action impossible' (1983/2000: 60).
Flusser says that this is a fallacy of what he calls postindustrial society – to
believe that photographs have the capacity to either be self-explanatory
or explain texts. Moreover, photographs are capable of denoting different things, depending on the setting wherein they are located. They are
signifiers shifting their meaning when migrating:

> The photograph of the moon landing, for example, can slip from an
> astronomy journal to a US consulate, from there onto an advertise-
> ment poster for cigarettes and from there finally into an art exhibition.
> The essential thing is that the photograph, with each switch-over to
> another channel, takes on a new significance: the scientific signifi-
> cance crosses over the political, the political into the commercial, the
> commercial into the artistic. (Flusser, 1983/2000: 54)

This renders the analysis of photographs a practice embedded in contingencies and local conditions; one may say, following Mikhail Bakhtin
(1981: 293–4), that the photograph is *heteroglot*, attaining its meaning in
association with other symbols and resources. This underlines Flusser's
(1983/2000) central idea that photographs are not primarily objects but
carriers of information; their intention is '[n]ot to change the world but to
change the meaning of the world. Their intention is symbolic', Flusser
suggests (1983/2000: 25). He continues:

> Photographs are silent flyers that are distributed by means of repro-
> duction, in fact by means of the massifying channels of gigantic,
> programmed distribution apparatuses. As objects, their value is neg-
> ligible; their value lies in the information that they carry loose and
> open for reproduction of their surface. (Flusser, 1983/2000: 56)

In Flusser's account, photographs are outcomes from the use of programmed apparatuses, providing a fixed set of opportunities; photographs are third-level abstractions and therefore need to be explained
rather than be regarded as representations of the world. In addition, they
are operating on an informational and symbolic level and can therefore
be circulated in various settings and communities. As such, photographs
are never innocent; they are always produced by symbolic-machinic
assemblage providing certain opportunities but also imposing specific
limitations.

In a classic essay, Susan Sontag articulates her concerns regarding the nature and effects of photography. Sontag says, in accordance with Flusser's (1983/2000) thinking, that one of the principal features of photographs is that we are capable of observing a great number of photos but we are less capable of interpreting and understanding what they actually mean or even what they portray:

> This very insatiability of the photographing eye changes the terms of confinement in the cave, our world. In teaching us a new visual code, photographs alter and enlarge our notions of what is worth looking at and what we have a right to observe. They are the grammar and, even more importantly, an ethics of seeing. Finally, the most grandiose result of the photographic enterprise is to give us the sense that we can hold the world in our hands – as an anthology of images. (Sontag, 1973: 3)

As we have increasingly learned to take photographs for granted as components of the reality of everyday life, Sontag argues, we tend to regard them as what transparently represents reality. While a painting can never be more than a 'narrowly selective interpretation' (Sontag, 1973: 6), there is 'something predatory in the act of taking a picture' because the photograph means 'having knowledge of them [subjects being photographed] they can never have' – 'it turns people into objects that can be symbolically possessed' (Sontag, 1973: 14). Sontag also addresses the function of photography to report social events and occurrences as it if was a neutral or detached medium depicting social reality. Sontag points especially the problem that a flow of photographs portraying human misery leads to the naturalization of suffering:

> The vast photographic catalogue of misery and injustice throughout the world has given anyone a certain familiarity with atrocity, making the horrible seem ordinary – making it appear familiar, remote ('it is only a photograph'), inevitable. At the time of the first photographs of the first Nazi camps, there was nothing banal about these images. After thirty years, a saturation point may have been reached. (Sontag, 1973: 20–1)

The problems with the extensive use of photographs are two-fold. First, photographs *per se* are never the neutral observations that their spokesmen may claim or that common-sense thinking believes. Instead, photographs are 'clouds of fantasy and pellets of information' (Sontag, 1973: 69). Second, the photographs themselves are incapable of explaining themselves and what they are portraying; they are 'inexhaustible invitations to deduction, speculation, and fantasy' (Sontag, 1973: 23). Sontag here claims that 'only that which narrates can make us understand' (1973: 23). In a passage echoing Kracauer's concern, Sontag says that industrial societies turn their citizens into 'image-junkies', which is 'the most irresistible form of mental pollution' (Sontag, 1973: 24). Even though the practice of photographing was in the hands of former painters until well into the second half of the nineteenth century (Kracauer, 1995: 53), Sontag refuses to refer to photography as an art at all; it is rather – like language – a medium in which art may be made (Sontag, 1973: 148). This connection between art and photography has been a standing concern in the analysis of photography. 'Photography has been', Barthes (1981: 30) says, 'and still is, tormented by the ghost of Painting'. In Barthes' view – diametrically opposed to Kracauer and Sontag's – photography is, contrary to language that by its very nature is 'fictional', 'authenticity itself': 'Language is by nature fictional; the attempt to render language unfictional requires an enormous apparatus of measurement. We convoke logic, or, lacking that, sworn oath; but the Photograph is indifferent to all intermediaries: it does not invent, it is authentication itself' (Barthes, 1981: 87). Such qualities may not have been firm ground for any claims of being art, but they have been useful in other domains of social organization. Gunning (1995), for instance, examines how the photograph was integrated into the police work and juridical procedures. The classic 'mug-shot' was a product of the latter half of the nineteenth century, when the police had learned to appreciate the new media of representation. Gunning underlines the importance of new juridical doctrines: 'The nineteenth century witnessed a rearrangement of the hierarchy of juridical proof, as the value previously accorded to witness testimony was replaced by the scientific reputation of the analysis of indices' (1995: 22). In this new doctrine, the body was conceived of in new terms, as what becomes immaterial and what may be circulated in the mobility of modernity. Here, the photograph became a legitimate means for safeguarding justice in police work and court procedures.

The literature on the photograph demonstrates some ambiguities in its attitude. On the one hand, it is 'hyperreal' in capturing more than is needed for the memory to function properly; on the other hand, it obscures and conceals in terms of failing to narrate its own images. Perhaps the photograph is best conceived of in the terms expressed by Sigmund Freud who spoke of the photograph and the gramophone (which will be discussed in the fourth chapter) as a 'materialization of memory', a view also advocated by Marshall McLuhan who thought of media as the extension of the human body. Freud writes:

> With every tool man is perfecting his own organs, whether motor or sensory, or he is removing the limits to their functioning. In the photographic camera he has created an instrument which retains the fleeting visual impressions, just as the gramophone disc retains the equally fleeting auditory ones; both are at the bottom material- izations of the power he possesses of recollection, his memory. (Freud, cited in Mowitt, 1987: 173)

At the end of the day, art is materialization, a portrayal of human think- ing and social practice; as such it may play an effective role in day-to-day organizing.

Art and organization

Introduction: Classifying art

One noticeable feature of this chapter is that there has been no artic- ulation of formal or lexical definitions of art. One of the reasons for this is that such definitional work is part of what Becker (1982) calls art worlds. Of course, there are a wide variety of definitions of the arts and related concepts such as 'artists', 'creative industries' and so forth (DiMaggio, 1987; Caves, 2000). Sociologists like Bowker and Star (1999) have shown that systems of classification and codification are central to the organization of the modern society – they are the infrastructure of everyday life, in many cases unattended to and thus taken for granted and rendered unproblematic. Just like scientists are trained to 'sort things out' (Roth, 2005; Sommerlund, 2006), artists are expected to define themselves in specific categories formulated by the regional, national or international administrative apparatus of the culture sector. Like all classification systems, these categories are inconclusive and 'leaky', not being able to fully compartmentalize separate categories of art. Naturally, hybrid forms of art, poorly adapted to pre-existing administrative pro- cedures, continuously emerge. However, before delving into procedures of classification and administration – a major concern for culture policy- makers, administrators and arts management researchers, as we will see – two definitions of art are presented, namely Dickie's (1997) 'Institutional theory of art' (cited in Macnaughton, 2007: 92) and DiMaggio's (1987). It is not assumed that Dickie's or DiMaggio's definitions are more adequate or useful than other formal definitions but they are used to demonstrate in what terms art and artists are defined. Dickie's definition includes five components:

1. A work of art is an artefact of a kind created to be presented to an artworld public.
2. An artist is a person who participates with understanding in the making of a work of art.
3. A public is a set of persons the members of which are prepared in some degree to understand an object which is presented to them.
4. The artworld system is the totality of all artworld systems.
5. An artworld system is a framework for the preservation of a work of art by an artist to an artworld public. (Cited in Macnaughton, 2007: 92)

DiMaggio, for his part, defines art accordingly: 'By *art work* I refer to high and popular cultural products in the visual arts, the performing arts, and literature' (1987: 441). Art is then defined and institutionally located in rather loose terms; both Dickie's and DiMaggio's definitions are capable of hosting a wide range of artistic activities and efforts.

One of the first types of organized artwork is the administrative and political work to formally define what art and artists are. DiMaggio (1987) examines what he calls *artistic classification systems* (ACS), typologies for classifying the arts, that may be studied, DiMaggio (1987) suggests, in four dimensions. First, art is '*differentiated* into institutionally bounded genres'. Second, 'they [ACSs] vary in the extent to which genres are ranked *hierarchically* by prestige'. Third, 'systems differ in the extent to which classifications are *universal* or differ among subgroups of members', and, fourth and finally, 'ACSs vary in the extent to which boundaries among genres are *ritualised*' (DiMaggio, 1987: 441, emphasis in the original). DiMaggio (1987: 449) also differentiates between three types of ACS: *commercial, professional* and *administrative* classifications. While commercial classifications are defined to satisfy commercial interests (e.g. the sorting of literature into genres in a bookstore), professional classifications are '[m]ost prevalent where the artistic field is relatively autonomous' (DiMaggio, 1987: 451), that is, when artistic work is monitored and controlled by artists and functionaries (e.g. curators and critics) in the artistic field. Administrative classifications, on the other hand, are:

> [d]istinctions among genres created by the state. Such classification has three forms: classification of art ancillary to the performance of routine state functions [separating art and 'non-art'], regulatory

policies that influence artistic classification indirectly, and explicit classifications in the administration of cultural policy. (DiMaggio, 1987: 451)

Heikkinen (2005), examining the use of administrative classifications, points out that such classifications are of central importance for artists because, in many Western countries, a significant number of artists are funded by the state, regional governments, or the municipalities, and these administrative and political bodies rely on the formally enacted categories and definitions of what counts as art and accompanying performance criteria (that is, how to distinguish between 'bad' and 'good' art). Heikkinen continues: 'The categorization marks the boundaries for what are to be included as areas of art or groups of artists, and the allocation of resources according to these categories marks the relative status of these areas' (2005: 330). Speaking more specifically of the four Nordic countries Denmark, Finland, Norway and Sweden, Heikkinen (2005) points at the similarities but also some differences between the cultural policies the four countries. In all four countries, the classification system is based on a complex interaction between a number of actors and institutions: 'The administrative definitions are generated through the interaction of several interests and actors, acting in the framework created by cultural policy, legislative and administrative regulations and the structural features of decision making' (Heikkinen, 2005: 330). The outcome is a national classification system formulated in order to guide decision-makers and administrators, but in fact also structuring the entire art field. Heikkinen shows that while, for instance, Sweden is content to use five categories of art (separated into the categories of 'author', 'visual arts', 'composers', 'musicians and singers' and 'theatre, dance and film'), Denmark has six categories, Finland thirteen, and Norway has enacted no less than twenty-four categories and subcategories to classify art and artists. Just as Bowker and Star suggest, no classification system is fully conclusive but it is always 'the product of continuing negotiation and exchange' (1999: 158). For instance, in Finland, the case of circus and vaudeville artists is an illustrative case. For a long period of time, this group of artists have been lobbying to be included in the formal categories but not until 1999 did the Arts Council of Finland set up a task force to investigate the request. Similarly, in the UK, photography did not qualify as art until the end of the 1970s and architecture even later (Roodhouse, 2006: 50). In Heikkinen's (2005) account, the arts, arts management and arts policy in the Nordic countries are what are jointly enacted in complex collaboration between artists' organizations and public and political bodies. The classification of the arts does not fall from the sky; it is socially enacted, thereby producing inclusions and exclusions that are abiding concerns and a source of ongoing controversies and struggles.

Roodhouse (2006), speaking of the UK and international standards, also addresses classification procedures. Contrary to Heikkinen (2005), he is very concerned about the ineffectiveness caused by inadequate or faulty definitions: 'At best, the data collected and used to inform management at micro and macro levels and to provide evidence for policymaking is inaccurate; at worst, it is seriously unreliable,' Roodhouse argues (2006: 48). Roodhouse (2006) lists a long range of definitions and classification procedures enacted in the UK and internationally, for instance by UNESCO, and shows how they, at best, overlap, but are never fully compatible, thus leaving room for local interpretation and application. In the recent interest in 'creative industries', defined by the British Department for Culture, Media and Sports in 1998 as 'those activities which have their origin in individual creativity, skill, and talent, and which have a potential for wealth and job creation through the generation and exploitation of intellectual property' (Roodhouse, 2006: 52), this confusion regarding the nature of the arts and the status of artists may be further propelled and accentuated. Roodhouse thus calls for a more integrated and comprehensive classification system, valid on both the international and national level. Roodhouse writes:

> [N]ot only do we have definitional confusion and inconsistencies at every level, but we also have confusion as a result [of] inconsistent, unreliable data and little comparable research. Other industrial sectors would not tolerate such a position, nor would managers, who rely on high quality management information to aid operational and strategic decisions. (2006: 56)

In summary, both Heikkinen (2005) and Roodhouse (2006) make us pay attention to the infrastructure of the art world, showing how what counts as art (thereby being qualified for public grants and financial support) is defined in social interaction between a number of administrative, political and representative bodies. Art is never, just like any other social practice, a self-enclosed and confined domain, but is instead what is fundamentally open towards social influences and interpretations.

Art and work

The first stream of work to be examined here is studies addressing the use of art in organizations. As has been known for centuries, art may play a political role in portraying the social order and its influential groups in positive ways. The church and the merging national states learned early to make use of art to produce desirable social effects. In modern times, the explicit use of art in propaganda was perhaps first widely used on a broad basis in the fascist European regimes in the interwar era. For instance, Lyotard (1991: 75) says that the Nazis operationalized Richard Wagner's (1849/2001) idea of a *Gesamtkunstwerk,* a 'total work of art' in their propaganda. What the Nazis and other fascist regimes sought to accomplish was, in Georges Bataille's (1945/1992: 159) formulation, a sense of 'transcendence', a celebration of fascist ideology as being 'universal'. Although the aesthetics of the fascist era is a notorious case, the concept of using arts and other means of representation to shape social reality was employed elsewhere during the interwar period and still lives on today (see e.g. Adler's [2006] recent paper for a particularly enthusiastic account of how 'creative' artists can help corporations maintain their 'competitive edge'). For instance, Gibson (2002) examines the New Deal cultural policy in the USA during the Depression years in the 1930s. Gibson, making references to Foucault's concept of 'governmentality', says that the architects of these policies '[h]oped to produce citizens capable of self-regulation in a way that would ensure their active and productive contribution to the nation' (2002: 280). Underlying the policies was then a 'welfarist rationality' constructing citizenry as 'consisting of free individuals responsible for their own self-management', very much in opposition to the fascist government-oriented ideology. Consequently, the Federal Art Project (FAP), inaugurated in 1935 as part of the New Deal programme, aimed at 'educating' its citizens to pursue liberal and democratic ends. Gibson writes:

> Art programs educated the citizenry to manage itself in relation to a certain set of desirable norms. During the 1930s in the United States, these norms were set in relation to the construction of a free citizen who had the capacities to participate in the democratic reformism of New Deal America. (2002: 281)

FAP had a number of objectives and the director, Holger Cahill, declared in 1935 that 'the aim of the project will be to work toward an integration of the fine arts with the daily life of the community, and an integration of the fine arts and practical arts' (cited in Gibson, 2002: 282). Gibson argues that FAP was 'atypical' for the New Deal programme in terms of operating 'not only for the immediate goal of financial relief, but with a greater social goal in mind' (2002: 282). At its peak, FAP came to employ more than 5,000 artists in various projects. Underlying the programme, notwithstanding the declaration not solely to evaluate short-term effects, was an educational credo and an instrumental view of the role of art in society. For instance, Irving Marantz, an FAP artist-teacher, commented that art was 'a great therapy that could turn juveniles (and by implication, other misfits) "into useful social beings"' (Gibson, 2002: 283). Art and art training programmes aimed primarily at schooling the citizens in widely agreed, socially enacted norms and values.

This instrumental view of art in society is addressed by other scholars examining 'arts and society' projects and programmes. Belfiore (2002; 92) argues that cultural policy supporting the political objective of 'urban regeneration' in European cities is shaped by the idea that public expenditure in the arts is justified by 'the advantages that they bring to the nation'. Examining more specifically the case of the UK, Belfiore (2002) cites a report issued by the British Department for Culture, Media and Sport (DCMS) in 1999, suggesting that 'art and sport, cultural and recreational activity, can contribute to neighbourhood renewal and make a real difference to health, crime, employment, and education in deprived areas' (DCMS report, 1999, cited in Belfiore, 2002: 93). Such policy statements are to be examined against the background of the economic and political changes in the UK in the 1980s, shaped by neoliberal Thatcherite politics and a postmodern concern regarding the definition, value and function of art. Here, the legitimacy of public funding of art institutions and artists was gradually undermined from a number of directions. Belfiore writes:

> The Arts Council was now faced with the task of justifying to the nation the fact that public money was spent according to the aesthetic judgment of small groups of people who could no longer claim the authority for higher artistic judgment ... In the new relativistic cultural climate, many felt that the Arts Council's attempts at bringing high art to the people – based on the assumption that it would 'do them good' – was the product of a paternalistic and patronising attitude that was no longer acceptable. (Belfiore, 2002: 94)

As a consequence, arts policy had to be articulated in new terms. In 1986, the British Arts Council, responsible for the public funding of art institutions in the UK, declared in a report that 'the arts, in partnership with the local authorities, could "bring new life to inner cities", create new jobs, and "help develop the skills and talents of ethnic minorities and other specific communities"' (Belfiore, 2002: 96). However, these visionary plans for merging social political objectives and culture politics were not easily implemented and put into practice. Unfortunately, Belfiore argues, the 'urban renaissance' hoped for by the Arts Council did not happen (2002: 96). Instead, urban renewal projects were criticized for representing 'a carnival mask' concealing and covering up persisting and growing economic and social inequalities in the population. Among other things that the policy-makers failed to take into account is the inertia of the arts institutions. While museums and art galleries, for instance, often fashion themselves with a vocabulary emphasizing the educational and liberating potentials of arts and art production, in fact, many such institutions have been, Tony Bennett argues, '[e]ffectively appropriated by social elites so that, rather than functioning as institutions of homogenisation, as reforming thought has envisioned, they have come to play a significant role in differentiating the elite from the popular classes' (cited in Belfiore, 2002: 102). Asking museums and art galleries to become political arenas, a function they traditionally, at best, play implicitly and as a secondary role, is to ask for a lot. Belfiore (2002), critical of the 'arts management' role in urban regeneration projects to date, argues that one of the principal concerns with such political ambitions is that they are perceived in overtly instrumental terms, thereby failing to see the full potential of the arts as a social resource. Belfiore concludes that one of the main problems when using art as a source of urban regeneration, operating on the basis of public subsidy and with specific, measurable social returns, is that art is used in an entirely instrumental manner:

> Degraded to the function of mere tool, arts become a matter of 'value for money'. One non-arts professional ... puts this baldly: 'I'm very positive about the use of the arts as long as it's not art for art's sake: it's a tool. You've got to have clear determined aim and objectives, and have an end product'. (Belfiore, 2002: 104)

A similar perspective is taken by García (2004) examining three art events in three cities: Glasgow's European City of Culture programme in 1990, Sidney's art festival in 2000, accompanying the Olympic Games, and an art festival in Barcelona in 2004. These three events were characterized by the arts playing, if not a central role, at least a significant role in the official presentation of the cities and their 'branding' as international art centres. However, again there is a divergence between political rhetoric and visionary articulations and the organization of the actual events. For instance, in Sidney, the ambition of the arts festival was to '[h]elp paving the way towards Aboriginal reconciliations', helping the Australians cope with their colonial history in a meaningful manner. This initiative was appreciated but was also criticized by representatives of indigenous people. For instance, film director Richard Frankland denunciated the 'tokenism surrounding most Aboriginal arts activity showcased within the frame of the [Olympic] Games' (García, 2004: 110). However, García (2004) identifies both positive effects and more lingering concerns regarding the showcasing of entire cities as cultural centres. First, it seems, especially in the widely acclaimed case of Glasgow's City of Culture year programme, that 'art programming' (to use García's term) provides a good platform for 'developing new or strengthening existing collaborations', and that art programming is in fact a critical factor influencing the image of the city or the region, thus 'improving perception of the place and attracting tourists and corporate visitors in the medium to long terms' (García, 2004: 114). On the more negative side can be counted the relatively marginal or complementary function of the arts programme in broader events: art programmes are 'frequently excluded from the event's mainstream promotions and receive insufficient funding to address refined objectives', García concludes (2004: 114). In addition, art programmes, in most cases located in city centres, appear to be events attracting primarily already privileged groups. In summary, using art in promoting particular events or when branding cities or regions is in García's (2004) account not an uncomplicated task. There is a great need for collaboration between various social actors and institutions in order to provide the arts with a more qualified role than being a token in a wider social arrangement or a procedure benefiting already privileged groups.

Speaking of a more practical and immediate organizational level, arts can in fact play a role in the creation of new social spaces previously devoid of arts. Macnaughton (2007) examines the arts in hospitals programme in the UK and, more specifically, studies the use of art in the James Cook University Hospital in Middlesbrough in northern England. Again, an instrumental view of the arts is what guides the policies and the rhetoric but in Macnaughton's (2007) account this does not suggest that such a view is failing to recognize the broader social significance of the arts. The hospital was decorated by a number of artists, working on the shared theme of the voyages of Captain James Cook, the great British explorer born in a small village just outside Middlesbrough. The newly opened hospital was a source of great pride for the local community and a number of interviewees articulated their views of the new hospital. While some were concerned about the costs and the idea of real-locating resources from the health care budget to more artistic pursuits, most of the interviewees liked the idea of using art in the hospital. For instance, a senior clinician (cited in Macnaughton, 2007: 98) pointed at the improved work environment as an immediate effect: 'You walk down the corridors and see all the pictures [and] you feel resuscitated having spent a morning in a busy clinic and that is extremely important'. One of the administrators pointed out that a new and aesthetically stimulating milieu had effects on morale:

> I think a brand new environment raises the morale of people who actually work there because, I think, with old and tatty [furnish-ings] you tend to become depressed and [adopt] a 'couldn't care less' attitude. But when something's nice and bright, I think it makes you feel better. Light and airy, to me, makes me feel better. (Member of hospital staff, cited in Macnaughton, 2007: 98)

In Macnaughton's (2007) study, arts management is given a productive and socially meaningful role as what is capable of bringing aesthetics into new domains and new settings. Not only did the new hospital serve as a landmark for the city of Middlesbrough but it was also designed to provide an environment that was appreciated by both patients and staff. Art here arguably serves a role similar to that articulated and hoped for by Friedrich Schiller; as what serves the greater public in meaningful and productive ways.

Working with art

The field of art provides a number of interrelated positions; one may produce art, distribute art, administrate art, or one may review art-work and write art criticism, etc. Like any other industry, the culture industry and, more specifically, the field of art includes a variety of pro-fessions, occupations and roles ranging from up-stream activities (e.g. the very production and retailing of art materials such as canvases and oil paints, or art schools and education programmes in universities and elsewhere) to the down-stream activities such as art gallery work and art criticism writing. All these activities share the quality of being organized and structured in accordance with specific managerial and administra-tive principles. In the following, some roles in the field of art will be examined in some detail.

Studies of artists' labour markets regularly show that there is an 'over-supply' of artists, especially in metropolitan areas. For instance, in the USA, over the period 1970–90, the number of artists grew at a rate of 127 per cent, a figure substantially higher than the regular civilian labour market, and the rate has continued to be high (Menger, 1999: 542). Adhering to a generic supply-demand equilibrium, artists therefore, despite being higher educated and younger than the general workforce, '[s]how higher rates of self-employment, higher rates of unemployment, and of several forms of constrained underemployment (nonvoluntary part-time, intermittent work, fewer hours of work), and are more often multiple job holders' (Menger, 1999: 545). In addition, there is a substantial 'income penalty' in the market, whereby artists earn comparatively less money than other occupational groups: 'The skewed distribution of artists' income is strongly biased towards the lower end of the range: Artistic careers are and remain risky,' Menger (1999: 553) contends. Notwithstanding these statistical facts, artistic work continues to attract newcomers.

The case of arts marketing

Boorsma (2002; 2006) examines the theory and practice of arts marketing, a 'sub-discipline' in marketing, concerned with fulfilling the 'wants and needs' of actual or potential customers and clients. Boorsma (2002) is critical of the conventional view of marketing and suggests that arts marketing needs to be conceived of in new terms: 'Without denying that the arts fulfil important human needs, it is obvious that this concept – "giving the public what it wants" – is unlikely to appeal to artists and arts organizations', Boorsma argues (2002: 66). The very nature of art, Boorsma says, is based on creativity and creativity cannot restrict itself to pre-existing demands: 'By definition it is impossible to create new – an original – aesthetic metaphor when the artist has to base the process of creation on the generalization about things potential customers want to see or hear' (Boorsma, 2002: 66). Therefore, what Boorsma (2002: 73) calls 'efficiency-oriented marketing' may in fact, rather than promoting the art works, obstruct the functioning of art. In Boorsma's treatment, arts marketing appears as an oxymoron, bridging two opposing processes. In a more recent publication, Boorsma (2006) suggests what she calls a relational view of art marketing wherein art is no longer seen as an 'autonomous phenomenon' but as what is in fact produced in collaboration with the art consumer, assigning him or her a 'co-creative role' in accomplishing artistic work: 'Under the relational view, arts marketing has a direct influence on the accomplishment of the artistic objectives and becomes responsible for the co-creative role of arts consumers' (Boorsma, 2006: 76). As Marcel Duchamp, the great modernist artist contributing to a radically new understanding of art, pointed out, 'it is the viewers who make the painting' (cited in Virilio, 2002: 27). On the basis of a reformulation of art as an autonomous object/phenomenon to being a *co-created event*, Boorsma (2006) proposes the following new definition of arts marketing:

> Arts marketing can be defined as the stimulation of exchange with selected customers, by offering service-centred support for the co-creation of artistic experiences and by building and maintaining relationships with these customers for the purpose of creating customer value and achieving the artistic objectives simultaneously. (Boorsma, 2006: 87, original emphasis omitted)

In a relational view of the arts social practices are redefined.

Managing artistic work

Another category of work in the artistic field is to serve as managing director for art institutions. In the winter of 2005–6, ten managing directors and regional government officials and political representatives in Sweden were interviewed as part of a larger research project examining creativity in bureaucratic organizations (for details of the study, see Styhre, 2007). The interviewees included three managing directors of two major state- and municipality-funded theatres and a smaller suburban theatre company, and three managing directors of two concert halls and an opera house. All the managing directors pointed at the complexities and ambiguities inherent in creative artistic work and emphasized how they had to follow what may be called their 'instincts' and their tacit knowledge when making decisions, thus supporting Sicca's (2000: 147) characterization of 'arts management' as a 'hybrid activity' involving 'aesthetic, management and social issues' and relying on a 'mutual exchange of expertise and experience' – 'the arts manager is an entrepreneur, administrator and leader rolled into one'. One of the theatre directors argues: 'I can only say one thing for sure about the planning of a theatre production: It never ends as first intended' (Interviewee, #1). There is always an openness towards changes in 'the production' (a term used by the interviewees to denote an artistic project such as a play or a series of concerts) until the premiere:

> No matter how much time you dedicate to the repetitions, it is that particular week when everything is tied together and one meets the audience. You talk about avoiding the moment of stress, and you may distribute that work over a period of three years, but there will still be that week where nobody is sleeping. (Interviewee #1)

On the other hand, artistic work demands a long planning horizon; the system does not tolerate quick changes: 'It takes three years from the planning to the premiere in an Opera House' (Interviewee #1). In addition, there were few instituted methods for evaluating quality and artistic creativity and neither the managing directors nor the politicians and administrators were eager to implement such methods. Instead, the nature of artistic work was conceived of as being what of necessity is resisting formal evaluations. The managing director of a concert hall said that defining quality in artistic work is 'a bit like defining God':

> When it comes to cultural activities, that is something you feel in the stomach. You can point at figures on audience statistics and you can show that the press has written this much about you ... but you really feel it in the stomach. That is the most important. You can work against all odds for a year if you have this feeling in the stomach that this will end well. (Interviewee #2)

He also thought that one must take into account that artistic work is not a 'regular commercial product', suitable for quantitative evaluations of quality: 'In an artistic activity, the core must be the message ... It is not a regular commercial product. It is a kind of ideology as well, almost like the Church ... One needs to be aware of what signals one sends' (Interviewee #2). This does not suggest that the managing directors indulged in some complacent 'art for art's sake' ideology; on the contrary, they were very concerned about the financial, political and artistic road marks they had to pay attention to. For instance, the managing director of a smaller suburban theatre company, located in a area characterized by its predominantly immigrant population, pointed at a number of failed productions where political or artistic objectives did not attract an adequate number of visitors:

> In 2003, we had a new manager ... His first production was *Hamlet*. That was the dream of his life: He had always dreamed of doing *Hamlet*. It was terrible. Why should this theatre do *Hamlet*? ... How should we be able to attract the youth [in the suburb] with a production like that? ... It was a disaster. (Interviewee #3)

The other example of a less successful production was when the theatre company decided to play August Strindberg's *Miss Julie* in Arabic, which eventually proved to be a failure because the theatre company did not manage to attract the focused group of visitors: 'We thought that "now we are making all people speaking Arabic a great favour", but it was actually quite the opposite. It was a catastrophe. There were no Arabic speaking visitors coming because we did not know how to make them come' (Interviewee #3). The ability to balance artistic, political and commercial interests and objectives was one of the major concerns for the managing directors. The balance between highbrow and middlebrow culture was especially a source of concern. The managing director of the prestigious city theatre [Swedish, *Stadsteater*] pointed at the gradually increased concern for ticket sales in cultural work:

> This is the tricky part ... We're not supposed to be concerned with either objectives or ticket sales, but that is something that has gradually gained ground the last 15–20 years in Sweden, that the owners have been more interested in ticket sales.
> Question: Is it [the repertoire] becoming politicised?
> Well, yes ... no, I do not think they are really acting responsibly if they are sponsoring culture ... This expectation regarding ticket sales implies a certain degree of self-censoring. We need to become a bit 'populistic' and play entertaining stuff. For instance, the city theatres are beginning to play musicals, which is attracting an audience. There is research suggesting that people not regularly visiting theatres, not visiting dramatic theatre or opera, are interested in musicals. (Interviewee #5)

For instance, in the opera house, ballets and dance performances attracted the smallest number of visitors while classic Broadway musicals like *Miss Saigon* or *Cats* generated significant ticket sales revenues and brought audiences from out of the city. Taken together, the cultural institutions relied on a small group of returning visitors, who were more predictable than, for instance, younger visitors: one of the theatre company directors said:

> Our experience is that when we play newly written drama, we are capable of attracting young adults to a larger degree. But the group of young adults is a very unreliable audience. We live off the returning visitors, those who already take advantage of the culture in society. (Interviewee #5)

Still, the managing directors were aware of the need to maintain the artistic quality and to develop the arts. For instance, the suburban theatre company director argued passionately about the need to bring new ideas into the field:

> The theatre must renew itself. It is *very, very important*. If forms of art become complacent and conserve a form of art that has been around for all times, then it will be bitter in ten years' time, because it is not

evident that the new generation favours theatre. During the golden age, until the 1970s, then there was not that much competition in the art sector as today. The theatre must renew itself, find new means. You may better speak of *scene-art* than theatre. In many places, music and dance is involved. It is important to lower the threshold to the theatre domain. (Interviewee #3, emphasis in the original)

Another source of concern was the governance of the cultural institutions, in Sweden heavily relying on state, regional and municipality funding and with only a small proportion of the income yielded by ticket sales. This system of financing produced a relationship between the managing directors and Arts Council officials and politicians that needed to be carefully managed. The managing directors and the officials declared their satisfaction with the arrangements and praised the mutual understanding and collaboration. Still, some of the managing directors pointed at the inherent tension in this relationship: 'Artistic activities are sensitive to the relationship between artists and politicians ... Especially the artists are concerned when politicians get involved. And some politicians do not know where the boundaries are' (Interviewee #2). The risk of 'self-censoring' was addressed in particular at times. The managing directors were aware of their reliance on state, regional and municipality funding, at the bottom line governed by democratically elected representatives, and thereby paid close attention to expectations articulated in the political system. For instance, one of the concert hall directors said that one needs to take into account both actual and potential visitors:

There are two groups that you need to interact with in tandem: those who come here and those who don't. A social institution financed by tax money needs to know that those who don't come here have a certain tolerance ... People are actually prepared to pay for something they never visit ... The day you feel the urge to come see a classic ballet, it is good that there is someone providing that. (Interviewee #2)

In some cases, political objectives were regarded as interfering with artistic objectives and ideologies, but in most cases there was quite a clear line of demarcation between politics and artistic endeavours. In general, the board of directors in the institution, including political representatives, did not intervene in the artistic work: 'Our owners do not intervene with the artistic matters, and neither does the board of directors. That is the responsibility of the managing director and the creative leaders. We are given an assignment but the content of the assignment is our decision' (Interviewee #5). However, at times, political objectives were brought into the cultural institutions. One of the theatre company directors was disgruntled over the increased burden of writing all the 'policy documents' requested from the authorities: 'We're expected to write action plans for diversity, for gender issues, and for discrimination, and God knows what: action plans for the handicapped, everything! There is a flow of assigned action plans making you exhausted' (Interviewee #1). Bearing in mind that cultural institutions are in general poorly equipped in terms of administrative support, this work normally ended up on the managing director's desk. In other cases, political and artistic objectives were aligned but formal regulations caused concerns for the directors. For instance, the theatre companies were asked to play so-called 'school theatre' for kindergarten to high-school children and, since the theatre companies were not allowed to charge the visiting schools more than a fraction (normally a few euros) of the cost-based ticket price, the school theatre activities were financially complicated to handle. From an artistic perspective, however, this assignment was not questioned in the least. A director argued:

> From a financial point of view, it is complete insanity to play for children but we do in fact get a couple of millions [Swedish crowns] from the state and the municipality every year to do that. It is an assignment. So [refusing to play school theatre] is like reasoning that 'the health care sector should only specialize in financially profitable illnesses, the rest they can just ignore'. (Interviewee #1)

In summary, managing cultural institutions such as theatre companies, concert halls and opera houses is a complicated managerial assignment, balancing – at least in the case of Sweden – political, artistic and financial objectives. The cultural institutions were in many cases located in a liminal space inbetween the 'market and the hierarchy', forced to both pay attention to ticket sales and other market-related issues and also be able to deal with the political and administrative processes and relations enacted in the system for funding of the arts. Managing directors are thus located in a complex field where many ideologies and objectives are intersecting. However, the passionate interest for the arts seem to be the glue that holds a loosely coupled system of practices, institutions, traditions and professional groups together:

> Q: How are the conditions for pursuing creative artistically qualified work today?
> A: It is probably as hopeless as during the last 2,000 years, but we [artists] are probably a viable breed. (Interviewee #1)

Working with art apparently has a long history of struggle for survival. The bricolage and the tinkering demanded in all arts management and culture work is also carefully accounted for in Lindqvist's (2003) study of 'exhibition enterprising' where six different exhibitions in Switzerland, the UK and Sweden were examined. In Lindqvists's (2003) study, not only artistic talent but also political *savoir-faire*, collaborative capabilities and administrative skills were highly useful resources enabling successful enterprising. In some cases, for instance, in the Swiss exhibition project where the internationally acclaimed artist Pipilotti Rist served as curator, the collaboration between the artist and the other co-workers did not run too smoothly, eventually making Rist resign from her position as curator. Like any other organized activity, exhibition enterprising demands its skills and competencies.

Summary and conclusion

In this chapter, the concept of art and its importance for perception and organization has been discussed from a variety of perspectives. Since the very concept of art and accompanying terms such as aesthetics, include components of ambiguity and, expressed in more affirmative terms, flexibility in the concept of art. Contrary to the sciences, carefully guarded by professional scientists and strong institutions such as universities, art is more susceptible to local interpretations and the common-sense thinking of the non-professional or amateur art consumer. Still, art serves a central role in society as commenting on and thereby shaping the social reality. As a consequence, art may serve as an organization resource in accomplishing organizational objectives.

3
Music: Auditory Perception and Organized Sound

Introduction

In this chapter, the concept of music will be examined as a social resource that affects perception in both organizations and contemporary and preceding societies. While literature and art has been widely used by social scientists and philosophers to denote abstract concepts and thoughts, music, embedded in the production, manipulation, structuring and organization of sounds, has been comparatively little explored and used in the social theory literature. However, there are examples of thinkers referencing music to render their thoughts intelligible. For instance, Nietzsche (1997: 232) – prior to his ardent critique in *Der Fall Wagner* – claimed that Richard Wagner 'philosophized in sound'. Other scholars paying close attention to the social function of significance of music include well-known studies such as Theodore Adorno's (2003) critical theory view of music – if nothing else, Adorno's scornful rejection of jazz is a often brought to public attention by his critics – and little referenced and lesser-known projects such as Henri Lefebvre's (2004) attempt to formulate what he called a *rhythmanalysis* of everyday life – a methodology emphasizing that day-to-day practices and undertakings follow a certain regularity and pattern similar to the components of music. Nevertheless, music is, as a series of scholars and thinkers have pointed out, both the most abstract and also the most concrete of the arts; music is possible to immediately perceive, yet its meaning and significance are not of necessity given as such. For instance, the Pythagoreans thought of music as metaphysics (McClary, 1987: 15) and still today music is often regarded as being more intangible and immaterial than other forms of art. Music then does not speak for itself but is a social accomplishment based on a long range of ideologies, epistemological beliefs and social conventions. In this chapter some of these beliefs and assumptions guiding and structuring the production and consumption of music will be examined.

This chapter is structured as follows. First, the concept of music will be discussed. Thereafter we turn to the new musicology literature to examine the social significance and meaning of music. Third, the relationship between perception and music is analyzed. In the next section, the use of music in organizing and what can be broadly labelled as 'music work' are discussed.

The concept of music

The concept of music denotes a wide range of individual and collective social practices generating rhythm, melody, harmony, or timbre for the purpose of ceremonial matters, social symbolism, or for mere enjoyment. According to some commentators, there is no single, unified definition of what music is (Bode, 2006: 581) but Merriam (1964), cited by Bode (2006), suggests three analytical dimensions when examining music; an *acoustic* dimension, a *behavioural* dimension and a *conceptual* dimension. Given these three dimensions, music can be defined, Bode suggests, as 'the cultural and social structuring of sound, materialized in the process of composing, performing and listening. Besides personal elements, the shared reference to specific cultural conventions is necessary' (2006, 581). While music has always been a significant component in everyday life, Western society has tended to professionalize music and stratify it into more and more detailed and narrowly defined categories or genres. One of the principal concerns for musicologists and music theorists is to identify and formulate the *meaning* of music. Goehr (1998: 47) quotes the anthropologist Lévi-Strauss on the matter:

> [M]usic is a language with some meaning at least for the immense majority of [hu]mankind, although only a tiny majority of people are capable of formulating a meaning in it ... [I]t is the only language with the contradictory attributes of being at once intelligible and untranslatable ... [M]usic [is] ... the supreme mystery of the science of [humanity]. (Claude Lévi-Strauss, cited in Goehr, 1998: 47)

One of the principal qualities of music *vis-à-vis* other forms of art is that music is what Nelson Goodman calls an *allographic art*. The visual arts, for instance painting, are representative of what Goodman calls *autographic art*. Autographic art resides on the idea of an indisputable original that cannot be replaced. For instance, Géricault's *The Raft of the Medusa* is an autographic piece of art, existing as one single and individual piece of art, located in the Louvre in Paris. On the other hand, *allographic art* is art where 'the application of the distinction between an original and a copy is not pertinent' (Dokic, 1998: 103). For instance, a composition (e.g. *The Magic Flute*) is performed (slightly) differently every time and the quality of the composition is not located in or derived from an original performance but in the qualities of the work. However, the distinction between autographic and allographic art is not watertight; for instance, in art photography the autographic qualities of the fine arts are eroded since it is technically possible to reproduce a photograph. In music, some recordings of compositions (e.g. Glenn Gould's recordings of Bach's work) are deemed unprecedented classics, thus giving music an 'autographic aura'. Still, music is, in contrast to the fine arts, entangled with the idea of *performance* and therefore it is more contingent, context-bound and locally constituted that the autographic arts.

The concept of music derives from the Greek term *mousikē*, meaning the 'cultivation of the soul' in Socrates's account (Goehr, 1998: 86). Sharing this affirmative view of music, Aristotle (1998) advocated musical training and drawing as part of the education (*paideia*) for children and young students in Book VIII of his *Politics*. Music has, Aristotle says, the ability to 'inspire souls' and 'inspiration is an emotion that affects the character of the soul' (1998, section 1340: 10). However, the term *mousikē* denoted for the Greeks something different from what we today call music. *Mousikē* did not belong to anything like the modern system of arts and the sphere of aesthetic values was not distinguished from that of ethical, religious, cognitive and practical values. Neither was music clearly separated from poetry and dance (Hamilton, 2007: 16).

As opposed to art, which may include a variety of material resources in visual art, sculpture, photographs, land art and installations, and so forth, music is essentially a 'physical' phenomenon closely associated with mathematics (by the Pythagoreans) and the natural sciences. It is also a commonplace belief that mathematical and musical talent are the only two clearly distinguishable domains of genius (Lévi-Strauss, 1979), related to one another in curious and – to my knowledge – not yet fully explored ways. Although music remains the predominant term, avant-garde composers have sought to move beyond the connotations of the term in order to open up new modes of composition. For instance, Edgard Varèse spoke of his music as 'organized sound' and later John Cage suggested the similar concept of 'organization of sound'. Although music tends, in the Western tradition, to be envisaged as being timeless and detached from social conditions, a fate shared with mathematics, music is in fact under the continuous influence of cultural, and above all, technological changes. For instance, the composition of a symphonic orchestra has not been the same over centuries but was largely a product of the nineteenth century. Instruments like the piano, the saxophone and, more recently, electric guitars and technological gadgets, including drum machines, sequencers, bass liners and computer software such as Cubase, are constantly opening up new audible universes. However, in order to make music a topic of investigation in organization theory and management studies, music needs to be turned into a social and cultural category influencing social practice and everyday work life.

One of the most thought-provoking works on the intersection between music and social science is Jacques Attali's (1985) *Noise*, a book written by a French economist, which is frequently referenced in the musicology literature. In the following, some of Attali's ideas will be introduced. As a point of departure, Attali (1985: 3) downgrades the institution and human faculty of vision in Western knowledge. The world cannot be understood by beholding; it is *hearing* the world that matters. It is noise (French, *bruits*) that is representative of social activities and accomplishments: 'Nothing essential happens in the absence of noise,' Attali (1985: 3) says. In Attali's view, it is the analysis of music and noise (*bruits* here not having as entirely negative connotations as *noise* has in English) that enables understanding and 'perceiving' the world; music is 'a tool for understanding' (Attali, 1985: 4). Attali also claims that the development of music denotes corresponding changes in society: 'Music is illustrative of the evolution of our entire society' (Attali, 1985: 5). For instance, 'Mozart and Bach reflect the bourgeoisie's dream of harmony better than and prior to the whole of twentieth-century political theory' (Attali, 1985: 5–6). Attali says that more than 'colors and forms', it is 'sounds and their arrangements that fashion societies'; with music, power and its opposite, subversion, is born. Therefore, 'in noise can be read the codes of life, the relations among men. Clamor, Melody, Dissonance, Harmony', Attali suggests (1985: 6). Moreover, music is not merely its sole performance but is simultaneously 'science, message, and time', a 'mode of expression' (Attali, 1985: 9). The economics of music have to be examined along three dimensions: the joy of the creator, use-value for the listener and exchange-value for the seller. However, it is not primarily the economic function of music that interests Attali but its recursive relations to society:

In Europe, during three different periods with three different styles (the liturgical music of the tenth century, the polyphonic music of the sixteenth century, and the harmony of the eighteenth and nineteenth centuries), music found expression within a single, stable code and had stable modes of economic organization: correlatively, these societies were very clearly dominated by a single ideology … music runs parallel to human society, is structured like it, and changes when it does. It does not evolve in a linear fashion, but is caught up in the complexity and circularity of the movements of history. (Attali, 1985: 10)

Attali argues that the music of an age is 'rooted' in the ideologies and technologies of the age, while at the same time music helps to reproduce these ideologies. The succession of economic and political codes is thus preceded and accompanied by comparative musical codes (Attali, 1985: 19). Music, 'inscribed between noise and silence', thus has as its function 'the creation, legitimation, and maintenance of order' (Attali, 1985: 30). Attali continues: 'Its primary function is not to be sought in aesthetics, which is a modern invention, but in the effectiveness of its participation in social regulation. Music … creates order.' For instance, Attali argues that tonal music took the place of religious belief prior to any ideology of political economy as 'the incarnation of an idealized humanity, the image of harmonious, nonconflictual, abstract time that progresses and runs its course, a history that is predictable and controllable' (Attali, 1985: 61–2); 'the entire history of tonal music, like that of classical political economy, amounts to an attempt to make people believe in a consensual representation of the world' (Attali, 1985: 46). In a time where deities became questioned or lost their function, music became consolation and was regarded as evidence of the higher meaning of human existence.

Attali also emphasizes the technological and organizational features of music. For instance, the construction of the piano and its popularization as the bourgeoisie instrument *par préférence* opened up new forms of composition. Beethoven, composing in the first half of the nineteenth century, was the first major composer to write pieces (e.g. his Sonata no. 106) for the piano (Attali, 1985: 35). More recently, Jimi Hendrix would be unthinkable without the advent of the electric guitar, an instrument he fully mastered and set the standard for in a manner similar to Liszt's contribution to the popularization of the piano. 'The form of music is always influenced by the transmitter and the medium,' Attali remarks (1985: 37). Attali also points at the importance of recording in providing what is fluid or not fully unified with an integrated and conclusive structure. Recording is, for Attali, a generalized procedure of inscription wherein control and order is imposed on a social formation:

> Recording has always been a means of control, a stake in politics, regardless of the available technologies. Power is no longer content to enact its legitimacy; it records and reproduces the societies it rules. Stockpiling memory, retaining history or time, distributing speech, and manipulating information has always been an attribute of civil and priestly power, beginning with the Tables of the Law. (Attali, 1985: 87)

Speaking of music, the practice of recording moved the power over music from the printing houses owning the right to publish the scripts of music and the entertainment entrepreneurs providing live music performances to the emerging record companies. When the phonograph was invented, it emphasized 'preservation' rather than 'mass replication' (Attali, 1985: 91). However, it took a long time to see the financial potential of the phonograph and the gramophone. Edison thought of his invention in terms of preserving speech and dictation rather than being able to reproduce recorded music and to provide entertainment. Only in 1914 was the first symphony recorded, even though Edison's patent dates from 19 December 1877. 'No one foresaw the mass production of music,' Attali concludes (1985: 92). Today, mass-produced music is one of the defining features of contemporary life; at least in urban settings, it is almost impossible to dwell without being exposed to music, in most cases music not personally selected but produced by organizations with commercial interests in mind. Attali argues that 'mass music' is a powerful factor in the integration and 'homogenization' of contemporary society; 'it becomes a factor in centralization, cultural normalization, and the disappearance of distinctive cultures' (Attali, 1985: 111). Muzak Inc. executive David O'Neill says: 'We don't sell music: we sell programming (cited in Attali, 1985: 112).' Music here plays the role of the *accompagnemang* of the social choreography. In addition, in the society of the spectacle, the ability to take part in mass culture becomes the lowest common denominator for human beings sharing existential concerns: when power is so abstract that it can no longer be seized and where the worst threat people feel is not alienation but solitude, conformity to the norm 'becomes the pleasure of belonging' and the 'acceptance of powerlessness takes root in the comfort of repetition' (Attali, 1985: 112, emphasis in the original omitted). In order to find a way out of the iron cage of mass-produced music and the individual's constant exposure to noise not personally selected, Attali speaks about composition as the individual's engagement in producing his or her own audible life worlds. Although this part of Attali's reasoning is the vaguest and least persuasive, he expresses his admiration for the Free Jazz movement of the 1960s represented by, for instance, Ornette Coleman and Cecil Taylor as a form of music that refuses to become commodified: 'Free jazz was the first attempt to express in economic terms the refusal of the cultural alienation inherent in repetition, to use music to build a new culture,' Attali remarks (1985: 138).

In Attali's account, music is what precedes social changes. It is also never 'innocent' but rather embodies and even reinforces specific ideologies and material conditions. Examining music thus gives valuable insights into the mechanisms of a particular society. Even though Attali is more of a speculative thinker than an empirically oriented historian or sociologist, he makes music a legitimate source of investigation within a broader sociological framework. As Edward Said (2001: 15) has pointed out, for instance, with reference to Foucault, there is a 'remarkable ignorance of contemporary intellectuals about music, whether classical or popular'. While social theory and philosophy has made use of art and literature as discussion points for broader theoretical discourses, music has for some reason been excluded. Perhaps the 'immateriality' of music, its abstract and almost 'physical' or 'mathematical' qualities, has been a decisive factor when choosing other cultural forms to examine. In addition, several musicologists and critical theorists such as Adorno (2003) have deplored that classical music no longer plays the central role in bourgeoisie education and life as it once did. The 'problems today', Adorno says in his characteristic tone, is that there is a 'collapse of all criteria for good and bad music, as they had been codified during the early days of bourgeois era. For the first time, dilettantes everywhere are launched as great composers' (2003: 7). A musicologist like Lawrence Kramer (1995: 5), for his part, says that '[b]y the mid-twentieth century, classical music had passed out of the public sphere'. Classical music increasingly plays an ornamental function, supplementing the commercial mass music on the radio and iPods. Perhaps one may argue that the culture of 'music connoisseurs' and 'music lovers' studied by Hennion (2002) is a reminiscent of these past bourgeoisie virtues.

To conclude: what we learn from Attali is that music plays a decisively larger role in social formations than is generally recognized. For instance, in the case of organization theory and management studies, the use of music is one resource among others in the very fabric of organizing.

The social meaning and function of music

One of the persistent themes in musicology and theory of music is the discussion regarding whether there is a meaning in music. As Edgard Varèse pointed out, music is both the most abstract and the most concrete of the arts; it is 'immaterial' while at the same time it is immediately perceptible for anyone as a physical phenomenon, as a vibrating string or the sinuous curves produced by wind instruments or the beat on a drum. As the noted director Daniel Barenboim argues in a conversation with Edward Said, 'music is ephemeral' – drawn back into silence like an object falling back to the ground by the force of gravity – and existing merely when it is performed. Unlike the written word, music only exists when it is created; when Beethoven wrote the 5th symphony, Barenboim argues (Barenboim and Said, 2002: 111), 'it simply existed as figment of his imagination and was subject to physical laws that he imagined only in his brain', but it did not come into being until an orchestra decided to play it.

In addition, similar to the visual arts and dance and cinema, music is not of necessity immediately meaningful for the listener. It can be beautiful, appealing, or disturbing but it may not be perceived as being located within pre-established systems of meaning in the same manner as literature, for instance. The musicologist Lawrence Kramer (1990), representing what has been called the *new musicology* (Leppert and McClary, 1987; Subotnik, 1996; for an overview and critique, see Hooper, 2006), takes the concept of meaning seriously in musicology analysis. 'As a practice', Kramer says, 'music should be subject to the same kinds of rigorous interpretations that we customarily apply to other cultural practices, be they social, artistic, technical, discursive, ritual, or sexual' (1990: xii). Kramer formulates four claims regarding music: (1) works of music have 'discursive meaning'; (2) 'these meanings are definite enough to support critical interpretations comparable in depth, exactness, and density of connection to interpretations of literary texts and cultural practice'; (3) 'these meanings are not "extramusical", but on the contrary are inextricably bound up with the formal processes and stylistic articulations of musical works'; and, finally, (4) 'these meanings are produced as a part of the general circulation of regulated practices and evaluations – part, in other words, of the continuous production and reproduction of culture' (Kramer, 1990: 1). Seen from this view, music is a totality of cultural artefacts that can be examined along the same analytical categories as any other cultural artefact. Kramer is especially critical of the Western tradition rendering music outside of reflection and meaning. Kramer quotes

Kant saying that ' [music] indeed speaks by means of pure sensations without concepts, and so does not, like poetry, leave something over for reflection' (Immanuel Kant, *Kritik der Urteilschaft*, cited in Kramer, 1990: 3). Kramer speaks of his project of identifying musical meaning as *musical hermeneutics*. There is, Kramer says, no 'fundamental difference' between interpreting a written text and a work of music (1990: 6). However, there is still a lack, Kramer claims, of 'techniques' for interpreting music. In a more recent book, Kramer speaks of musical meanings in terms of 'communicative action' that is embedded in a continuous texture of 'psychological, social, and cultural relations': 'Music – and in this it is no different from more explicitly semantic modes such as narration and visual depiction – means not primarily by what it says but by the way it models the symbolization of experience,' Kramer says (2002: 7).

Susan McClary (1987) shares with Kramer (1990; 2002) the view that music, like literature and the visual arts, has for various reasons been located within a 'separate sphere', replete with pseudo-religious rituals and attitudes' (McClary, 1987: 15). She continues: '[F]rom the very early times up to and including the present, there has been a strain of Western culture that accounts for music in non-social, implicitly metaphysical terms' (McClary, 1987: 15). The status of music as what is somewhat marginal, supplementary or additional to other human accomplishments, most notably science, is to some extent derived from the privileged position of vision in the Western tradition. The human faculty of hearing is also the most vulnerable of the senses, McClary argues, because the ear cannot be closed or used selectively: 'one can avert one's eyes from the décor of an elevator but not one's ear from the Muzak'. Music and sound thus 'tend to slip around and surprise us' (1987: 16). Music is both fluid and fluxing and outside of our full control at the same time as it is historically embedded in metaphysics rather than social practices. McClary (1987: 17) points at another factor making the field of musicology a domain concerned more with universals and truths than social accomplishments, namely the divergence between the professionals that know all the theory about music and the layperson who merely listens but with limited insight into broader theoretical frameworks:

> [W]e have a priesthood of professionals who learn the principles of musical orders, who come to be able to call musical events by name and even to manipulate them; and, on the other hand, we have a laity of listeners who respond strongly to music but have little conscious critical control of it ... Neither the priest nor the consumer wants to

break the spell: to reveal the social grounding of that magic. (McClary, 1987: 17)

Kramer (2002) demonstrates with a great number of references to the history of music how individual works, genres and composers have been examined as representatives for different social and cultural relations. For instance, Beethoven's 'Moonlight' Sonata (published in 1798) became a veritable success because it was interpreted as being a romantic piece of music that fitted into the predominant heterosexual matrix of the nineteenth century (Kramer, 2002: 38–9). Moreover, the nineteenth century brought the first cases of idolatry when Franz Liszt toured Europe and North America and rendered concert hall audiences spellbound with his virtuoso piano technique and his ecstatic appearance. In the 1850s, during the Swedish opera singer Jenny Lind's American tour, Jenny Lind sofas, sausages and pancakes were merchandized (Kramer, 2002: 90). A similar business emerged around Liszt, whom the Danish author H.C. Andersen referred to as 'the Orpheus of our day' in the 1840s. In Kramer's analysis, music is not detached or separated from everyday life experiences and beliefs but is, on the contrary, what is brought into the very centre of human existence: 'We make sense of music as we make sense of life. And since we make sense of life only amid a dense network of social, cultural, and historical forces, musical meaning inevitably bears the traces, and sometimes blazons, of those forces' (Kramer, 2002: 163). For the untrained ear, musical meanings are not immediately available for interpretation. For instance, Kramer (2002) discusses John Coltrane's recording of Ira Gershwin's *Summertime* (on his record *My Favorite Things*) in terms of being what Kramer calls a *debricolage:*

> My notion of debricolage remains the element of inventiveness but replaces real scarcity with a fictitious or travesty scarcity. Debricolage adapts old material to new uses for reasons of desire, not of need. Instead of assemblage, its basic principle is disassemblage, and what it disassembles are the norms and forms of dominant culture. In debricolage, these appear in bits and pieces, but so articulated that their original wholeness remains perceptible; they are not just strewn about, but carefully disassembled. (Kramer, 2002: 245)

Summertime is, Kramer says, a classic song in the urban bourgeoisie songbook, composed by the Jewish New Yorker Ira Gershwin. In Coltrane's interpretation, the song is expressing, Kramer suggests, some of the concerns of a black man living in a non-egalitarian or racist culture; it is a 'rearticulation' of the bits and pieces of the song while its wholeness is perceivable. Coltrane's greatness as a saxophone player is his ability to pay homage to the original song while rephrasing some of its content and adding a certain sense of what Freud (1955) called *Unheimlichkeit*, a sense of concern and uncanniness. The meaning of Coltrane's song lies then both in its performative function – the black man decomposing the great American bourgeoisie songbook – and in its actual performance as a delicate piece of jazz.

McClary (1987) offers another example of how music attains new meanings in the course of time and under the influence of continuous interpretations and evaluations of an oeuvre. First, McClary examines the 'tonal procedures' in composition as being representative of a bourgeoisie ideology, assuming that tonality, that is, the favoured form of composition of a ruling class during a certain period of time, represents 'eternal, universal truths'. The dynasty of Great Composers begins with J.S. Bach, who gives the impression, McClary argues, '[t]hat *our* way of representing the world musically is God-given' (1987: 58). But no composition can make claims of being eternal and universal but is instead always a product of particular times and specific cultural, social and economic conditions. The role of the musicologist is to re-contextualize musical work and to inscribe meaning into music not through references to universals but to particularities. Composition must be brought down from the celestial heights to earth and the life world of the composer and his (or, in a few cases, her) audiences and contemporaries. Not even Bach, the quintessential musical genius beside Mozart, was unaffected by dominant doctrines of his day. McClary (1987) emphasizes at least three different traditions of composition being brought together and rearticulated in Bach's work:

> [T]he styles Bach assembles are not simply different with respect to surface mannerisms: each has its own peculiar quality of moving through time. To combine in a single composition the on-rushing goal orientation of the Italian opera or concerto with the more sober, static, contrapuntctual ideal of the German Lutheran repertory and the motion-arresting graces of French dance is to produce in time a highly conflicted procedure. Yet Bach's genius lies in his ability to take these components that are highly charged – both ideologically and with respect to dynamic musical impulse – and to give the impression of having reconciled them. (McClary, 1987: 20)

The Italian opera and concerto, the German contrapunctual composition and French dance were integrated in Bach's project to compose music in the praise of God. Claiming that Bach's work is capable of grasping universal truths is ignoring the accomplishments of Bach when bringing into harmony a series of heterogeneous elements. McClary (1987) argues that, far from representing universal values or aesthetics, Bach's composition represents an 'audacious synthesis of all available cultures' – with Germany at its centre – that was not very likely to have pleased many of his contemporaries – 'not even most Germans'. Bach was instead canonized as representing pure order only *after* the codes on which his 'semiotic strategies' had relied and their 'accompanying social context' had 'become inactive'. Therefore, the universality of Bach's composition, McClary says, was achieved only at the expense of specific, concretely articulated meaning (1987: 55).

Max Weber, familiar with the density of German culture, says that the 'pietists' – among whom Bach counted himself – suspicion of music in religious practice prevented them from fully appreciating Bach's work, a work today celebrated as being among the most accomplished contributions to the human arts. This is for Weber a somewhat ironic twist in the history of music:

> It is tragicomic that J.S. Bach's music, which corresponds to his intense religious piety and despite a strict dogmatic relationship bears an unmistakable flavor of pietism, was in his own domicile suspected by the pietists and unappreciated by the orthodox. (Weber, 1958: 111)

Obviously, the work of even the greatest composers cannot be properly understood unless one abandons mythologies and hagiographic accounts and delves into the working procedures and enacted worldviews of the composers. Similarly to scientific work, composition rarely if ever takes place in a social vacuum but is instead representative of a particular society.

Kramer's (1990; 2002) work on musical hermeneutics and musical meanings and McClary's (1987) studies of classic composition are representative of the broader change in musicology to move away from positivistic, formalistic and overtly technical analyses and to embrace a broader social science framework. DeNora (2000) represents a complementary, sociological view of music and a tradition of thinking that is critical of what she calls the 'semiotic view of music'. In the semiotic view, music is analyzed in terms of its innate composition and structure and is largely dislocated from its 'context of application', its use in everyday life. DeNora (2000) argues that musicologists such as Lawrence Kramer and Susan McClary, no matter how brilliant the analyses they are capable of articulating, represent such a semiotic view. DeNora states her position: '[S]emiotics risks a kind of covert objectivism, a presumption that music's meanings are immanent, inherent in musical forms as opposed to being brought to life in and through the interplay of forms and interpretations' (2000: 22). The most extreme form of semiotic analysis is for DeNora (2000) Theodore Adorno's notorious rejection of popular music – most notably jazz – solely on the basis of structural analyses and thinly veiled personal preferences. Rather than engaging in a lifeless examination of musical form and matter, DeNora calls for a broader sociological account of the use of music in everyday life, and especially the use of music as what Foucault calls a 'technology of the self' and as a 'device for social ordering':

> Music is not merely a 'meaningful' or 'communicative' medium. It does much more than convey signification through non-verbal means. At the level of daily life, music has power. It is implicated in every dimension of social agency ... Music may influence how people compose their bodies, how they conduct themselves, how they experience the passage of time, how they feel – in terms of energy and emotion – about themselves, about others, and about situations. (DeNora, 2000: 17)

For instance, discussing the use of music to constitute meaning in work, Korczynski (2007: 258) suggests that music is a 'potentially rich medium through which to explore people's experiences at work'. Music is, Korczynski (2007) continues, a 'transgressive medium of communication' allowing expression of sentiments that would perhaps not be permitted in 'other formats'. For instance, in shanties sailors could sing out grievances to the ship's captain or slaves could mock figures of power in their songs. Music may thus play a social function to regulate social relations and provide arenas for transgression or what may be called 'carnivalistic symbolism', that is, 'symbolic action' temporarily overturning the social order, thereby paradoxically reproducing the predominant social system. Seen in this view, music is a 'technology of the self' bridging agency and social structure.

Sociologists and so-called ethnomusicologists engage in systematic research unravelling a wide variety of musical uses and applications. Among other things, music attains its social meaning and function in actual use in real life situations; in aerobics classes, in shopping malls, in public spaces, in the personalized audible universe provided by iPods and other MP3 players, making activities such as urban commuting a less wearisome experience. In the sociological view of music – similar to

Wittgenstein's claim that the meaning of a word derives from its performativity – the meaning of music is its use. Schatzki (2002: 58) elegantly captures such a view of meaning: 'Meaning ... is carried by and established in social practices ... Meaning is not a matter of difference, abstract schema, or attributional relativity, but a reality laid down in the regimes of activity and intelligibility called "practice"'. The social meaning of music can never be explained *a priori* but must always be sought in its use in everyday life, DeNora (2000) contends.

The secularization and rationalization of music

Even though music today is not only in every man and woman's possession but is also one of the most pervasive features of contemporary urban life – it is becoming virtually impossible to escape music *in toto* – the trajectory from clerical church music to the lounge music and muzak of the department stores and public spaces has been long and non-linear. Leppert (1993) argues that prior to the Renaissance, the 'codification of music' – that is, 'the development of music theory, methods of composition, and performance practices' – was the concern of ecclesiastical writers and musicians. For instance, organ-builders and organists were originally monks or technicians from monasteries (Weber, 1958: 115). During the Renaissance, social elites in secular society became increasingly interested in the social distinction value of music: 'What for churchmen had been an issue of orthodoxy, in elite secular society was increasingly one of differentiating self and class. Music, that is, could help stabilize and authorize hierarchical social position and the various means by which it is gained and held' (Leppert, 1993: 44). Elias (1993), writing about Mozart, emphasizes the 'utility' of art in traditional societies: 'Human art in earlier times had a less specialized function in a wider social context – for example, as images of gods in temples, as adornment for the tombs of dead kings, as music for banquets and dancing. Art was "utility art" before it became "art"' (Elias, 1993: 47). In the new emerging social relations, music came to signify new qualities; music became a resource, a form of cultural capital in the hands of the leading economic strata in the Italian commercial centres (Tomlinson, 1993). During the Renaissance, the opera was developed under the name of *opera seria*. Monteverdi's *Orfeo* (first performed in 1607 and published in 1609), is commonly regarded as the first modern opera (Weber, 1958: 111). Until the mid-nineteenth century, concert halls and opera houses became the locus wherein the bourgeoisie demonstrated their cultivation and refinement. During the period after the Renaissance, musical instruments were both developed and attained their present form and a new hierarchy of instruments was established. For instance, in the eighteenth century, three types of viols were established from the rich variety of instruments: the viola, the violin and the cello (Weber, 1958: 108). As a consequence, the wind instruments that had dominated the orchestra in the Middle Ages and during the Renaissance were gradually displaced by stringed instruments. Instruments dominating during the Middle Ages – a lutenist, for instance, earned three times the salary of a violinist and five times that of the bag-piper in Queen Elizabeth's court (Weber, 1958: 111) – were gradually replaced by new instruments. Perhaps the most decisive step to make music a bourgeoisie domain, detached from folk music, was the invention (or rather the stabilization of a standardized form) of the piano. The development of the piano took place in Italy and Germany but the indoor salon culture of middle and northern Europe enabled a broader reception of the piano than in the Mediterranean region:

> The development of the hammer piano occurred by stages partly in Italy (Christoferi), partly in Germany. Italian culture (until the threshold of the present) remained alien to the indoor culture of the Nordic Europe. Italian ideals lacked the influence of the culture of the bourgeois-like home. They retained the ideal of *a capella* singing and the opera. The arias of the opera supplied the demand for easily comprehensible and singable tunes. (Weber, 1958: 120)

By the beginning of the nineteenth century, the piano had become 'a standard commercial object produced for stock' (Weber, 1958: 122). For Evens (2005), the piano is 'a uniquely European instrument' as it reflects 'European music and a Western rationality sensibility': 'eighty-eight keys corresponding to eighty-eight playable pitches. Push the key and the mechanism responds, sounding the note until the button is released' (Evens, 2005: 85). The piano thus embodies a rational ideology and its emphasis on standardization and predictability. Leppert (1993) emphasizes the cultural and symbolic function of the piano in the Victorian culture:

> In Victorian culture the piano functioned in sound and sight alike as an analogical referent to social harmony and domestic order. Its sonorities, whether potential or realized, served as the aesthetic metaphor simultaneously connecting and justifying between public and private life – between the outside world of the Industrial Revolution and the protected inner sanctum of the Victorian bourgeois

home, between men and women in their social relations, and (in some ways more important) between bourgeois desire and erotic capacity, on the one hand, and their sublimation (a tense and contradictory process), on the other. (Leppert, 1993: 139)

Among the bourgeoisie, playing the piano was regarded as effeminate and paintings from the time rarely display men by the instrument (but frequently young women). The decorative function of the bourgeoisie woman was complemented by her ability to entertain the family with piano sonatas. To this day, at least in Northern Europe, taking piano lessons is part of a proper bourgeoisie upbringing. In Leppert's (1993) account, the piano serves as what Sigmund Freud calls a *transitional object* wherein sexuality and desire can be played out without threatening the social order. Leppert (1993: 141) writes:

The piano, as the predominant musical instrument of its time among the hegemonic classes, reflected and produced associations, both sonoric and visual, between pleasure, sexual desire, hatred, murder, and women. One cannot understand the histories of nineteenth-century music – its production and reception, in the salon or the concert hall – without taking account of these associations.

Notwithstanding the symbolic and psychological functions of the piano, its establishment as a bourgeoisie household item led to changes in compositional practice. Beethoven is generally regarded as the first major composer to write pieces for piano; Chopin the first composer to restrict himself entirely to the piano; Liszt became the first superstar pianist. Or in Weber's (1958: 122) colourful formulation, 'in Liszt the instrument skill of the great virtuoso elicited from the instrument all that had finally been concealed of expressive possibilities'.

Another indication of what Weber (1958) calls the rationalization and professionalization of music and the emergence of a music industry is pointed at by Elias (1993), suggesting that Mozart, the paragon of musical genius, struggled to create a position outside the European courts where he could serve as a 'freelance composer'. Elias (1993: 36) correctly notes that, in comparison to, for instance, writers or painters, musicians and composers are 'more dependent on the collaboration of other people'. In Mozart's time, it was the European courts that could provide an environment and resources where such collaborations could bear fruit. According to Elias (1993: 43), Mozart sought to compose music for 'the anonymous market, for a public which is by and large the artist's equal' rather than for 'particular patrons, usually social superiors'.

Unfortunately, there was no such European freelance market during Mozart's lifetime and the end of his life was spent in acute poverty because of his inability to please the demands of the courts where he served. Elias notes that Mozart was in fact living in a society where a liberal and open market for music were on the verge of becoming established; Beethoven, born in 1770, almost fifteen years after Mozart, managed to achieve, not easily but with far less trouble, what Mozart hoped to accomplish, that is, to liberate himself from the dependence of court patronage. Beethoven was thus able to 'follow his own voice in his composition', that is, writes Elias, to follow 'the immanent sequential order of his inner voices rather than the conventional taste of his customers' (Elias, 1993: 39–40). Seen in this view, Mozart is a deeply tragic figure, unable to release himself from the social conventions and constraints of the cultural and socio-economic order of his time. Rather than being able to exploit his full potential, Mozart remains encumbered with the demands to respond to the tastes and preferences articulated within the intricate European court system. From Beethoven onwards, composition and music largely served a market constituted by and operated by concert halls, professional orchestras and individual entrepreneurs and composers rather than the European courts or the church. Music gradually became an industry producing its own companies and corporations, star performers and well-known composers. Music was rationalized from being an obscure activity pertaining to the clergy's religious ceremonies to a culture industry in the making.

In the period from the Renaissance to the mid-twentieth century, being capable of evaluating and enjoying music and – primarily for the women (playing piano) but also for men (playing a stringed instrument such as the violin) – mastering an instrument was part of, to use Gay's (1984) phrase, the 'bourgeoisie experience'. In the twentieth century, when the leisure societies of the bourgeoisie were replaced by entrepreneurial ideologies and when mass-produced music and a veritable music industry had gained a foothold in the economy, the bourgeoisie virtue of taking part in music was marginalized. Music's value as cultural capital depreciated and the bourgeoisie was gradually transformed from active producers of music to consumers and spectators.

Gendering music

Susan McClary (1991: 9) examines musicology from a gender theory perspective and declares that '[o]ne of the principal tasks of feminist music criticism would be to examine the semiotics of desire, arousal, and sexual pleasure that circulate in the public sphere through music'. Feminist analyses of music are rare because the ideology of musicologists assume that music is in essence universal and transcending more mundane social concerns such as the relation between men and women and the broader gendered structure of society (Shepherd, 1987; Cusick, 1998). 'Music is generally regarded as a neutral – a *neuter* – enterprise', McClary (1991: 139) says, 'again because of the desire not to acknowledge its mediation through actual people with gendered bodies'. For instance, a great visionary like Arnold Schönberg in his *Theory of Harmony* longed for a 'musical discourse that is, like the angels, asexual' (McClary, 1991: 12). McClary states her position:

> Throughout the history of the west, music has been an activity fought over bitterly in terms of gender identity. The charge that musicians or devotees of music are 'effeminate' goes back as far as recorded documentation about music, and music's association with the body (in dance or for sensuous pleasure) and with subjectivity has led to its being regarded in many historical periods as what was understood as a 'feminine' realm. Male musicians have retaliated in a number of ways: by defining music as the most ideal (that is, the least physical) of the arts; by instating emphatically on its rational 'dimensions'; by laying claim to such presumably masculine virtues as objectivity, universality, and transcendence; by prohibiting actual female participants altogether. (McClary, 1991: 17)

There are reasons to believe that music has been regarded as effeminate for a significant period of time. The Italian monk Guido d'Arrezzo, for instance, declared almost a thousand years ago (c. 1025) that '*temporibus nostris super omnes homines fatui sunt cantores*' ('In our time the silliest of all men are the singers') (cited in Goehr, 1998: 136). Not only are 'masculine' ideologies of interest to musicologists, but they have also had more direct social consequences. For instance, McClary (1991: 17) says, musicologists like Linda Austern and Richard Leppert have demonstrated that 'one reason the English have produced so little music is that they – more than their German and French neighbors – have associated music strongly with effeminacy'. For the British, music was an essentially a feminine matter. In addition, McClary (1991: 18–19) points at the relative lack of female composers and complements her argument by suggesting that the few examples of music composed by women have 'often been received in terms of the essentialist stereotypes ascribed to women by masculine culture'. She continues: 'it [music composed by women] is repeatedly condemned as pretty yet trivial or – in the event that it does not conform to standards of feminine propriety – as aggressive and unbefitting a woman'.

McClary provides a number of examples of how ideas and beliefs about femininity affect composition. Her first example is Monteverdi's *Orfeo*, wherein the character Euridice is presented as a frail young girl through certain tonalities commonly associated with women (and especially younger women). McClary writes:

> I am not suggesting that Monteverdi wrote inferior music for Euridice or that this is what he thought of women. But his musical construction of 'maidenhood' is informed by what his audience would expect to hear as the utterance of a young girl. The tiny speech, painstakingly composed out of the available rhetorical devices to produce *anti*-rhetoric, might well have been more difficult to accomplish than the flamboyant oratory of the Orfeo character. (1991: 44)

Next, McClary studies the illustration of mad women in music during three periods. These are Monteverdi's nymph (1638), Donizetti's Lucia (1835) and Strauss's Salome (1905). McClary notices that these characters are presented very differently in terms of the style of the composition. The scientific view of and common-sense beliefs regarding the nature of madness were altered during this period of time (Foucault, 1967), as well as the nature of composition. Thus the emotional turmoil of Monteverdi's nymph and Strauss's Salome are expressed in different musical terms. As a consequence, the idea of what counts as normal feminine behaviour and how this is rendered as musical form is historically contingent. Music and composition, therefore, are not detached from the social fabric and predominant ideas regarding the relation between men and women and what qualifies as normal behaviour. Third, McClary discusses Bizet's *Carmen* as a product of a turbulent time at the threshold of modernity wherein dominant ideas regarding class, gender and sexuality were rendered problematic and renegotiated. For McClary, Bizet manages to bring together and address all these new concerns in his opera:

> [I]rreconcilable contradictions were erupting in many domains in 1870s France: the limits and reversal of imperial expansion were beginning to become evident, and both women and the working class were organizing to demand their economic, political, and cultural rights. Liberal humanism's commitment to universal rights were strained when it became a matter of sharing privileges with

women, the working class, or the colonialized – upon all of whom the privileged were dependent. This tension between liberal overextension and the need to assert control even informs the terms of musical discourse itself … *Carmen* manages to dramatize every single one of these issues in a way that is most compelling. (McClary, 1991: 54–5)

Above all, Bizet is capable of making sexuality an issue of investigation. Sexuality is perhaps one of the greatest drives and sources of desire for human beings, but previous composers brought other passions and affects into the domain of music prior to Bizet's work. Nietzsche (1997: 241) says, for instance, that Beethoven 'was the first to let music speak a new language, the hitherto forbidden language of passion'. For McClary (1991: 151), music is an extraordinarily powerful medium because most of the listeners have 'little rational control over the way it influences them'. Thus, the Cartesian mind–body split predominant in the Western epistemology for centuries leads to a 'paradoxical attitude' towards music; at the same time, music is regarded as 'the most cerebral, nonmaterial of media' while it is also the medium the 'most capable of engaging the body' (McClary, 1991: 151). McClary argues that classical music – no less than, say, pop – is bound up with the issue of gender construction and the 'channelling of desire'. Just like its popular counterpart, classical music presents a wide range of competing images and models of sexuality, whereof some 'seem to reinscribe faithfully that often patriarchal and homophobic norms of the cultures in which they originated, and some of which resist or call those norms into question' (McClary, 1991: 54). Human life is not only based on pure reason and cognitive faculties but also on the embodied passions and sexuality. The general tendency to think of music as a *neuter*, a neutral enterprise rather than human expression and a celebration of human life, has prevented a gendered view of music. McClary has shown that there is no such neutral position but every form of composition is anchored in social conditions, which in themselves represent various gendered preferences and *modus operandi*. Engaging in a theoretical project to reveal and trace all the connections between composition and the gendered beliefs of historical periods means to relocate music within its proper realm, that is human lives and social conditions, rather than assuming again some innate metaphysical constitution of music. Music is not transcendence, it is a representation of the human condition and, more specifically, McClary (1987) says, a representation of gendered human conditions.

Proper music versus noise/repetition: the social construction of boundaries of music

Another source of concern in the musicology literature and the writing addressing music is the line of demarcation between music and non-music and between various genres. Such disputes are articulated in periods of change and where new influences gain recognition in the domain of music and composition. In the first half of the twentieth century, representatives of the Vienna School such as Arnold Schönberg, Anton Webern and Alban Berg developed and refined dodecophony composition (also known as 'twelve-tone music') wherein old tonalities were abandoned. More recently, visionaries such as Edgard Varèse in the USA (discussed in greater detail below) and Karlheinz Stockhausen in Germany envisaged composition in new terms. What was of particular interest for these new composers was to explore new sonorities such as the noises of the contemporary, modern society. As the British composer Henry Cowell points out, noise *per se* is not in some innate opposition to music but is in fact what constitutes the idiosyncratic tone of an instrument:

> [T]here is a noise element in the very tone itself in all our musical instruments. Consider the sound of a violin. Parts of the vibration producing the sound are periodic, as can be shown by a harmonic analyzer. But others are not – they do not constantly re-form the same pattern, and consequently must be considered noise. In varying proportions all other instruments yield similar combinations. A truly pure tone can be made only in an acoustical laboratory, and even in there it is doubtful whether, by the time the tone has reached our ear, it has not been corrupted by resonances picked up on the way. (Cowell, 2006: 23)

The 'noise components' in the beginning of musical tones, often no longer than a few milliseconds in duration, are referred to as 'attack transients' and enable the aural identification of a musical instrument: according to Russo and Warner:

> Without these noise components it is virtually impossible for listeners to differentiate between, for instance, a clarinet and piano tone sounding at the same frequency, because their pitched or 'steady-state' portions (comprising most of all instrumental tone's duration) happen to be timbrally similar. (2006: 49)

Experimental avant-garde composers like Stockhausen showed early interest in further exploring such noise, previously neglected or excluded from the domain of music. Stockhausen speaks of 'coloured noise' being filtered from 'white noise', the totally unstructured sphere of signals.

'White noise' can be described as the simultaneity of all audible vibrations. It sounds like the roar of the sea. From this 'white noise' we can filter out frequency bands using all sorts of electrical filters – hence coloured noises (consonants like *sh*, *f*, *s*, *ch* etc. are such 'noise spectra). The sound continuum between the 'pure tone' and 'white noise' can – for now – be defined such that the 'pure tone' is the narrowest 'noise band', or *vice versa*, that 'white noise' is the densest superimposition of 'pure tones'. (Stockhausen, 2006: 375–6)

Coloured noise represents specific spectra that can be used in composition. While more conventional composers may show little interest in bringing new elements of noise into music, a substantial amount of popular music, from the genres of jazz to contemporary heavy metal, electronica and hip-hop have explored ways of elaborating on noise. The feedback and distortion of electric guitars in the 1950s and 1960s, the use of scratching and sampling of noisy sounds in hip-hop and the white noise and 'clicks' in recent laptop-generated electronica are examples of how noise is brought into music to accomplish new sonorous effects. 'What is noise in the old order is harmony in the new,' Attali (1985: 35) contends. Another characteristic of popular music is the emphasis on repetition. In classical composition, there are naturally elements of repetition (e.g. the refrain, the ritournello, the recurrent theme) but in popular music one may identify what McClary talks about as a 'gradual but pervasive African-Americanization' throughout the twentieth century (McClary, 2006: 295). American popular music, fundamentally embedded in African folk music and the social conditions of the slave economy, rests on blues and jazz, as the two principal traditions emphasize the *beat* of the music, the circulatory repetition of drum figures: 'In black culture, repetition means that the thing circulates (exactly in the manner of any flow) . . . There is an equilibrium. In European culture, repetition must be seen to be not just circulation and flow but accumulation and growth' (James A. Snead, cited in Cox and Warner, 2006: 286). As we will see, the line of demarcation between music and non-music gradually eroded in the twentieth century. Prominent among the new composers is the French-American Edgard Varèse, whose ideal of composition will be examined next.

Renegotiating the concept of music: Edgard Varèse's 'organized sound'

Edgard Varèse was born in Paris in 1883 and studied composition in France before he emigrated to the USA in 1915 and settled in Sullivan Street in Greenwich Village, New York City, where he died in 1965.* While Varèse is commonly portrayed as a typical modernist, cosmopolitan, intellectual avant-garde composer, he actually spent long periods in Europe throughout his life and introduced much European composition in the USA (Davismoon, 2004). Henry Miller dedicated a chapter in his *The Airconditioned Nightmare* to Varèse. Here, Varèse was portrayed as a major composer sadly little known to the American public. Personal accounts of Varèse sketch a vivid, humorous and charismatic person, open to new impressions and ideas, engaging in variety of artistic and scientific projects, and a personal friend of a number of major culture personalities of his time (Ouellette, 1968; McMillan, 2004; Jaër 2004; Risset, 2004). For Jean-Claude Risset, Varèse 'was a fiercely independent mind, unwilling to accept any system, any orthodoxy, any paternalistic or autocratic authority' (Risset, 2004: 38). Today, Varèse stands out as a major contributor in contemporary modern music. Varèse was among the first to bring new sound elements into music. Prior to Varèse, however, Hector Berlioz (1803–1869) experimented with sounds through mixing 'single instruments from dissimilar families (flute, harp, cello harmonics and a mute trombone)' (Trieb, 1996: 179) and through the location of orchestral choirs in the performance space. Varèse admired Berlioz's compositions, for instance *Symphonie Fantastique* and *Harold In Italy*, because Berlioz had been (in Varèse's formulation) 'passionately interested in *sound*' (Trieb, 1996: 179). However, Varèse wanted to advance music further and adopt the sounds of the modern times – vehicles, factory whistles, the noise of industry. In 1913, the Italian futurist Luigi Russolo published the book *The Art of the Noises*, theorizing the influence of what was previously regarded as noise in music: 'Ancient life was all silence. In the 19th century, with the invention of machines, Noise was born. Today, Noise is triumphant and reigns sovereign over the sensibility of men' (Russolo, 1986: 23). Even though Varèse refused to be associated with the futurists and was only modestly impressed by their experiments, he

---

* The works of Edgard Varèse include the following compositions: Bourgogne (1908), Amérique (1921), Offrandes (1922), Hyperprism (1923), Octandre (1924), Intégrales (1925), Arcana (1927), Ionisation (1931), Ecuatorial (1934), Density 21.5 (1936), Déserts, (1954), La Poème électronique (1958) and Nocturnal (1958). Many of Varèse's compositions prior to his emigration to the USA in 1915 were destroyed in a warehouse fire in Berlin in 1913.

belonged to a generation exploring the new soundscapes of modernity. For instance, in 1916, Erik Satie's *Parade* 'mixed the sound of the type-writer with the instruments of the symphonic orchestra' (Trieb, 1996: 175). Influenced by such recent experiments, Varèse claimed he wanted to '[m]ake music of the streets, the sounds of the streetcars, the bells on horses' (Varèse, cited in Clayson, 2002: 80). However, this does not imply that Varèse unconditionally wanted to add elements of noise to his compositions. Instead, sound was in Varèse's view to be controlled and monitored in detail: 'While Varèse was fascinated by the physics and acoustics of sound as such, that did not imply that sound in its raw form already had sufficient physical structure to give satisfying musical structure or form to the composition' (Pape, 2004: 20). Pape continues:

> Like an alchemist seeking to transform metal into gold, Varèse wanted to transform raw sounds into music. He was looking for 'the secrets hidden in noises and sounds' ... He wanted to open the possibilities of timbre and intensity, to exit from the impasse of the tempered system. (2004: 23)

Throughout his career, Varèse remained faithful to this credo. When his first major work, *Hyperprism*, premiered in New York City in 1923, the review in *New York Herald* wrote that 'the name of Edgard Varèse will go down in musical history as the man who started something' (Clayson, 2002: 103).

While many modernist composers brought new elements and new instruments into their work, Varèse was concerned that there were no proper instruments yet invented capable of producing the sounds he envisaged. Varèse also spoke of composition as an 'art-science': 'The emotional impulse that moves the composer to write his scores contains the same elements of poetry that incites the scientist to his discoveries,' Varèse argued (cited in Clayson, 2002: 133). Already in 1917, Varèse declared his impatience with the conservatism of European classical music and hoped for scientific achievements to serve as an impetus for a renewal of modern music: 'Our alphabet is poor and illogical. Music, which should be alive and vibrating, needs new means of expression and science alone can infuse it with youthful sap' (Varèse in 1917, cited in Risset, 2004: 31). This does not mean that Varèse was ignorant of past contributions. On the contrary, Varèse introduced a number of Euro-pean composers to an American audience and had great knowledge about medieval choral works, for example. Bernard (1987: xv) writes: 'Varèse was an innovator, but one who worked with a firm grounding in the musical past and with an informed grasp of the limitations imposed by his heritage.' Nevertheless, Varèse was hostile towards contemporary European *neoclassicism*; he thought of many of his contemporary European composers as being backward and conservative, stuck in their admiration for past achievements. Varèse, for his part, thought of Mozart, for instance, as being 'boring' (Jaër, 2004: 60). Varèse argued:

> [I] realized that Europe was drifting back to neoclassicism or rather what is so-called ... You cannot make a classic; it has to become one with age. What is called classicism is really academicism, the influence we want to combat as an evil thing, for it stifles spontaneous expression. (Varèse, cited in Lanza, 19944: 61)

One of the principal differences between the European neoclassicists and Varèse was that the latter refused to acknowledge any closed and regulated system. For Varèse, one must invent one's own rules and the 'musical space' has to be open: 'I think of musical space as open rather than bounded, which is why I speak about projection in the sense that I want simply to project a sound, a musical thought, to initiate it, and then let it take its own course' (Varèse, cited in MacDonald, 2003: 139). For instance, even though Varèse appreciated Schönberg's deconstruction of the tempered system in his dodecaphony, 'he considered it a great tragedy that Schönberg, having freed music from tonality, subsequently sought refuge in a system' (Bernard, 1987: xvii). For Varèse, the artist needs to reinvent new rules every time one creates; one must not succumb to any predefined system. Therefore, Varèse was more influenced by modern science than musicological doctrines and stale systems. Trieb (1996), examining the collaboration between the Dutch electronic company Philips, the Swiss architect Le Corbusier and Varèse in a project for the Brussels Exposition in 1958, emphasized Varèse's affirmative view of science. First, Varèse was dissatisfied with the limits of the existing musical instruments and therefore he sought for new means of producing sound. Second, Varèse thought that the modern composer should not feel '[h]ampered by the orchestra's fixed palette of instruments and the sounds they make (Trieb, 1996: 175). For instance, Varèse used sirens in his work *Ionization* to explore the '[b]eautiful parabolic and hyperbolic curves, which seemed to me equivalent to the parabolas and hyperbolas of the visual domain' (Clayson, 2002: 42). Varèse's vision of modern music represented what Gaston Bachelard spoke of as an 'epistemological break' in the sciences; not only did he want to incorporate new sounds and compose along new lines of thinking, but the very notion of 'music' as such was abandoned. Rather than speaking of music, Varèse favoured the notion of *organized sound*:

> As the term 'music' seems gradually to have shrunk to mean much less than it should, I prefer to use the expression 'organized sound', and avoid the monotonous question: 'But is it music?' 'Organized sound' seems better to take the dual aspect of music as an art-science, with all the recent laboratory discoveries which permit us to hope for the unconditional liberation of music, as well as covering, without dispute, my own music in progress and its requirements. (Varèse, cited in Miller, 1945: 171)

Varèse thus strongly emphasized the scientific features of his work: 'I tell people I am not a musician. I work with rhythms, frequencies and intensities' (Clayson, 2002: 143). What is of particular interest here is Varèse's emphasis on collapsing the distinction between noise on the one hand, and sound and harmony on the other.

> Sound and noise. There is no difference between sound and noise; noise is sound in the course of creation. Noise is due to non-periodic vibration, or vibration too complex in structure, or a duration too complex in structure, or a duration too short to be analysed or understood in the ear. (Varèse, cited in Trieb, 1996: 176)

Again, Varèse speaks of noise in strictly scientific terms, in term of 'non-periodic vibrations', 'duration' and 'perception'. Varèse's artistic vision elaborated on the possibility of exploring the listener's ability to capture what is prior to cognition; 'an excess of reason is mortal to art', Varèse argued (Clayson, 2002: 95). Varèse was under all circumstances sceptical about harmony and 'tunes'. 'Tunes are merely the gossips of music,' Varèse claimed (Clayson, 2002: 143). Above all, Varèse expressed the vision of his music in a vocabulary intersecting with a philosophical or a scientific language. Bernard (1987: xix) points out that Varèse '[p]referred to speak analogically, not analytically, of his music, often with reference to physical phenomena'. However, this does not mean that Varèse thought of his music as being representative of anything but itself: 'Music being a special form of thought can, I believe, express nothing but itself' (MacDonald, 2003: 137). Nevertheless, Varèse employed concepts reminiscent of a geometrical discourse in mathematics, including notions like 'sound-masses', 'planes' and 'counter-points':

> When new instruments will allow me to write music as I conceive it, the movement of the sound-masses, of shifting planes, will be

clearly perceived in my work, taking the place of linear counter-point. When these sound-masses collide, the phenomena of penetration or repulsion will seem to occur. Certain transmutations taking place on certain planes will seem to be projected onto other planes, moving at different speeds and at different angles. There will be no longer the old conception of melody or interplay of melodies. The entire work will be a melodic totality. The entire work will flow as a river flows.

We have actually three dimensions in music: horizontal, vertical, and dynamic swelling and decreasing. I shall add a fourth, sound projection – that feeling that sound is leaving us with no hope of being recollected back, a feeling akin to that aroused by beams of light sent forth by a powerful search-light – for the ear as for the eye, that sense of projection, or a journey into space. (Varèse, cited in Trieb, 1996: 181–2)

When speaking of his composition *Intégrales* (1925), Varèse uses an explicitly geometrical image of 'spatial projection' to capture the idea of sound projection (Ouellette, 1968: 83). Even though Varèse did not conceive of himself as an 'iconoclast' but merely as being '[i]nterested in finding new means by which I could compose with sounds outside the tempered system that existing systems could not play' (Clayson, 2002: 10), his contribution to music, composition and musicology remains a radical critique of predominant doctrines. Such doctrines institute a line of demarcation between noise and melody, mere sound and proper music, art and science, instruments and non-instruments. For Varèse, such a separation is intolerable because it fails to recognize that the experience of sounds and music in the modern world is never fully devoid of what we for the lack of a more adequate term call *noise*. Michel Serres (1982; 1995b) emphasizes that, ontologically speaking, noise is what is primordial and what always surrounds us; one must not think there are pockets of not-yet-eliminated noise, but, on the contrary, noise is what predominates in the world. All human accomplishments are struggles against noise, Serres says. Varèse shared this view and refused to eliminate this register of sounds from his music – his 'organized sound'.

Needless to say, such a vision of music demands a certain amount of patience and a long-term perspective. Varèse thus refused to succumb to what Karlheinz Stockhausen, another eminent explorer of the boundaries between music and everyday life sounds, called the 'the lazy dogmas of impossibility' (Clayson, 2002: 94) and awaited the emergence of electronic equipment to fulfil his vision. Pape (2004) outlines Varèse's project:

> Varèse hoped the new instruments he envisaged would help realize his vision of moving sound masses and shifting planes. Sound would transform into another, moving at different speeds and angles. For Varèse, music existed normally in three dimensions: horizontal, vertical, and that of growth and decay. He proposed a fourth dimension, that of sonic projection in space, which he conceived of as a voyage in space for the ear and for the eye. Ultimately, he conceived his organized sound as geometric forms that were moving in space according to their own laws at varying speeds, varying angles, and with varying rotations. (Pape, 2004: 22)

Unfortunately, when Varèse was introduced to new technology, for instance the computer at the Bell Telephone Laboratories in New York City with which he collaborated during the 1960s, he was often disappointed because the technologies were deemed to be 'too inflexible' (McMillan, 2004: 7). However, despite the lack of technological progress, Varèse remained faithful to his ideas. Nietzsche (1979: 39) said (of himself) in *Ecce Homo* that 'some people are born posthumously'. Such claims are not wholly inadequate when examining Varèse's work. Pape (2004: 19) contemplates this position: 'Edgard Varèse was a visionary composer whose clairvoyance into the future of music was so far-reaching that he could only suffer the fate of so many other visionaries: to be either ignored or attacked'. 'When Varèse died,' Risset reports, 'Pierre Boulez wrote: "Adieu, Varèse, adieu! Votre temps est fini, et il commence" [Farewell, Varèse, farewell! Your time is over and it begins]' (2004: 28). Le Corbusier, another major modernist contributor, points at the poor reception of the work of people whose '[t]ime has not yet come' (Nietzsche, 1979: 39): 'Varèse is a great name in modern music. Look at the case of Picasso, he fought for 50 years, and today he has become the lighthouse of modern painting. Look at the "The Rite of Spring" by Stravinsky, booed for hours' (Le Corbusier, cited in Trieb, 1996: 193). Such is the predicament of the avant-garde: '[T]he artistic vanguard knows that it has no readers, no viewers, and no listeners,' Jean-François Lyotard notes (Lyotard and Thébaud, 1985: 10). However, the avant-garde, dependent on their ability to navigate without any map or any direction but individual ideas and visions, is placing the burden on the audience to be able to understand what cannot yet be understood. For instance, Varèse's contribution to the Philips pavilion at the Brussels exposition in 1958 was riddled by a series of conflicts and disputes and the Philips management team had little opportunity to fully understand Varèse's work, a composition entitled *Poème électronique*. Somewhat paradoxically, Varèse's firm stance against conventional music helped the Philips managers digest his contribution: 'When the Philips directorship learned that Varèse termed his work "organized sound" they were much relieved; what they had heard in the one-minute demonstration in February 1958 was not what they would call music' (Trieb, 1996: 249). Again, by definition, avant-garde work cannot be properly received. Yet Varèse refused to think of his work – or the work of any other for that matter – of being 'ahead of its time': 'Contrary to general notion, the artist is never ahead of his own time, but is simply the only one who is not way behind' (Varèse, cited in Risset, 2004: 34).

The case of Edgard Varèse is informative because it underlines the connections between thinking, composition, new technology and emergent vocabularies to describe and signify new ideas in composition. Varèse foresaw a future where new instruments would enable the fulfilment of his visions, but he was disappointed with the new technologies developed. However, Varèse helped formulate a new vision and a new vocabulary for composition, thus underlining the associations between music composition and other human endeavours. If nothing else, his term 'organized sound' stands out as an important term when understanding the emergence of both contemporary composition and the modern music industry.

Music and new means of perception

As Edgard Varèse thought, among others, music is both the most abstract of arts, embedded in physics and the ultimate matter of being, and the most concrete, that which everyone with proper hearing abilities can immediately perceive and approve or disapprove. Still music demonstrates a separation of first- and second-order structuring similar to art; the first-order perception of music does not of necessity mean that adequate second-order observations may be formulated. In the decisive move from music merely serving a ceremonial or social function to art for art's sake, the need for second-order observations grows. Umberto Eco (1957/2006) is here speaking about the *open work* as what is demanding the listener to fill in the gaps and inconsistencies of the composition:

> A classical composition, whether it may be a Bach fugue, Verdi's *Aida*, or Stravinsky's *Rite of Spring*, posits an assemblage of sound units which the composer arranged in a closed, well-defined manner before presenting it to the listener. He converted his idea into conventional

symbols which more or less oblige the eventual performer to reproduce the format devised by the composer himself. Whereas the new
musical works referred to above [works of Karlheinz Stockhausen,
Luciano Berio and Henri Pousseur] reject the definitive, concluded
message and multiply the formal possibilities of the distribution of
their elements. They appeal to the initiative of the individual performer, and hence they offer themselves, not as finite works which
prescribe specific repetition along given structural coordinates, but as
'open' works, which are brought to their conclusion by the performer
at the same time as he experiences them on an aesthetic plane. (Eco,
2006: 168–9)

In the open work, the listener is facing a 'multiple polarity' of sounds
from which he or she must allow 'a center to emerge from the sound
continuum'; 'Here are no privileged points of view,' Eco (2006: 172) says,
'and all available perspectives are equally valid and rich in potential'.
The open work thus demands a form of co-production on the part of
the listener. Needless to say, the open work represents a more systematic
form of listening'.

It is not only new forms of composition that demand new listening capacities; the technological development in the field of music also
opens up new sonorities. As has been pointed out with the example of the
piano, not being developed to its present form until the early nineteenth
century, musical instruments are continuously modified and enhanced.
Bijsterveld and Schulp (2004) refer to the concept of *organology*, that is,
'the study and knowledge of musical instruments', and discuss a number of examples of how musical instruments are modified. Over time,
even within well-established groups of instruments, there is a continuous technological development. Taylor (2001) points at the clarinet
as another example of an ongoing technological trajectory similar to
that of the piano in terms of being continuously subject to changes
and refinement: while the so-called Boehm-system clarinet was com-
pleted in the mid-1840s, today serving as a standard for the instrument,
clarinetists are 'constantly experimenting' with different reeds, ligatures
and mouthpieces, all of which have their own histories. Therefore, not
all clarinetists, not even classical clarinetists, use the use Boehm-system
clarinets and the term *clarinet* – not even the *soprano clarinet in B-flat*,
the most common clarinet today – does not refer to a 'single, final, technological artifact' (Taylor, 2001: 7). A clarinet is an instrument that is
constantly modified and improved to suit various interests and uses.

Bijsterveld and Schulp (2004) notice a significant conservatism in the
field and therefore, they argue, innovators are regularly representatives

of what they call the 'creative marginality', individuals that must, to use Latour's (1988: 69) phrase (speaking of Louis Pasteur) demonstrate a 'mixture of audacity and traditionalism' (Bijsterveld and Schulp, 2004: 667). This creative marginality is rarely represented by composers but usually rather skilled yet marginal figures such as music teachers and instrument builders, who identify what they regard as annoying short-comings of particular instruments. New versions of instruments or new instruments are generally not immediately recognized and adopted but instead innovators make much use of what Bijsterveld and Schulp (2004) call *strategies of reconciliation:*

> The *strategies of reconciliation* used by the instrument makers themselves were of two kinds. One was to change the *design* of the instrument so as to bring the innovation closer to tradition (innovation → tradition). The other was to rely on *rhetoric* such that the tradition appeared closer to the innovation (innovation ← tradition). An example of the first kind involved 're-conventionalizing' the appearance of the instrument. (Bijsterveld and Schulp, 2004: 665)

New instruments cannot – just like epistemic things in scientific work – be expected to 'speak for themselves', but must be carefully narrated and related to the previous tradition. Instruments are here claimed to either represent a continuation of the predominant register of instruments, or the tradition *per se* is translated into what suits the new instrument. The life of the newly invented instrument is thus precarious; it may be recognized on a broad front and in fact displace older instruments (as in the case of the fretted electric bass guitar) or remain a curiosity in the pantheon of musical instruments (as in the case of the theremin, Sconce, 2000: 119–20). Taylor points at the social and technological changes that have affected the broader public's access to music:

> With each historical technological breakthrough, each technological shift, there are changes in the social organization. The invention of movable type in the early sixteenth century meant that music could escape its former boundaries of the centers of power and move farther than it had before; a 'musical public' was born. Composers climbed the ladder of social respectability; and, by the late eighteenth century, copyright protected their works. The early nineteenth century saw that rise of the composers as artists, as genius ... With music publishing, people could take music home and make it for themselves (which practitioners of orally transmitted music had always done, of

course). But with the gramophone, people by and large stopped making music on their pianos and other instruments at home and started buying it instead, ready-made, turned into consumers rather than producers by the modern Western inventions of talent, genius, and masterpiece. (Taylor, 2001: 4–5)

Even though it took some time to fully see the commercial potential of the gramophone and other media for music reproduction, once they became established as household appliances they led to the gradual erosion of playing as a bourgeoisie skill. The most recent example of a technology that is affecting both how music is created and composed, distributed and consumed is the emergence of computer-based technologies. Digital technologies are used for recording both analogue instruments and for mixing and mastering music and for online distribution of, for example, mp3 files. The composer R. Murray Schafer points at the new opportunities:

> Since the invention of electroacoustical equipment for the transmission and storage of sound, any sound, no matter how tiny, can be blown up and shot around the world, or packaged on tape or record from the maker of the sound. Sounds have been torn from their natural sockets and given amplified and independent existence. (2006: 34)

Although some writers hope that access to digital technology may make broader groups of individuals take part in music production (Taylor, 2001: 5), to date it is primarily the distribution and consumption of music that have been debated. Emerging social practices like file-sharing have been fiercely debated in the new millennium as posing a threat to the artists' copyright, established for centuries.

Music and organization

Introduction

In organization theory and management studies, Pritchard, Korczynski and Elmes (2007) note, music and musicology are addressed in three distinct literatures: (1) the empirically focused literature on 'the role and impact of recorded music in work environments'; (2) a literature 'that asks us to consider what scholars can learn from music about managing and organizing'; and (3) a literature that asks what shared 'structures and processes' 'create patterns in both music and work' (Pritchard, Korczynski and Elmes, 2007: 5). The first body of literature includes studies in the fields of human relations theory and human resource management practice and demonstrates how music can be used as an organizational resource to accomplish desired ends. For instance, early proponents of scientific management such as Frederick W. Taylor's disciple Frank Gilbreth (1911) discuss a case where the workers in a Cuban cigar factory listening to music while working substantially improved their productivity. In this literature, music is what serves as a social lubricator, making social systems run more smoothly. In addition, in the domain of marketing the use of music to relax the shopper and make shopping a pleasant experience is an early example of a function of music in a social engineering project. Second, a body of research includes studies of record companies, entertainment venues, rock festivals, opera houses and a long range of organizations and firms living off music production and consumption. It is noteworthy that such studies do not need to draw on a musicology framework – that is, music *per se* is nothing more than an organizational product no different from financial derivate instruments, health care services or dairy products – but may instead rely on mainstream organization theory. Such studies include, for instance, Arian's (1971) study of organization change in the Philadelphia Orchestra, Murningham and Conlon's (1991) study of group dynamics and de-paradoxification work in twenty professional British string quartets, or Maitlis's (2005) study of sensemaking in a symphonic orchestra. In the third body of literature, music and musicology serve as a domain from whence metaphors are extracted and brought into organization analysis to make sense out of organizational or managerial events and occurrences. Here concepts and expressions such as 'harmony', 'jazz improvisation', 'being tuned' and so forth are used as metaphors or metonymy underlining practices aimed at accomplishing tonality in a disharmonic system. Similar to the great European tradition starting with Bach, harmony and tonality are praised qualities of the social order. In the literature on jazz improvisation, as a useful metaphor for capturing how complex innovation work is conducted, there is an emphasis on individual deviations from the scripts, but otherwise these metaphors tend to privilege harmony over other sonorities.

In the following, the use of music in organization will be examined from a number of perspectives. It will distinguish between *music at work* in terms of being either what is used to handle managerial or human resource management concerns (i.e. monotony or boredom) and *music work* wherein a range of professionals and experts work to perform, record, distribute, or promote various forms of music. In addition, the use of music as a tool for social engineering and the shaping of the public sphere will be examined. Here the literature on the use of music in retailing and at events is attended to, showing that music is a significant means for structuring and influencing everyday modern life.

Music at work

Work is a fundamental human activity and naturally popular music pays close attention to such everyday human experience (Linstead, 2006). Beside love and eroticism, work is a persistent theme in popular culture and various genres of music are no exception to the rule. What has been noticed by commentators is that there is a significant difference between genres and time periods. For instance, in mainstream rock music, Rhodes (2007) argues, the relationship between work and the working subject is complicated and sketched in rather bleak terms. 'It is rare to find any rock songs that celebrate a dogmatic, idealized, or utopian notion of work and organization. When rockers sing about work, they sing about the problems people have with it,' Rhodes writes (2007: 25). While rock music formulates critical views of working-class experience, American hip-hop and rap music, a genre consumed by a broad variety of social groups, addresses the *Weltanschauung* of urban coloured communities (George, 1998; Chang, 2003). In these communities, historically less favoured than the American white working class, Rehn and Sköld argue (2005), there is little of the *ennui* that Rhodes (2007) finds in the rock music genre lyrics. Instead, rap music – more specifically, the subgenres of rap examined by Rehn and Sköld (2005); (Lena, 2006, identifies no less than thirteen different subgenres of hip-hop music) – celebrates material resources and extravagant consumerism. Hip-hop and rap is a genre filled with *joie de vivre* and celebrations of conspicuous lifestyle preferences. While rock music is often based on realism, deploring daily efforts at dead-end jobs and providing little or no hope for a better future, hip-hop and rap music is escapist in terms of refusing to recognize the social structures of a society characterized by poverty, unequal distribution of life chances, and forms of immediate and unobtrusive discrimination. Society, work and the economy are thus conceived of in opposing ways in different popular music genres.

In this section, the literature on music at work will be addressed. Pritchard, Korczynski and Elmes (2007) summarize previous research in Table 3.1 overleaf.

It is outside the scope of this chapter to review all of the periods. Instead, a number of studies pointing at the many uses of music will be examined.

Table 3.1 The broad pattern of the role of music in the regulation of work and the types of research in four periods

	Role of music in the regulation of work	Extent of music's role and typical forms of work affected	Main body of research
Preindustrialization	Workers sing as they work, sometimes to coordinate and pace labour	True for many manual occupations. Examples include sailors' shanties and slave songs	Research of social historians and folklorists
Industrialization	Tendency to associate imposition of industrial discipline with musical silence	Evidence of isolated examples of musical culture existing in some factories	Research of social historians
Fordist industrialization	Centrally distributed broadcast music serves to relieve boredom in Taylorized workplaces	Widespread introduction of broadcast music in factories with low-skilled work from the 1940s onward in the UK and the USA	Research of management-oriented industrial psychologists. Largely ignored by industrial sociologists
Postindustrialization	Individualized modes of music consumption allow individuals to use music in a range of ways at work. Broadcast music in service settings	Limited research suggests that iPod use is more prevalent in high-tech workplaces among 'knowledge workers'	Extremely limited extant research on individuals. Research in service settings primarily centres on music's effect on consumers rather than workers

Source: Adapted from Pritchard, Korczynski and Elmes, 2007: 8.

The use of music in Cadbury and Rowntree confectionery factories and the BBC's Music While You Work *programme*

In the interwar period, industry psychologists directed attention towards music as a means of reducing the negative consequences of repetitive and monotonous work. As early as 1929, the National Bureau for the Advancement of Music published the book *Music in Industry* by Kenneth Clark, suggesting that music in industry is 'no longer an experiment' since 'its efficacy has been practically demonstrated under varying conditions and in nearly every field of industrial activity' (Clark, 1929: 1). Clark here advocates music, like so many followers after him, as what provides a true win-win opportunity for owners and management on the one side and employees on the other. 'It is the good fortune of music in industry that while it does increase the efficiency of the employee and thus greatly benefits the employer, it also brings a great deal of personal happiness to the worker who takes part in it', Clark announces (1929: 8). In Clark's view, music is capable of increasing productivity, providing a common ground for executives and 'the working force' – Clark here lists a number of CEOs and holders of management positions being engaged in various amateur music activities – 'improving' the morale of the workers, and increasing productivity. For the workers, music is beneficial because it 'counteracts the monotony and fatigue of the job' but also 'opens up awareness of self-expression' (Clark, 1929: 18–19). In Clark's early account, music effectively serves the role of the 'oil in the machinery' (the title of the first chapter). Clark (1929) then continues to review how music has been used in a number of sectors of the American economy, including music in 'great stores' in a range of American cities, 'at manufacturing strongholds' including the steel business, automotive industry, textile plants and oil refineries, and in 'business offices'. Clark's (1929) account of the various uses and the value of music in industry is a clear statement in favour of music and testifies to an instrumental and functionalist, yet humanistic, belief that music is capable of producing many benevolent and desirable effects.

One of the first more systematic scientific studies of music at work was Wyatt and Langdon's 1937 study of music in work settings, providing 'scientifically testable' claims of music's 'industrial potential' (Jones, 2005). Over a period of twenty-four weeks, Wyatt and Langdon tested the effects of six differing 'temporal programmes' including 'dance music', 'foxtrots' and 'waltzes' on twelve women making paper crackers in a confectionery factory. Wyatt and Langdon theorized music's effects in terms of 'psychological stimulation', capable of relieving boredom and alleviating the 'awareness of monotonous conditions' but without 'distracting visual and cognition attention' (Jones, 2005: 727). Music thus provided new opportunities for shaping the working environment for the equal benefit of workers, management and owners. Wyatt and Langdon also found significant positive effects in their experiments: 'In general ... the type of music played under the varying conditions of this experiment produced an increase in output during playing period ranging from 6.2% to 11.3%' (Wyatt and Langdon, 1937: 38, cited in Jones, 2005: 727). Such results spawned a substantial body of new research. In 1943, after just a few years of research in this domain, the industrial psychologist Burris-Meyer (1943) declared that 'auditory stimuli' could produce various embodied and mental effects on the part of the listener:

> By auditory stimuli, we can control metabolism. We can increase or decrease muscular energy. We can increase respiration. We can increase or decrease pulse rate ... We can change the threshold of sensory perception, and this is very important in precision work. We can reduce, delay, or increase fatigue. By the control of these phenomena it is possible to establish a physiological basis for the generation of emotion. (Burris-Meyer, 1943: 262, cited in Jones, 2005: 727)

Other writers, like Benson (1945), were capable of providing detailed recommendations on what music to play in work settings: 'Hawaiian music, waltzes, and South American music is very good work music,' Benson (1945: 25) remarks. Moreover, Benson (1945: 29) continues, 'to date, scientific surveys have led us to believe that classical music should not be played in a factory, either during work or rest periods'. At the same time, Benson (1945: 19) warns that there is 'no foolproof method' to know when to play what kind of music. Still, there are some general recommendations that are applicable: work music is 'most beneficial' when it is 'easily recognized, easily sung, and easily heard'. Therefore, Benson (1945: 23) continues, the recordings played in the factory or workplace 'must have a definite melody line, a steady rhythm, and as nearly as possible a constant volume level'. Above all, Benson is convinced that music is of great value for industrial organization:

> Those employers who have installed broadcasting systems have learned that by playing music during a certain number of minutes out of each work period, much of the wasted energy and time is counteracted or is spent more beneficially. Instead of leaving their bench or machine, workers are more apt to be found whistling or singing (at their work), singly or in groups, to the music, or, if there is a rest

period, dancing to the music. This break in the monotony, this getting rid of excess energy or pent-up emotions does more to alleviate fatigue and overcome irregular work habits than trying to make the employee work in time to the music. (Benson, 1945: 22–3)

Music became an integral part of the managerial system in the inter-war period and the World War II years, a tool complementing previous managerial practices capable of both producing less strenuous work conditions and increasing productivity.

In the remainder of this section, two studies conducted by Marek Korczynski and his colleagues will be discussed in some detail. The first study examines the use of music in the Cadbury and the Rowntree confectionery factories in Yorkshire in England in the interwar period. Both the Cadbury and the Rowntree families were Quakers and ran their companies in accordance with a paternalistic credo. For instance, Edward Cadbury was worried that the repetitive factory work would stunt the growth of younger workers and therefore he advocated singing as 'a form of physical exercise' (Robertson, Korczynski and Pickering, 2007: 217). However, this did not mean that factory workers could sing as they liked; instead, the Cadbury board minutes suggest, the singing should be done 'systematically'. However, this 'systematic' and regulated use of music in an industrial context was a new phenomenon – an 'experiment' in Cadbury's own term. In the Rowntree factory, a similar policy was enacted and was greatly appreciated by the employees. The company magazine reported in January 1922: 'The half-hour singing . . . is looked forward to and enjoyed by all concerned . . . By general consent . . . the half-hour is a pleasant one, according to more than one of the girls, is the shortest in the day' (cited in Robertson, Korczynski and Pickering, 2007: 218). The use of music was framed in highly gendered terms. Many of the most repetitive and static jobs in the factories were undertaken by women. The assumption was that women – in general infantilized through being associated with 'youthful labour' – suffered more than men from the fatigue of factory work and therefore benefited more from the music. Still, oral histories suggest the female co-workers appreciated the music. They were not, Robertson, Korczynski and Pickering (2007: 228) argue, 'passive recipients of music but active agents who continue to refer to music in narrating their own work histories'. However, part of the official reasoning for using music was to increase productivity. One woman's narrative reflected how music supported her work: 'You could work like billy-o with it, you know' (Robertson, Korczynski and Pickering, 2007: 225). The right music could, for instance, provide a rhythm for the performance of repetitive tasks like packing. In addition, music could also give the sense of having more energy and resulting in more productive work. At the same time, there is a subversive element in music that may be threatening for management. Many labour movements and religious movements – the Salvation Army being perhaps the most well-known case – used music to create a sense of unity (Hall, 2001). A more recent example is Dennis's (2007) study of the Australian Police Department in the city of Grayville (a pseudonym), which used the police brass band to handle emotional strains in police work and to build better relations with the Grayville community. However, the collective singing of songs during strikes suggests that there is a certain potency of protest in music. 'The sound of a room full of women singing together at volume would have been a formidable force,' Robertson, Korczynski and Pickering note (2007: 226). It is therefore unsurprising that singing was banned in the early days of Cadbury and that some overlookers at Rowntree stopped music in the interwar period, since 'actively engaging with singing (or perhaps dancing) could be disruptive to both productivity and general factory discipline' (Robertson, Korczynski and Pickering, 2007: 226). In summary, music was introduced in the two British chocolate factories on basis of both philanthropic and financial objectives in line with the predominant paternalistic culture of the two firms. The music served a purpose to release some of the strains of work and to help the employees deal with a monotonous workday. Still, music was structured and managed to suit the interests both of labour and management, and the workers were given permission to sing during certain periods of the workday but only music that was regarded as appropriate.

Korczynski and Jones (2006) studied the BBC's *Music While You Work* programme and its effects on factory work during the World War II years. They emphasize that initiatives like *Music While You Work* represented a break with the previous treatment of music under industrial capitalism. They point at the exclusion and prohibition of traditional forms of music in the emerging disciplinary factory regimes:

> The relationship between music and work was changed dramatically by the advent of industrial capitalism. In pre-industrial times, it was common for people in many occupations to sing as they laboured . . . The shanties sung out by sailors as they hauled ropes for the setting of sails are perhaps the best known of these work songs in Britain . . . Music and work were mutually constituted to a significant degree, with the rhythm and pace of one informing the rhythm and pace of the other. The imposition of factory discipline, however, meant the

proscription of musical expression at work pushing music and work to exist in binary opposition to each other ... Manchester spinners in the mills of the early nineteenth century, for instance, would be fined for even whistling at work. (Korczynski and Jones, 2006: 146)

While the first uses of gramophone to broadcast music in workplaces may have occurred in the 1910s, it was not until the war years that broadcast music was employed in both British and North American factories (Korczynski and Jones, 2006: 148). Korczynski and Jones (2006: 154) argue that attempts to 'humanise the workplace', a political project influenced by the American Human Relations tradition founded by Elton Mayo at Harvard University and financially backed by the Rockefeller Foundation (Guillén, 1994; O'Conner, 1999), were launched in an attempt to avoid 'disturbing the essentials of Taylorism'. Such activities thus centred on research on better ventilation and lighting systems, and 'the creation of "optimum" rest breaks systems'. Korczynski and Jones continue:

> Central here were attempts to reform elements of work in a way that would lead to both greater efficiency *and* to higher levels of satisfaction among the workforce. But, ultimately, such reforms, at the margins of the basic Taylorist organisation of work, were only worthwhile if they did increase efficiency. (2006: 154)

Music While You Work was one such attempt to increase efficiency and worker satisfaction. In a memo issued by the BBC on 10 July 1940, it was stated that the music broadcast should have the following characteristics: '(a) rhythmical music, (b) non vocal (*familiar vocals now accepted*), (c) no interruptions by announcements, (d) *maintain volume to overcome workshop noises*' (Korczynski and Jones, 2006: 149, emphasis in the original). This music was, in other words, composed and performed, similar to the Muzak Corporation's musical programming, to provide a smooth work pace with few interruptions and disturbing effects. Such declarations were not based on aesthetic preferences but were embedded in clinical research conducted by industry psychologists. In a report published in 1943, a BBC executive reported such clinical research results: 'Research has proven conclusively that music acts as mental "tonic", relieves boredom and encourages the tired worker, promotes happiness, improves health, lessens nervous strains, and gives increased production' (Reynolds, 1943: 4, cited in Korczynski and Jones, 2006: 157). However, there were limits to the willingness to satisfy worker expectations. In the report *Fatigue and Boredom in Repetitive Work*, published in 1937, for instance, '[i]t was found that many (twenty-eight out of sixty-eight) workers had waltzes as their favourite type of music. But waltzes were found to be one of the types of music least conducive to increased output' (Korczynski and Jones, 2006: 155). Even though the *Music While You Work* programme was not designed to satisfy workers' preferences and needs but to enhance productivity and reduce boredom and fatigue, it became a success in terms of number of factories and workplaces broadcasting the programme. In the BBC's survey of the fifth year of the series, published in 1945, it was announced that 'over 9,000 major industrial organizations are now relaying the programmes through their factories' (Korczynski and Jones, 2006: 148). Even though there are good reasons to believe that the *Music While You Work* programme did in fact accomplish some of the dual objectives of increasing efficiency and worker satisfaction, Korczynski and Jones argue that the initiative was 'primarily a top-down exercise in which the workforce and their representatives played at best secondary roles'. They continue:

> In particular, the absence of a central role played by the trade unions in pushing demands for factory music is telling. Also, the evidence showed clearly that there was a significant degree of mediation in the type of music played, and an absence of workforce voice regarding decisions over the duration of the music played. Given this, it is hard to see the development of factory music as a straightforward accommodation between capital and labour in mid-twentieth century Britain. (2006: 160)

Rather than being an example of the aligning of the interests of capital and labour, Korczynski and Jones (2006: 161) argue that '[t]here was a sense of *paternalist* accommodation between capital and labour partly underpinning the development of factory music'.

Another more positive view of the working subject's active use of music to endure stressful work conditions is Korczynski *et al.*'s (2005) historical account of female factory workers' singing in British munition factories during World War II. Just like the factories broadcasting *Music While You Work*, the female factory workers were exposed to a similar managerialist and paternalist ideology – for instance, the song 'Deep in the Heart of Texas' was banned from the *Music While You Work* programme in 1942 because it was a 'participatory song' and 'its inclusion disrupted production – too many workers downed tools to clap hands in appropriate places' (Korczynski *et al.*, 2005: 190) – but the female workers did make use of music to suit their own interests and demands: 'The women workers did not just do the tasks allocated to them in a docile manner, whilst passively listening to music. Rather they actively and creatively used music to survive as humans in the de-humanized context of soul-destroying jobs' (Korczynski *et al.*, 2005: 195).

During World War II, music was brought back into the workplace, but it was not, as Korczynski and Jones (2006) and Korczynski *et al.* (2005) show, primarily propelled by humanist ideals but as being an additional production factor in the hands of management. However, at times factory workers managed to appropriate the music, making it a source of liberation and Joy rather than being merely a component in a social machinery preoccupied with efficiency and output.

Company songs and the community

Another example of paternalist uses of music to shape employees' behaviour and preferences is the use of company songs. El-Sawad and Korczynski (2007) study the 'IBM Songbook' in use at IBM in the interwar period and up to the 1950s, when the Songbook became obsolete. The founder of IBM, Thomas J. Watson Sr, nourished a firm paternalist ideal and conceived of himself and publicly placed himself in the role of the father figure for his employees. Watson Sr was himself fond of music and appreciated singing, despite the fact that biographers portray him as 'tone deaf and unmusical' (El-Sawad and Korczynski, 2007: 86), and the Songbook suited his paternalistic leadership at IBM. This paternalist ideology, abounding with 'father and family' metaphors and narratives, is apparent in the Songbook. The Songbook itself was based on well-known folk tunes and popular songs – in many cases songs used by radical unions – provided with lyrics celebrating the employing company, IBM executives, the accomplishments of the sales force and so forth. El-Sawad and Korczynski (2007: 83) review the Songbook: 'The 51 songs classed as main company songs include Song Number 1 (the IBM anthem, 'Ever Onward'), songs 3 to 11 (songs in praise of corporate executives including three songs devoted to Watson Sr), Song 16 (the IBM 'Anniversary Song') and Songs 67 to 106 (a mixture of songs extolling IBM dogma, celebrating products, praising sales records, and geared to a number of different collectives at IBM – IBM engineers, factory foremen'. The lyrics were not articulating subtle beliefs but were rather direct and unobtrusive celebrations of the company and its leading men. Some examples:

> We're co-workers at IBM – all one big family.
>
> (Song 67, 'The IBM Family')

Who are we? Who are we?
The International Family
We are T.J. Watson men
We represent the IBM.

(Song 76, 'The IBM slogan') (Both cited in El-Sawad
and Korczynski, 2007: 83)

IBM, happy men, smiling all the way
Oh what fun it is to sell our products night and day

(Song 74; cited in El-Sawad and Korczynski, 2007: 86)

'Through song', El-Sawad and Korczynski (2007: 85) say, 'IBM employees would sing praise to IBM, to senior leaders, and, not least, to Watson Sr himself.' Of the main songs, 65 per cent refer to the belief about the superiority of IBM products, and 31 per cent of the songs address the recognition of product sales and promotion (El-Sawad and Korczynski, 2007: 86). El-Sawad and Korczynski carefully account for how their analytical categories such as 'paternalism', 'evangelism', 'sales', and 'work ethics' are addressed in the songs. The Songbook served, El-Sawad and Korczynski (2007: 89) suggest, both as a medium for disseminating predominant beliefs and norms and as 'a mnemonic in the creation of social memory':

Through song, employees were instructed on how to think, what to feel, and what to do. They should unite, sing praise, all hail, pay homage, and proudly cheer IBM and its senior executives. They should revere, honor, follow, and serve forever their leaders. They should sell. They should feel loyal, faithful, and proud; love, honor, and adore IBM, its products, its senior executives, and last but certainly by no means least, Watson Sr. (El-Sawad and Korczynski, 2007: 87)

However, after World War II, old cultural forms gradually became obsolete and unfashionable. For instance, the Nazis' use of music at rallies, at their marches, and in mass displays of coordinated athletic movements had undermined the desirability of using music in social bonding and in 'consolidating group solidarity' (El-Sawad and Korczynski, 2007: 100). In addition, the folk tunes and popular songs rearticulated in the IBM Songbook eventually lost their cultural significance as new forms of music emerged:

[B]y the time of the first IBM Songbook was printed in 1931, the music was already out of step with the popular music of the time in the United States – jazz and swing. As the 20th century advanced, it became harder and harder for management to find contemporary music that had strong connotations of the collective. (El-Sawad and Korczynski, 2007: 101)

As Maney (2003: 120, cited in El-Sawad and Korczynski, 2007: 99) remarks, the IBM Songbook gradually became a document of past cultural forms and public preferences: 'The generation of employees who listened to Elvis Presley on the radio had little interest in publicly singing outmoded tunes about the company. Nobody thought to write IBM lyrics set to the tune of *Heartbreak Hotel*. The songs faded out.'

Although Thomas J. Watson Sr's preference for paternalist songs may appear as an amusing historical fact, inextricably entangled with social, cultural and economic conditions long since gone, the use of company songs and similar collective cultural expressions have in fact survived until rather recently. For instance, Graham's (1994; 1995) study of a so-called Japanese Subaru-Isuzu transplant in the USA shows that the Japanese sought to adopt an American culture and developed a company song named 'Team Up For Tomorrow' that was played at formal ceremonies and gatherings at the factory. Even though Graham (1994; 1995) reports widespread scepticism towards such cultural manifestations, it is telling that seemingly outmoded uses of music appear to reappear at times. Moreover, paternalism may not be ages away but continue to emerge in new forms (Fleming, 2005).

Organizing the public sphere: the concept of muzak and its contemporary forms

In the following section, a case bringing together the second and third type of studies will be examined: the case of the Muzak Corporation, which invented what may be called the 'musical programming' of social life. Muzak is of great interest for organization theorists and management students because it is both a financially successful company and the outcome of great entrepreneurial skills and a foremost example of what Weber spoke of as the rationalization of society. Lanza (1994: 32) reports that the market for household radio receivers boomed in the 1920s and 1930s in the USA. In 1924, one third of America's furniture budget was spent on radios and by 1930, 40 per cent of American households had a radio; in 1940, 82 per cent of the households featured a radio. Music gradually became the background sound of most homes during the interwar period. During the period, the Muzak Corporation, founded in 1934 by the former military general Owen Squire, developed and marketed its own versions of 'functional music' (Lanza, 1994: 40).

The Muzak Corporation saw early the need for an anchoring of their product in scientific evidence, pointing at immediate social benefits, and engaged researchers to prove the value of the product: Lanza reports:

> Following an early Stevens Institute of Technology study in the 1930s (which found that 'functional music' reduced absenteeism in workplaces by 88 percent, with 53 percent reduction in early departures), industrial psychologists started taking Muzak very seriously and conducted similar, more elaborate tests. (1994: 43)

Muzak was part of what Shenhav (1999) refers to as the 'craze of efficiency' brought by the engineering ideology enacted by the emerging engineering class gaining a foothold in American society from the end of the nineteenth century (see Veblen, 1904, for an account of the social consequences of the movement). Shenhav (1999: 96) accounts for the breadth of this 'efficiency craze':

> The spread of the efficiency craze in America spilled over – by acts of translation – to seemingly unrelated domains, colonializing religious, moral, and political thought. Feminists began to apply the principle of efficiency to the home ... Protestant churches were receptive to the idea, and in New York a Church Efficiency Committee was established ... Gilbreth [one of F.W. Taylor's disciples] extended motion studies of musicians, baseball players, fencers, and oyster-openers. (Shenhav, 1999: 96)

At that time, music was a domain of yet unexploited potential to be further explored. One of the binding principles of Muzak products was that the music should be devoid of 'factors that distract attention – change in tempo, loud brasses, vocals' (Lanza, 1994: 48). The researcher Richard L. Cardinell (cited in Lanza, 1994: 48), engaging in research commissioned by Muzak, argued: 'The worker should be no more aware of the music than of good lighting. The rhythms, reaching him subconsciously, create a feeling of well-being and eliminate strain.' Not only were Muzak's products used in factories and 'back-offices' to soothe the employees but they were also used to manipulate the behaviour of consumers and customers. For instance, a regular day at a restaurant may use the following 'sequencing programme':

> A typical sequencing program for restaurants complemented the daily eating ritual. The breakfast hours (7–9 am) offered cheery sunrise melodies and caffeinated rhythms. From 9 am to noon, background filler whetted appetites until the official lunch diet of

light classical and spicier strains was served. After more filler begin-ning at 2 pm, cocktail tunes came on at 5 pm to mix with piano and such exotic condiments as vibraphone. The discreet and qui-etly classical dinner hours from 6 to 9 pm provided sustenance in anticipation of the evening dance protocol, which permitted increased volume and tempo the closer midnight encroached. (Lanza, 1994: 42)

Muzak's innovative use of music eventually proved to be useful in social-engineering projects and military activities. For instance, military research in US Army Human Engineering Laboratories on radar detection showed that 'the subjects hearing a Muzak program proved to have a .27 of a second faster reaction time than those exposed to nothing but the white noise of a small fan' (Lanza, 1994: 151). However, there are also some amusing anecdotes of how the programming did not always work to full satisfaction. Lanza reports:

Military vigilance workers may have performed better with Muzak's standard format, but workers employed in the world's oldest profes-sion at a brothel in Stuttgart, Germany, grew concerned because their uptempo Muzak 'Light Industrial' selections were not getting clients in and out fast enough to secure a profitable turnover. The proprietors had to make a special request for livelier music on their second and fourth quarter-hours. (1994: 152)

Notwithstanding such 'programming failures', Muzak was ranked forty-three among the world's largest companies in the late 1960s and early 1970s; total Muzak earnings exceeded $400 million per year (Lanza, 1994: 149). Although Muzak's musical programming today seems overtly manipulative – the novelist Vladimir Nabokov flatly described it as 'abominably offensive' – the ideas formulated by Muzak executives and their collaborating academic researchers are now widely present in soci-ety. Virtually no public space fails, in one way or another, to design an audible space of preference. At the end of the 1970s, Muzak even launched its first own-broadcast satellite, providing new opportunities for global distribution of light musical entertainment. Muzak's contribu-tion to social organization represents a generalized form of management of audible space with the intention to coordinate and structure social reality for the benefit of everyone; more pleasant restaurant dinners, less boring elevator rides, a soothing atmosphere in the supermarket and a more alert military defence are some of the desired and often accomplished outcomes.

Radano (1989), seeking to examine muzak in more affirmative terms than social scientists regularly do, agrees that the very idea of muzak is to 'enforce a sense of musical certainty and conformity'. Muzak is therefore wholly devoid of what Walter Benjamin (1973) called the 'aura' of an artistic work, a sense of unicity and authenticity. Through the use of precise means of style devoid of information and surprise, that is, 'a distinct lack of abrasive tone colors, harmonic ambiguity, rhythmic complexity', muzak helps to stabilize and structure social spaces into 'congruous ordered assemblages' (Radano, 1989: 456). Such capacity to familiarize and structure social space is, as we will see, highly valued when designing contemporary shopping spaces. However, even though the musical performances of muzak are overtly bland, Rodano argues that muzak exploits a tradition of thinking articulated in the European avant-garde, namely that of eliminating the distinction between the artist and the listener. Radano (1989: 457) notes that muzak places the responsibility for creating a meaningful experience in the 'realm of the receiver', thus 'circumventing the dichotomy of artist and listener'. Muzak thus poses a 'double threat' to traditional artistic standards and authority. First, it is representative of how mass culture has appropriated modernist and avant-garde aesthetics, which in turn has helped reshape how 'everyday Americans' think about and interpret the arts; second, muzak represents a populist ethos that rejects the notion of the artist and the 'autonomous art work' (Radano, 1989: 458). Muzak is, thus, in all its blandness and suavity, radical in terms of appropriating the projects of decentring of the arts and the artist, themes shared in artists and composers as diverse as the early French avant-garde artists, the group of Dada artists and the composer John Cage. In muzak, it is no longer the artist and his or her work that matters but the actual experience of the music; it is in its essence populist in terms of demanding very little, almost nothing, from the listener. Muzak thus supports Adorno's (1934/1978: 270–1) declaration that 'the concept of taste is itself outmoded'. Taste presupposes cultural training and discipline; muzak demands no such skills and capacities. It operates to constitute, in Radovan's formulation, a 'simple being'.

Contemporary muzak: music and atmospherics in retailing

While muzak may today be regarded as being obsolete and antiquated – the very use of the term muzak to denote the presence of kitsch and overtly commercial products in the domain of music suggests that such is the case – the dominating idea of muzak, the behaviourist belief in the ability to actively 'shape' human behaviour through music, remains viable in marketing research and marketing practice. For instance, in a study conducted by the BBC where listeners were asked to keep diaries and carefully record all music, including bird song, ring tones and radio jingles, they listened to during a twenty-four-hour cycle, it was found that, on average, an individual was listening to two hours and forty-six minutes of chosen music as against one hour and sixteen minutes unchosen (White, 2007). Attitudes towards the unchosen music were 38 per cent negative, 28 per cent positive and 34 per cent neutral. Even though the results were ambiguous and could equally support arguments put forth by the pro- and anti-muzak lobby, in contemporary society every individual is exposed to twenty-nine minutes of unchosen, negatively experienced music every day.

In the corporate 'conquest of cool' – in Frank's (1997) apt phrase – and the emergence of 'hip consumerism', major corporations seek new and unexploited bands to fashion their commercials with 'credible' soundtracks. For instance, in Sweden the band Oh Laura won the 'Song of the Year' Grammy award in 2007 for the song 'Release Me', which was featured in a Saab commercial. The band was largely unknown to the wider Swedish or international audience prior to the use of their music to market the vehicle. Trading money for credibility is becoming the great opportunity for bands and artists of various genres. In Hollywood, many films, especially those marketed to younger audiences, are accompanied by soundtracks filled with selected songs supporting the core product, giving it the right 'buzz' in the focused group of consumers. On a more mundane level, in everyday retailing, music serves a similar function. Yalch and Spangenberg use the concept of 'atmospherics' to refer to the '[d]esign of an environment through the use of colors, lighting, sounds, and furnishing to stimulate perceptual and emotional responses by consumers, and ultimately affect their behavior' (Yalch and Spangenberg, 1990: 60). Music plays a central role in providing an adequate atmosphere, or 'sound environment', to please shoppers. However, as Yalch and Spangenberg (1990: 60) argue, 'despite widespread beliefs that music enhances a retail environment and thus results in increased store traffic, greater satisfaction and higher sales, a literature review revealed minimal direct evidence supporting these beliefs'. A great number of studies have aimed at proving the effectiveness of music in creating a pleasant shopping experience (Garlin and Owen, 2006): '[E]xperimental studies of consumers subject to music shows that background music has a positive effect on consumer spending and turnover ... Background music tends to reduce frustration at queuing and waiting and supports the adoption of helpful forms of behavior (e.g., offering to do volunteer work)', Pritchard, Korczynski and Elmes (2007: 11) conclude.

Yalch and Spangenberg's (1990) own study indicates that shoppers in fact do respond 'psychologically and behaviourally' even though few shoppers consciously notice the presence of the music. Even though the results provide only weak indicators in favour of the use of music in retailing, Yalch and Spangenberg maintain that 'atmospherics remains an area of environmental psychology offering great potential for improving the efficiency and effectiveness of retail and service operations' (1990: 62). Similar weak indicators are reported by Garlin and Owen's (2006) meta-analysis of a significant number of studies of the use of music in retailing. Results suggest that music has a small but significant effect on the shoppers' well-being and slow music is proved to make them spend longer at the venue than faster music. In addition, higher volume is perceived negatively. The study concludes that slow, familiar, low-volume music may be helpful in shaping consumer behaviour (see also Alan, 2006).

DeNora (2000), advocating what may be called a 'practice-based view of music' (see Schatzki, Knorr Cetina and Savigny, 2001), shows that music is in fact a 'social force' shaping the social space through the deliberate use of various types of music in different settings. Social space is, in DeNora's (2000) account, not only architecturally and technologically spatialized but space is also produced (in Lefebvre's, 1991, sense of the term) through musical arrangements. In retail outlets, DeNora (2000: 134) says, '[m]usic serves as part of a collection of cultural resources that can be used to create scenic specificity'. She continues: 'In conjunction with window displays, décor, assistants dressed in employee-discounted merchandise and, indeed, the merchandise itself, music is a means of delineating retail territory, a way of projecting imaginary shoppers on to the aesthetically configured space of the shop floor' (2000, 135). In a study of the use of music in eleven shops on the high street in an English city, DeNora and her colleague found that music was used not only to affect customer behaviour but also to help the employees do the 'emotional work' expected from them, for instance, in terms of acting as 'co-shoppers' influencing the 'purchase behaviour' of customers: 'We noted numerous examples of staff behaving as if they were co-shoppers, "confessing" to customers their own shopping difficulties and dilemmas in a cosy, gossipy manner' (DeNora, 2000: 139). In general, the study points at a number of strategic uses of music in the public sphere, actively attempting to shape and create social space and individual behaviour.

Sterne's (1997) study of the Mall of America in Bloomington, Indiana, USA, the second-largest mall in North America by the time of the study, addresses a number of themes discussed by DeNora (2000). For Sterne (1997: 23), referencing Henri Lefebvre's *The Production of Space* (1991), music is a 'form of architecture'; rather than simply filling an empty space, the music 'becomes part of the consistency of that space'. Sound is an integral component of the building's infrastructure, always present in various forms in different parts of the mall. Music is here 'programmed music', music designed to serve as an 'architectural element' that supports the commercial interests of the shops in the mall – the mall is after all 'a built space devoted to consumerism' (Sterne, 1997: 25). Such programmed music (appearing in the form of background or foreground music) is music that is 'stripped of any distinctive elements' (Sterne, 1997: 30), representing a 'style devoid of surprise' in Radano's (1989) apt formulation. Music is here used to create a sense of pleasure and well-being, aimed at prolonging the time spent in the mall. In addition, each shop or restaurant in the mall uses music to actively cultivate the 'business image considered most appealing to whatever demographic group of customers they hope to attract' (Sterne, 1997: 35). For instance, shops attracting middle-class adult shoppers play different music than youth-oriented retailers. Sterne (1997) examines a number of retailer chains and how they actively use musical programming. For instance, Victoria's Secret, a lingerie retailer, plays European classical music (e.g. Wiener classics and Romantic works in the German tradition), signifying cultivated refinement and sophistication and a general sense of 'Europeanness' that Sterne suggests is credible in North America, supposedly appealing to the middle-class shoppers the store is hoping to attract. Sterne (1997) argues that the music here has a 'metonymic effect'; it works as a form of décor for the shopping experience and suggests that one needs a 'cultivated, refined sensibility to enjoy all that Victoria's Secret has to offer' (Sterne, 1997: 37). In Sterne's account, the Mall of America is a social space highly structured around the various sounds signifying the entrance and departure from specific domains of the mall, for example, the movement from stores to the galleria and from stores aiming for youthful customers to stores attracting other groups. The mall is a 'soundscape', carefully regulated and monitored. Music is also a component of the integrated architecture of the mall and is therefore an indispensable part of the design of the mall. In both DeNora's (2000) and Sterne's (1997) studies, the music is never 'innocent' but is always laden with meaning and implicit objectives. It bears the mark of consumerism.

In conclusion, the use of music is not a very powerful tool when shaping social spaces; it nevertheless plays a small but significant role in a totality of strategies and tactics mobilized when constructing agreeable and pleasant shopping experiences. In comparison to other, more contemporary and aggressive applications of music (for instance, the all-too-annoying phenomenon of the commercial distribution of ring signals for mobile phones, ranging from the latest R'n'B tune to digitalized Wiener classics) the use of background music in retailing is barely noticeable and, arguably, rather harmless. If it shapes consumers' behaviour, it probably happens subconsciously.

Music work

Another body of literature addresses the organization of a number of professions, expert groups and specialists working with music as their field of formal training and expertise. Musicians, music teachers, producers, music critics, concert hall directors, rock club and music festivals managers, instrument builders, sound and recording technology engineers and so forth, are in their own idiosyncratic ways trained in mastering specific practices pertaining to the production, distribution and consumption of music in various forms. For instance, Bowen and Stiehl (1992) discuss the management and work procedures of the San Francisco rock band Grateful Dead's road management organization as a corporation satisfying all the demands for an 'excellent company' in the sense laid down by Tom Peters and Robert Waterman (1982): strong corporate culture, dedicated and skilled co-workers, sound financial performance, profit-sharing programmes including all co-workers and so forth. In the following, the case of sound engineers will be examined, showing that their work relies on substantial tacit knowledge and communicative skills that are learned by doing and in formal education programmes.

Horning (2004) studies the development of sound engineering as a professional practice from the early days of acoustic sound recording, from the end of the nineteenth century until the 1920s, to today's technoscientific sound laboratories saturated with advanced engineering technology. Sound recording in the acoustic paradigm is a craft based upon the engineer's ability to locate musicians and singers in the recording room space, enabling a satisfying mix of sounds on the final record being cut. These skills included both sound and sight because the recording included visual inspection of the records:

> Judgment about where to position the instruments and voices, as well as knowing how to 'read' the grooves of the record (since playing the wax master ruined it), the recordist had to visually inspect the grooves to make sure no instrument was too loud, indicated by groove

spacing, were critical skills learned only by trial and error. Yet as one early expert noted, not all possess the necessary skills, and some could never learn 'the necessary knack of recording'. (Horning, 2004: 706)

In the course of technical development and the institutionalization of the culture industry, the recording studio became more technologically complex, enabling musicians and producer-engineering teams to explore and create new sounds rather than merely capturing sounds that were at hand. The invention and commercializing of electric guitars and electric basses in the 1950s and the development of early synthesizers such as Keith Moog's new innovations brought new media to the domain of music recording. Robert E. McGinn (cited in Horning, 2004: 708) argues that electrical recording transformed recording 'from a predominantly craft-based enterprise relying on cut-and-try methods to a mature profession grounded increasingly in scientific, mathematical, and systems engineering methods and knowledge'. Horning argues that sound engineers are dependent on their tacit knowledge, knowledge that, after Polanyi's (1958) coinage of the term, denotes 'things you know but cannot fully articulate', that is, central competencies and know-how that escapes available regimes of representation and articulation (see also Sudnow, 1978). One such form of tacit knowledge is the use of microphones when recording instruments and voices (Horning, 2004: 710). Different microphones (including different quality brands such as Sennheiser or Neumann, and many models and types) respond differently to different instruments and frequencies; selecting the microphone is thus pivotal when producing the desired sound. The microphone is thus the medium bridging – but also shaping – the sound of the instrument or singer and the technological apparatus constituted by a long series of interrelated technological artefacts. Knowing how to bring artistic skills and expectations, technological artefacts and mathematically and theoretically grounded ideas regarding the frequencies of the sound waves and their interferences into harmony is the mark of the professional sound engineer. Since tacit knowledge is by definition what resists signification, what remains mute, sound engineers struggle to establish a shared vocabulary grasping the sound they want to create, both in intramural or esoteric (in its non-pejorative sense of the term) communication with other sound engineers but also in conversations with musicians (which may or may not master the esoteric vocabulary) and – from the view of the sound engineers – other laymen. As Edward Said (2001: 40) notes, 'the letters and words of literary texts are of course denotative; they share a common, and overlapping, discursivity with spoken language . . .

Music is not denotative and does not share a common discursivity with language.' Music is not transparent for everyday language and therefore a means of translation has to be agreed upon. Porcello (2004), himself having extensive experience of sound engineering work, addresses the difficulties facing both professional sound engineers and novices in the field. He points at the value of what he calls 'aural perception classes' in formal sound-engineering education programmes:

> In an aural perception class, students do not only learn how to hear sound; in studying the electrical and acoustic principles underlying limiters, compressors, equalizers, and so forth, not only do they learn how sound waves are modified and their effects on achieving a balanced musical mix; when studying circuits, they do not simply memorize information and electrical current flow. In each case, they simultaneously learn a complex technical discourse – a way of talking about and hence conceptualizing the relevant phenomena – then translating them into significant communicative resources to be deployed in situated sessions studio work. (Porcello, 2004: 738)

Porcello (2004) provides excerpts from his conversation studies of the dialogues between professional sound engineers and musicians and between professional sound engineers in a music-studio setting. Naturally, the conversation between peers runs smoother and with 'more economy', that is, fewer things need to be articulated to convey the message. However, when discussing what sound a drummer in a rock/funk/jazz fusion band would prefer, a long range of linguistic resources are used to create a sense or mutual understanding and commitment. For the outsider, the words and sounds articulated may be complicated to decode, but apparently the two interlocutors manage to make sense out of expressions like 'no muffling', 'lots of ring', 'tight sound', 'hollow', 'nggggg' and 'tsing tising', 'bop, bop, bop, instead of bahpmmmmm, bahpmmmmm, baphmmmmm' and so forth. Porcello lists five linguistic resources used in the conversation:

1. *Singing/vocables*. 'Phonetic and phonological work' used 'to mimic' musical sounds', e.g., 'hm', 'pz', 'dz'.
2. *Lexical onomatopesis*. 'Words that bear at least a partial acoustic resemblance to the sound to describe, but which are simultaneously metaphors that more abstractly describe the sound'.
3. *'Pure' metaphor*. 'Words such as "pitch-bend", "tight" or "deep" are used to describe timbral characteristic, but do *not* bear any acoustic

similarity to the sound in question (which distinguishes them from lexical onomatopoetic words)'.
4. *Association*. 'Associations involve citing other musicians, recordings, sounds, time periods, and so forth, in search for a common frame of reference from which to describe the timbres in question, and, implicitly, where this band will fit into the larger world of musical styles and commodities'. These associations function "indexically", involving other styles, musicians, or production technologies'.
5. *Evaluation*. 'Is used to establish a mutual sense of solidarity between two interlocutors'. (Porcello, 2004: 746–7)

The conversation is thus filled with advanced uses of a variety of linguistic resources. When communicating with peers, sound engineers are prone to use a stock of ready-made phrases denoting specific sounds and effects. For instance, product names 'become shorthand descriptors of the acoustic features that result from their performance or use', Porcello (2004: 748) says: 'Musicians regularly talk about sound in terms such as "Telecaster sound" versus a "Stratocaster sound", an "Ampeg SVT [Bass] sound", a "Hammond B3 [organ]"'. Learning to master this vocabulary and, more importantly, being able to relate signifier (e.g. 'Telecaster', a common electric guitar model produced by the Fender guitar company) and specific sounds (signified) being produced by the artefact (instrument, microphone or technological instrument, for example, a compressor or an equalizer) comes with formal training and learning by doing. Just like the wine-taster must both learn to taste the wine and account for it and finally manage the taste to correspond as transparently as possible with his or her verbal articulations when describing the taste of the wine (including idiosyncratic references to, for example, 'vanilla', 'leather', 'berries', etc.), so must the sound engineer be able to bridge concepts and sounds and bring them into harmony. The concept of tacit knowledge, substantially debated in organization theory and the domain of knowledge management, is here a handy term for capturing this specific skill.

Summary and conclusion

In comparison to other forms of art, music has been comparatively little used in social theory to illustrate various abstract ideas and lines of reasoning. As musicologists like Susan McClary and composers like Edgard Varèse have pointed out, music is simultaneously a most concrete and a most abstract art. Concrete in terms of being immediately perceived and complicated to shield off; abstract in terms of never speaking for itself but always open to interpretations and various intellectual or emotional responses. Nevertheless, music has always played a significant role in both religious and secular ceremonies and from the Renaissance onward it gradually became a source of cultural capital for the elites. In the nineteenth century, musical training was a *sine qua non* of any bourgeoisie upbringing: stringed instruments, preferably violin, for the boys and piano for the girls. During more recent times, in the period of modernity and late modernity, music has continued to serve as an important tool in structuring and shaping society; equally marketers, industry psychologists and many other professional groups have made music a resource to exploit in their pursuit of the desired social order. Seen in this way, music was never innocent; whether it was composed in the glory of the Lord, as in the case of Johann Sebastian Bach serving the clergy in northern Germany, or being distributed as Muzak musical programming services, music plays a role as a means of perception that is part of an organizational setting that constitutes a variety of resources and practices. Music is an integral part of organizing.

4
Media: The Remediation of Image and Sound

Introduction

> The inhabitants of London could now order ... sipping their morning tea in bed, the various products of the whole earth and reasonably expect their delivery upon his doorstep; he could, at the same moment, and by the same means, adventure his wealth in the natural resources and new enterprises of any quarter of the world, and share, without exertion or even trouble, in the prospective fruits and advantages. (John Maynard Keynes, cited in Morley, 2007: 236)

In 1900, John Maynard Keynes, the great Cambridge economist, praised a new invention, the landline telephone, and tried to foresee its social and cultural significance. Although written more than one hundred years ago and before the tidal wave of new media brought by the twentieth century, Keynes's enthusiasm shares many qualities with more recent praises for new media. We have been told a thousand times by columnists, IT entrepreneurs, politicians and self-declared experts and media pundits with vested interests that information and communication technologies will once and for all alter our lives and make it easier, more comfortable and more exciting (Broddy, 2004: 165–6). Such media hype has been exposed by May (2002) and Mosco (2004), for instance. May (2002) expresses his scepticism regarding the coming 'information society' or 'information age' and Mosco (2004) explores the mythologies of cyberspace as a texture of narratives envisaging a bright and unproblematic future (see also Markeley, 1996; Ullman, 1997; Helmreich, 1998; Stivers, 1999). Contrary to such ideas about media being *absolument moderne* and representing the most advanced forms of technology, Coyne (1999) argues that there is a flair of 'romantic medievalism' surrounding what he calls the 'digital narrative':

> Digital narratives often present computer skills as mysterious arts, analogous to romantic conceptions of medieval alchemy and black arts. Computer programs and computer networks are labyrinthine. Computer systems involve the interconnections of software and hardware components, many of which were designed and manufactured by others and so are mysterious 'black boxes', even unpredictable and irrational ... The ingredients of romantic medievalism are there: labyrinthine progression, hierarchies of place and status, irrational interventions through the forces of magic, powerful and irrational forces, and the acquisition of power and victory by magic but appropriated through superior reason. (Coyne, 1999: 38)

In addition, as Sconce (2000) demonstrates, virtually all new media such as the radio and the television have been accompanied by persistent folksy beliefs and stories about the 'supernatural' and eerie capacity of media; voices from spirits can be detected in the white noise of radio transmissions, television sets may have the capacity to distribute messages 'from the other side' (for instance, the 1970s horror movie *Poltergeist* where the TV screen played a central role) and so forth. Quite recently, a series of horror movies from Japan (e.g. *The Ring*) have exploited and further developed such public beliefs, renewing the genre of horror movies through de-familiarizing everyday technologies such as mobile phones and computer screens. The uncanny has been associated with new media, from as early as the invention of electricity:

> Electricity remains a somewhat uncanny agent in popular thought even today, making it a prime component in the continuing metaphysical presence attributed to contemporary media. From the initial electromagnetic dots and dashes of the telegraph to the digital landscapes of virtual reality, electronic telecommunications have compelled citizens of the media age to reconsider increasingly disassociative relationships among body, space and time. (Sconce, 2000: 7)

In Sconce's (2000) account, new media are never devoid of public belief and concerns but are always located within predominant beliefs.

In either case, representing something really new or being derived from traditional thinking, media are not unaffected by predominant beliefs and ideologies. However, new media tend to be surrounded by hype and it is only after a substantial period of time, when the media are naturalized – when they become 'banal', as Mosco (2004) says – that media become truly powerful:

> The real power of new technologies does not appear during their mythic period, when they are hailed for their ability to bring world peace, renew communities, or end scarcity, history, geography, or politics; rather, their social impact is greatest when technologies become banal – when they literally (as in the case of electricity) or figuratively withdraw into the woodwork. (Mosco, 2004: 19)

In this chapter, media will be discussed as what, to use a concept from Heidegger, *enframes* perception in organizations. Crary (1999), albeit not making references to Heidegger, captures this sense of the term nicely:

> [I]t is not inappropriate to conflate seemingly different optical or technological objects; they are similarly about arrangements of bodies in space, techniques of isolation, cellularization, and above all separation. Spectacle is not an optic of power but an architecture. Television and the personal computer, even as they are now converging towards a single machinic functioning, are antinomadic procedures that fix and *striate*. They are methods for the management of attention that use partitioning and sedentarization, rendering bodies controllable and useful simultaneously, even as they simulate the illusion of choices and 'interactivity'. (Crary, 1999: 74–5)

Perception is therefore, as Paul Virilio, among others, has emphasized in a series of publications (e.g. Virilio, 1989), mediated and thus images and sounds are – in the predominant information technology regime – digitalized and what Bolter and Grusin (1999) call *remediated*, translated from one form into another (see also Mitchell, 1992). Media are what essentially shape, influence and structure human perception in everyday life. Goodwin (1995), studying the use of advanced scientific media in the work of oceanographic research, emphasizes the 'organization of perception':

> The organization of perception is not … located in the psychology of the individual brain and its associated cognitive processes, but is instead lodged within, and constituted through, situated endogenous practices. Such perception is a form of social organization in its own right. (Goodwin, 1995: 256)

Perception is then what takes place in the very borderland between man and machine, in the zone where 'wetware', software and hardware constitute a functional assemblage. Moreover, the production and circulation of images and sound, the topic of discussion of the two previous chapters, are strongly influenced by new media and digitalization (Evens, 2005; Greffe, 2004). New media are here generally synonymous with digital media. Evens (2005: 65) defines digital media in formalistic terms: 'Logically, the computer is a huge network of intersecting pipes, and each intersection either allows the electricity to pass or prevents it. It is this condition – this general principle of operation according to an abstraction whose rules are immanent to its code – that defines a technology as digital'*. Media are what are capable of creating, arranging, storing and distributing images, texts and sounds. Therefore, they need to be examined as key organizational and social resources, strongly shaping and structuring human perception.

This chapter is structured accordingly. First, the concept of media is discussed. Second, various forms of media are examined. Third, the connections between media and so-called posthumanist thinking are delineated. Thereafter, the use of media in organizations is accounted for and, finally, some concluding remarks are presented.

The three world views of media

The concept of media (or more specifically, *new* media) is here not to be confused with the mass media (newspaper, radio, television, etc.) but

---

* It is very complicated to formulate comprehensive definitions of media such as information technology. In their review of the papers published in *Information Systems Research* over a decade, Orlikowski and Iacono (2001) found that there is a lack of detailed conceptual elaboration on the concept of information technology *per se* in the literature. In addition, Orlikowski and Iacono (2001) suggest that the 'IT artefact' is made up of '[a] multiplicity of often fragile and fragmentary components, whose interconnections are often partial and provisional and which require bridging, integration, and articulation in order to make them work together' (Orlikowski and Iacono, 2001: 134). Furthermore, the IT artefact is not static but dynamic; new materials are invented, different features developed, and users adapt the artefact in new and unpredictable ways. Given these contingencies and 'context-specificity', Orlikowski and Iacono (2001: 135) argue that there is '[n]o single, one-size fits all conceptualization of technology that will work for all studies'. In this chapter, media will be conceived of, following Orlikowski and Iacono's (2001) recommendations, as an ensemble of material and non-material resources that are strongly shaped by their use in social settings. Media are then temporal stabilizations of assemblages of material resources and social practices.

instead denotes the assemblage comprising the selected message, technology, inscription procedures and other components in the production and circulation of texts, images and sounds. Media is then a complex theoretical construct drawing on a number of disciplines such as technology studies, informatics and computer science, and a range of disciplines in the humanities (Hansen, 2006). Krämer (2006: 93) argues that media are 'first and foremost cultural techniques that allow one to select, store, and produce data and signals'. Gitelman (2006) defines media in broad terms and recognizes the historical constitution of media:

> I define media as socially realized structures of communication, where structures include both technological forms and their associated protocols, and where communication is a cultural practice, a ritualized collocation of different people on the same mental map, sharing or engaging with popular ontologies of representation. As such, media are unique and complicated historical subjects. Their histories must be social and cultural, not the stories of how one technology leads to another, or of isolated geniuses working their magic on the world. (Gitelman, 2006: 7)

Traditionally, media have been conceived of as what is linked to 'signs', 'communication', or 'information', but today media are more and more thought of as capable of selecting, storing and producing signals (Krämer, 2006: 97). Such a view of media brings media studies together with a broader posthumanist framework wherein human beings are little more than carriers of information in the form of signals. Such posthumanist images will be examined in greater detail later in the chapter. Katherine Hayles (2002), a professor of English at the University of California, is one of the most prominent representatives of the field of media studies. She emphasizes the intersection between representation and technology and how it is becoming complicated to separate them:

> [W]ithin the humanities and especially in literary studies, there has traditionally been a sharp line between representation and the technologies producing them. Whereas art history has long been attentative to the material production of art objects, literary studies have generally been content to treat fictional and narrative worlds as if they were entirely products of the imagination. (Hayles, 2002: 19)

Hayles argues that one needs to examine what she calls *inscription technologies* to understand a particular representation. An *inscription technology* is a device that is capable of 'initiating material changes that can be read as marks' (Hayles, 2002: 24, original in italics). Examples of inscription technologies include telegraphy, film, video, medical devices such as X-rays and CAT scans. All these technologies produce marks that can be decoded and thus serve as representations for actual (as in the case of medical technology, representing the human body) or fictional (as in the case of the typewriter or computer software producing fiction) realities. Hayles claims that one must not ignore the role of inscription technologies when studying representations: '[M]y claim is that *the physical form of literary artifact always affects what the word (and other semiotic components) mean*' (Hayles, 2002: 25, emphasis in the original). More specifically, when speaking of literary texts, the principal media are what Hayles (2002: 26) calls *writing machines*: '"Writing machines" names the inscription technologies that produce literary texts, including printing presses, computers and other devices. "Writing machines" is also what technotexts do when they bring into view the machinery that gives their verbal constructions physical reality'. For Hayles, conventional literature theory has been satisfied with focusing on the text *per se*, the representation of the writer's work, and has virtually ignored or excluded the materiality of the text; the technological and physical properties of the text. In the present period, literature theorists not only examine printed books but also representations entangled with other media. For instance, computer-based technologies are used to produce texts and representations appearing on the computer screen downloaded from the internet. Internet homepages are new forms of representation embedded in the material assemblages including representation, hardware, software, servers, cables and connections and so forth. Text and materiality are simultaneously produced, Hayles (2002) says:

> Materiality thus emerges from interaction between physical properties and a work's artistic strategies. For this reason, materiality cannot be specified in advance, as if it preexisted the specificity of the work. An emergent property, materiality depends on how the work mobilizes its resources as a physical artifact as well as on the user's interactions with the work and the interpretative strategies she develops – strategies that include physical manipulations as well as physical frameworks. In its broadest sense, materiality emerges from the dynamic interplay between the richness of a physically robust world and human intelligence as it crafts this physicality to create meaning. (Hayles, 2002: 33)

Bolter (1991: 11) speaks of this convergence of text and materiality as the emergence of a *writing space*, a concept denoting '[f]irst and foremost all the physical and visual fields defined by a particular technology of writing'. In Bolter's account, it is the computer that is the new media *par préférence*; 'Writing is the creative play of signs, and the computer offers us a new field for that play. It offers a new surface for recording and presenting texts together with new techniques for organizing our writing. In other words, it offers us a new writing space' (Bolter, 1991: 10). One of the great challenges for media theorists is, Bolter says, to explain that computers are no less natural or no more artificial than writing with pen and paper (1991: 37); both these technologies are media capable of storing and transmitting information.

Hypertext and electronic writing

In media studies, representations (or any other significant 'signal', to use Krämer's [2006] phrase) and various technologies or material resources (e.g. paper in the case of newspapers and books) are brought together into a functional unity that cannot be examined on the level of its constituent parts. This co-alignment of representation (e.g. writing) and technology is also of central importance for Landow (2006) discussing the concept of *hypertext*, that is, a 'text composed of blocks of texts ... and the electronic links that join them' (Landow, 2006: 3). Ted Nelson first coined the concept of *hypertext* in 1974, denoting 'non-sequential writing'. Since hypertexts are *coded texts*, they are also infinitely variable; once one changes the code, one changes the text (Landow, 2006: 36). For Landow, being very enthusiastic about emerging opportunities, hypertexts are capable of providing '[a]n infinitely recenterable system whose provisional point of focus depends on the reader, who becomes the truly active reader in yet another sense' (Landow, 2006: 56). He continues: 'one of the fundamental characteristics of hypertext is that it is composed of bodies of linked texts that have no primary axis of organization'. Hypertexts thus uproot the conventional text in two related ways: first, by removing 'the linearity of print' – 'one damn thing after another', in Bowker's (2005) formulation – thus freeing 'the individual passage from one ordering principle – sequence' (Landow, 2006: 99); second, by 'destroying' the notion of a 'fixed unitary text'. This does not means, Bolter emphasizes, that hypertexts are 'chaotic'; instead they are '[i]n a perpetual state of reorganization' (1991: 9). Everett (2003) proposes the concept of *digitextuality*, the merging of the term *digital* and Julia Kristeva's concept of *intertextuality*, to denote the intersections between forms of media, both traditional ('old') media and digital ('new') media. Media always operate on layers of information structured into images, texts and codes, and Everett (2003) seeks to show how these 'informational entities' are interrelated and entangled in the day-to-day use of media. Landow (2006) approves the new fluid nature of the hypertext and assumes this will enable new ways of reading and establish new subject positions moving beyond the traditional author–reader axis. Similar ideas are formulated by Bolter (1991), speaking about 'electronic writing' as what is in contrast to traditional printed books: 'The printing press was a great homogenizer of writing, whereas the electronic technology make texts particular and individual. An electronic book is a fragmentary and potential text, a series of self-contained units rather than an organic, developing whole' (Bolter, 1991: 9). Moreover, as Derrida points out, this 'electronic writing' is not solely based on 'the phonetic-alphabetical model' but is '[i]s increasingly hieroglyphic or ideographic or pictorial as well' (Derrida and Stiegler, 2002: 103–4). Rajagopal (2006) also addresses the capacity of new media to cast off the linearity of printed texts, privileging vision and excluding other senses, and to recreate a new sense of presence:

> If print redefined the boundaries of a community of experience in abstract linguistic terms, divorced from the sensory immediacy of a given context, electronic media redefine the boundaries again. They can transcend a given linguistic field with sounds and images that recreate the sense of presence with oral communication. (Rajagopal, 2006: 284–5)

Electronic writing can mobilize more resources than the conventional writing of the printed book. While writers like Landow (2006) are enthusiastic about opportunities of the new hypertext media, Espen Aaseth (2003), a Norwegian scholar and 'founding father of studies of non-literary textuality' (Landow, 2006: 252), is explicitly critical of what he calls 'hypertext ideology' and its emphasis on the 'teleological myth of media convergence' (cf. Everett, 2003) wherein '[a]ll old media come together in the dawn of the high-tech era and are subsumed by the new digital supermedium' (Aaseth, 2003: 416). Rather than being one single unified medium, as implied by various media theorists (e.g. Landow, 2006), various hypertext media have as little in common as printed documents such as 'telegrams, lecture notes, and restaurant menus' (Aaseth, 2003: 416). Aaseth continues to claim that 'the functional difference' between old and new media, paper and digitality, 'could not be drawn clearly' (2003: 418). This distinction is problematic because, Aaseth argues, some paper media have more in common with some digital media than certain digital media have with each other. As a consequence, the analogue/digital distinction in media theory is 'overrated' and 'uninformative and breaks down under scrutiny,' Aaseth concludes. This position is not uncontroversial and Aaseth is consequently thoroughly criticized by Landow (2006: 250–2) for being uninformed and biased.

Speech, writing and code

The distinction between the traditional modes of writing based on linearity, sequence and fixity and the 'electronic writing' of the hypertext, being in a state of perpetual reconfiguration and resisting any linear order is, notwithstanding Aaseth's (2003) critique of, a central theme in the media studies literature. Hayles (2005) even speaks about speech, writing and code as three complementary 'worldviews'. Also Poster (2001a) recognizes such a tripartite distinction:

> Every age employs forms of symbolic exchange which contain internal and external structures, means and relations of significations. Stages in the mode of information may be tentatively designated as follows: face-to-face; orally mediated exchange; written exchanges mediated by print; and electronically mediated exchanges. If the first stage is characterized by symbolic correspondences, and the second stage is characterized by representation of signs, the third is characterized by informational simulations. In the first, oral stage the self is constituted as a position of enunciation through its embeddedness in a totality of face-to-face relations. In the second, print state the self is constructed as an agent centered in rational/imaginary autonomy. In the third, electronic state the self is decentered, dispersed, and multiplied in continuous instability. (Poster, 2001a: 6–7)

Speech and writing have developed their own specific media; code is the code of computer languages being mastered by a narrow group of experts, computer programmers and is what is on the verge between representation and technology. While speech and writing are capable of being used in a freer and creative manner to express a range of emotions and ideas, code is what is entangled with its performativity – *it is what it does*: Ellen Ullman, software engineer says:

> We can use English to invent poetry, to try to express things that are hard to express. In programming you really can't. Finally, a computer program has only one meaning: what it does. It isn't a text for an academic to read. Its entire meaning is its function. (Cited in Hayles, 2005: 48)

However, no use of programming languages is wholly devoid of non-functionalist aspects. Piñeiro (2007), discussing the 'aesthetics of computer programming', also emphasizes this 'rational' nature of computer language and computer code:

> Programming is a highly rational activity, and it fits very well into the general opinion of what a rational endeavour is. Programs are logical structures, and computers can only execute direct commands. Therefore, there is absolutely no room for interpretations or vague sentences or explanations. Programming languages are logic, objective, and clear ... In short, programming is as rational as its gets. It is based on perfectly objective interactions with machines that have very detailed predetermined behaviour and do not allow for any sort of vagueness. (Piñeiro, 2007: 106)

In Piñeiro's (2007) account, the 'code worldview' is not unaffected by aesthetic values: 'Regardless of the restrictions forced upon human activity,' Piñeiro writes, 'if there is as much as an ounce of creative work involved or permitted, aesthetic concerns will thrive' (2007: 105). Thus, there are 'beautiful programs and there are ugly programs, and there are many opinions about what it is that makes a program beautiful' (Piñeiro, 2007: 106). More specifically, there is a certain beauty in 'the precise fit' between the 'huge numbers of data elements' that are integrated in the program. 'A precise fit' is thus a source of pride and beauty, and is, without doubt, Piñeiro says, 'a question of skills, patience, time and stable technical specifications' (2007: 112). Just like any other profession, computer programmers are eager to earn recognition from peers and colleagues, and such recognition includes the informed and credible evaluation of one's work. Piñeiro (2007: 119) concludes:

> Why would programmers want to write beautiful code? The immediate answer is: programmers do not perceive code as only a virtual machine that does things but also as their creation. Their relationship to code is more that of creator than of technician to machine. Their code then speaks of them: not only of their skills but also their personal preferences in things like coding style, programming language and designing strategies. (Piñeiro, 2007: 119)

The worldview of the code is then not strictly rational, grounded in indisputable logic, but is also a source of aesthetics and beauty.

No matter if the code is strictly functional or imbued with aesthetic concerns, it is inherent to much everyday media; it is the infrastructure *par excellence* in contemporary society. Dodge and Kitchin (2005) show how media based on code produce and constitute everyday social space. Elevators, trains, electric door locks, mobile phones, surveillance cameras, etc., are media/technologies based on code. Code is thus the underlying regime of writing – the *infrastructure*, to use Star and Bowker's (2002) phrase – of media. Dodge and Kitchin (2005) explain the concept of code:

> Code consists of instructions and rules that, when combined, produce programs capable of complex digital functions that operate on computer hardware. We therefore use the term code in a restricted sense to refer to the rules and instructions of software rather than broader notions of codes as sociocultural structures and technical/legalistic protocols of ordering and control, such as national laws, international treaties, etiquette, standards, systems of measurements, institutional customs, and professional codes of conduct. (Dodge and Kitchin, 2005: 163)

Code includes a variety of languages and applications, varying '[f]rom abstract machine code and assembly language to more formal programming languages, applications, user created macros, and scripts' (Dodge and Kitchin, 2005: 163). Dodge and Kitchin also distinguish between 'coded objects' (e.g. alarm clocks), 'coded infrastructures' (mail, phones, television), 'coded processes' (e.g. the use of Automatic Teller Machines [ATMs]) and 'coded assemblages' (e.g. the processes of billing, ticketing, check-in, baggage routing and security checks at an airport). Dodge and Kitchin (2005) provide four narratives of how individuals living in London are affected by coded media and technologies in their day-to-day lives, from waking up in the morning (to the signal of a coded alarm clock) until bedtime when the coded television set is switched off. For Dodge and Kitchin, social space is not *a priori* (as suggested by Kant in his *Critique of Pure Reason*) but is instead the outcome from, using a concept from the French philosopher Gilbert Simondon (1992), an onto-genetic 'transductive process' wherein space is rendered meta-stable and operative 'for the time being'. Space is, to use Lefebvre's (1991) term, 'produced'. 'Code and human life are produced through or folded into each other, taking the form of coded practices,' Dodge and Kitchin (2005: 178) conclude. For instance, electric signs at the bus stop indicating whether the bus is late help the individual being on the way to work fashion and structure the social space. Electronic messages submitted and displayed on the screen may, for instance, help make the decision whether to walk the distance or to take another bus if the regular bus is delayed. Code and coded media are thus, Dodge and Kitchin suggest, constantly intervening in the individuals' 'spatial practices': 'Code is bound up in, and contributes to, complex discursive and material practices, relating to both living and non-living humans and technology, which work across scales and time' (Dodge and Kitchin, 2005: 164). Burrows and Gane (2006: 802) express the idea accordingly: 'Digital media are not rendering physical places unimportant (the so-called "end of geography" argument), but rather are structuring and restructuring the spaces we inhabit and consume in everyday life, in vital, but often unseen ways.' Media, in many if not most cases embedded in code, are thus remediating social reality and helping to disseminate images, texts and sound, but are also inherent to the very production of social space.

Media and the subject

'Electronic media', today primarily represented by a number of computer-based technologies but previously dominated by such as the telegraph, the telephone and the radio, are the objects of analysis for media theorists. Marshall McLuhan, one of the first great proponents of media theory and media studies as an individual domain of research and analysis, frequently speaks of electronic media as 'extensions of the central nervous system' (McLuhan, 1997: 121). McLuhan argues that the virtually limitless extension of electronic media imposes a great source of stress on humans because now they are continuously 'on line' and in connection with the outside world. Human life thus becomes a continuous struggle to collect information:

> When we put our central nerve system outside us we returned to the primal nomadic state. We have become primitive Paleolithic man, once more global wanderers, but information gatherers rather than food gatherers. From now on the source of food, wealth and life itself will be information. (McLuhan, 1997: 124)

In addition, McLuhan argues that electronic media represents a rupture with the linearity of previous media – a theme shared with many media theorists – most notably book and printing technology. The multiplicity of electronic media is no longer engaging vision in a linear procedure but is instead mobilizing all senses in more immersing experiences:

> The ways of thinking implanted by electronic culture are very different from those fostered by print culture. Since the Renaissance most

methods and procedures have strongly tended towards stress on the visual organization and application of knowledge ... Literacy stresses *linearity*, a one-thing-at-a-time awareness and mode of procedure ... But electronic media proceed differently. Television, radio, and the newspaper (at the point where it was linked with the telegraph) deal in *auditory space*, by which I mean the sphere of simultaneous relations created by the act of hearing. We hear from all directions at once; this creates a unique unvisualizable space. The all-at-once-ness of auditory space is the exact opposite of linearity, of taking one thing at a time. (McLuhan, 1997: 122)

For McLuhan (1997), the emerging non-linear media constitute the human subject differently than linear media do; given that media are extensions of the human central nervous system, the subject is becoming distributed in the media system in which he or she belongs. The entanglement of media and subject-positions, brought into attention by McLuhan (1997; 1964; 1962), is addressed by a number of media theorists. Bolter (1996) does not share McLuhan's view of media as extensions of the human body but he underlines media's implications for the subject. Again, the duality linear/non-linear media is invoked. While older media such as the printed book in fact *are* texts, graphic domains, that are 'stable and monumental' (Bolter, 1996: 110) and only occasionally contain complementary illustrations, new media based on code and new forms of visuality constitute 'new writing spaces':

Word processing, numerical and textual databases, (verbal) electronic mail and newsgroups, and hypertext constitute a new writing space. Electronic writing, particularly hypertext, challenges some of the qualities of the printed or handwritten self. The self in electronic writing space is no longer the relatively permanent and univocal figure of the printed page. The electronic self is instead unstable and polyvocal. (Bolter, 1996: 112)

Bowker (2005: 102) says that Elizabeth Eisenstein's (1983) work on printing – discussed in more detail below – emphasizes 'a certain kind of packaging algorithm for knowledge', that is, 'the linear time of the narrative in coordinate space (left to right, top to bottom, forward in time as you read). In electronic writing space, fundamentally embedded in cybernetic principles, this algorithm does not apply; instead, there is a need for 'enfolding knowledge into itself'. For Bolter (1996), the Cartesian view of the subject is intimately bound up with printed media and its linear algorithm. The gradual emergence of media drawing on and privileging other forms of visuality is eroding the basis for the predominantly Western cognitive subject:

> Writing in general and print technology in particular have contributed to a series of related definitions of self in the period from the Renaissance to the 20th century: the self has been regarded as an autonomous ego, the author or the text that constitutes one's mental life. Virtual reality and cyberspace suggests a different definition. The self is no longer constructed as an autonomous, authorial voice; it becomes instead a wandering eye that occupies various perspectives, one after another. This virtual eye knows what it knows not through the capacity for abstract reasoning, but rather through empathy, through the sharing of the 'point of view' of the object of knowledge. (Bolter, 1996: 106)

Thus new media are not unambiguously separated from the constitution of subjectivity and cognition but are instead operating as a set of resources enabling the constitution of subject-positions. Bolter (1996) argues that the increased emphasis on new forms of visuality in media demands a new view of the subject: 'Virtual space is the abnegation of the space of personal cognition that Descartes envisioned. That space was pure ego, abstracted from the visual and the sensual. Virtual space, cyberspace, is one of pure, if utterly artificial, sense perception' (Bolter, 1996: 113). For Bolter, rather than subjects being the privileged locus of perception, perception is what precedes the subject; subject-positions derive from modes of perception, or what Jay (1996) calls 'scoptic regimes'.

Friedrich Kittler is another eminent media theorist who has written extensively on media and their influence on the constitution of the subject. Kittler too speaks of media in somewhat different terms than McLuhan and his writings are a highly original blend of historical overviews, literary passages and theoretical analyses. Kittler is generally treated as a poststructuralist writer and his media analysis is heavily indebted to both Jacques Lacan and Michel Foucault. Kittler (1990) examines what he calls the two *discourse networks* of 1800 and 1900. During the course of a hundred years, a series of new media was developed. If nothing else (e.g. being the century of colonialism, industrialization and the era of ideologies), the nineteenth century was the age of media innovation. Media innovations gave in turn birth to, or a new legitimacy to, a series of institutions and social practices that together formed discourse networks. Kittler defines the term *discourse network*:

> The term discourse network ... designates the network of technologies and institutions that allow a given culture to select, store, and process relevant data, Technologies like that of book printing and the institutions coupled to it, such as literature and the university, thus constituted a historically very powerful formation, which in the Europe of the age of Goethe became the condition of possibility for literary criticism. (Kittler, 1990: 369)

In Kittler's view, the situation in the year 1800 was radically different from that of the year 1900:

> Besides from mechanical automations and toys, there was nothing. The discourse network of 1800 functioned without photographs, gramophones, or cinematographs. Only books could provide serial storage of serial data. They had been reproducible since Gutenberg, but they became material for understanding and fantasy only when alphabetization had become ingrained. (1990: 116)

At the turn of the eighteenth and nineteenth centuries, humans were accustomed to use a limited number of media, most noteworthy the printed book, but electronic media and media mobilizing vision and the capacity of hearing were not yet widely available. In the nineteenth century, a number of media innovations appeared: the typewriter, the telegraph, the photograph and cinema. The nineteenth century was arguably 'a century of vision' wherein new forms of observations, inspection and seeing were established and instituted. These new media not only produced new social practices but also provided new subjectivities or means for what Foucault calls *subjectification*. Kittler (1999; 1997) examines the three media innovations the typewriter, the gramophone and cinema on the basis of Jacques Lacan's psychoanalytical theories. Before examining Kittler's complex argument, some elementary Lacanian theory will be introduced. However, it is beyond the scope of this text to account for a more detailed and sophisticated overview of Lacan's work. Rather than using the three instances *the superego, the ego* and *the unconscious* in the well-known Freudian topology (Freud, 1940/2003), Lacan talks about the three categories of *the symbolic, the imaginary* and *the Real* (commonly spelled with a capital R). The superego, constitutive of the subjectivity of the human agent, is based on *the symbolic*, the use of language and symbols in everyday speech and conversations; 'the *symbolic* is a closed system of differences. As the law of signification, it can be assimilated to language and, in its purified form, to mathematical language. It corresponds approximately to Freud's *superego* and its grounding for discernability and difference,' Leupin (1991: 119) writes. On the contrary, *the imaginary* is not based on linguistic interchanges between individuals but is instead the 'register' or 'dimensions of images' (Lacan, 1989: xi) that the human agent mobilizes when constructing the image of the ego. The ego is therefore not grounded in 'other-directed interactions' such as conversations, but is rather the production within the human agent's own 'conscious or unconscious, perceived or imagined world' (Lacan, 1989: xi). Leupin explicates Lacan's position: 'The *imaginary* is the system of projections and identifications; it replaces the Freudian *ego* and is defined by its intersubjective specularity. It is fundamental to the binary mode of similarity and dissimilarity and the dialectics of intersubjectivity' (1991: 11). In Ritzer's (1997: 134) account, the imaginary is 'the order in which the individual experiences herself as a whole and complete subject'. Finally *the Real*, one of Lacan's most complicated terms corresponding to Freud's unconscious, not to be confused with reality. The Real is instead a concept that coordinates the relationship between the imaginary and the symbolic. Lacan refuses to formulate a conclusive definition of the Real but renders it as what is essentially and by definition impossible to represent and formalize (Leupin, 1991: 11). The Real is thus outside the available regimes of signification and therefore cannot be pinned down into categories (Leupin, 1991: 6). Coyne (1999: 224) suggests that for Lacan the Real is 'the primal realm enjoyed by the child prior to the mirror phase', that is, before the first six to twelve months when the child starts to recognize him or herself in the mirror, seeing oneself as unified but also split into a 'me' and 'I'. Among many other implications for psychoanalysis, Lacan's emphasis on the constitutive nature of language for psychological instances, effectively captured by what has become something like a Lacanian slogan, the claim that 'the unconsciousness is structured like a language' (see also Arnaud, 2003: 1137; Fink, 1995), has contributed to the decentring of the subject in poststructuralist thinking, a recurring theme in the literature influenced by continental philosophy: 'For him [Lacan] language does not repeat the subject's preexisting intentions or ideas, the subject no longer constitutes language or functions as its master, but conversely, is constituted as a subject by language,' Grosz notes (1990: 97).

As has been pointed out by many commentators (Homer, 2005; Ritzer, 1997; Fink, 1995), Lacan's vocabulary is filled with purposeful ambiguities and elusiveness, making his thinking both intriguing and complicated to fully capture. However, Kittler (1999) uses the Lacanian vocabulary to examine the nature of new media, corresponding to the following scheme: typewriter/symbolic; cinema/imaginary; phonograph/the Real. Kittler summarizes his argument:

> Only the typewriter provided writing as a selection from the finite and arranged stock of its keyboard ... In contrast to the flow of handwriting, we now have discrete elements separated by spaces. Thus, the symbolic has the status of block letters. Film was the first to store those mobile doubles of humans who, unlike other primates, were able to (mis)perceive their own body. Thus, the imaginary has the status of cinema. And only the phonograph can record all the noises produced by the larynx prior to any semiotic order and linguistic meaning ... Thus, the Real ... has the status of phonography. (Kittler, 1999: 16)

Later on Kittler continues: 'The typewriter cannot conjure up anything imaginary, as can cinema; it cannot simulate the real, as sound recording; it only inverts the gender of writing. In so doing, however, it inverts the material basis of literature' (1999: 183). The written text and its mechanization – ardently criticized by Heidegger, saying that 'mechanical writing deprives the hand of its rank in the realm of the written word and degrades the word to a means of communication' (cited by Kittler, 1999: 199) – belong to the realm of the symbolic. It is difficult to draw too farfetched conclusions from Kittler's intricate analysis without ending up walking on thin ice, but one implication may be that new media are having constitutive effects on the subject, essentially a 'lacunary apparatus' (Lacan, 1998: 185), something that is already 'lost' and what is in a process of being simultaneously both decomposed and reassembled (Fink, 1995). Media such as the typewriter, cinema and the phonograph are thus in various ways 'interfering' with the constitution of the subject – media and subject are bound up and interrelated in various ways. More specifically, media operate and function on the level of the psychological topology of the subject. Seen from this point of view, there are no media 'external' to the subject but instead media are always constitutive components of the subject in contemporary society. The Cartesian self discussed by Bolter (1996) is then little more than a myth or an ideology of the detached position of the *cogito*. Expressed differently, media are not detached from human lives but are instead capable of creating new subjectivities and new perspectives on the subject; media imply 'self-observation' (Kittler, 2006: 42) and they 'determine our condition'.

Some media theorists are less interested in the broader psychoana-lytical implications but emphasize media as cultural products and the recursive relation between media and society; they jointly constitute one another in intricate manners. Bolter and Grusin (1999) introduce the three concepts of *immediacy, hypermediacy* and *remediation* in their analysis of media. *Immediacy* denotes a style of visual representation 'whose goal is to make the viewer forget the presence of the medium (canvas, photographic film, cinema and so on)' and to make him or her believe that he or she is in 'the presence of the object or representation'; *hypermediacy* is, on the other hand, defined as a style of visual represen-tation 'whose goal is to remind the viewer of the medium'; *remediation,* finally, is '[t]he formal logic by which new media refashion prior media forms'. Immediacy aims to mask the media for the viewer. '*Immediacy* is our name for a family of beliefs and practices that express themselves differently in various times among various groups ... The common fea-ture of all these forms is their belief in some necessary contact point between the medium and what it represents,' Bolter and Grusin write (1999: 30). The most classic example is *trompe l'oeil* paintings (Lep-pert, 1996) or the 'photorealistic painting' of Vermeer or the Swedish artist Ola Billgren wherein the observer is enticed to believe that there is in fact no medium but merely an actual reality observed. A more recent example is virtual reality technologies that seek to create imme-diacy in their applications. Successful immediacy creates a seamless web between media and reality. Hypermediacy represents the opposite strat-egy wherein media or images are bundled into one single assemblage that continually reminds the viewer of the presence of the media. Bolter and Grusin (1999: 9) exemplify with a CNN news homepage arranging 'text, graphics, and video in multiple panes and windows' and joining them with 'numerous hyperlinks' to constantly remind the viewer that CNN is providing the information. Bolter and Grusin (1999) argue that digital media are strongly based on the presence of hypermediacy; the interface, and its arrangements of menus and icons, is aimed at creat-ing a sense of a comprehensive and self-enclosed mediated environment enabling effective work. In a hypermediated environment, there is no escape from media; media are always present and observable. Bolter and Grusin point at the differences between the logic of immediacy and hypermediacy:

> In digital technology, as often in the history of Western represen-tation, hypermediacy expresses itself as multiplicity. If the logic of immediacy leads one either to erase or to render automatic the act

of representation, the logic of hypermediacy acknowledges multiple acts of representation and makes them visible. (1999: 33–4)

Finally, remediation is the logic of relocating a previous medium into a new domain. For instance, to use an everyday example, CD records printed to look like vinyl records – see for instance the hip-hop act Gang Starr's record *Moment of Truth* (1995) – homepages designed to look like an open (printed) book, or the sampling of (analogue) instruments such as a grand piano or an acoustic guitar in digital synthesizers, are three examples of how familiar formats are exploited to naturalize a new medium. Remediation is often neglected or taken for granted because we fail to notice a transfer or even translation of a representation from one medium into another. E-books and sound files (e.g. in the mp3 format) are two other examples of remediations that are becoming part of every-day life. Bolter and Grusin's (1999) vocabulary provides a set of tools for examining how media penetrate everyday lives and for demystifying the functioning of media. What they underline is that media tend to come in many guises and employ different logics. At times, media are conspicuous and visible, while at other times they can be brought into the texture of the social fabric.

Formalistic principles of media

Manovich (2001) offers a comprehensive overview of the field of new media and formulates a set of formalistic principles of media. In his view, new media represents a 'convergence of two separate historical trajecto-ries' – *computing* and *media technologies*. Manovich (2001: 20) traces these two trajectories to the 1830s, when Charles Babbage invented his 'Ana-lytical Engine' and Louis Daguerre developed the daguerreotype, the first photographic image. The polymath Charles Babbage's Analytical Engine was the first programmable machine and therefore a forerunner to our computers: Manovich explains:

> The engine contained parts of the key features of the modern digital computer. Punch cards were used to enter both data and instructions. The information was stored in the Engine's memory. A processing unit, which Babbage referred to as a 'mill', performed operations on the data and wrote the results to memory; final results were to be printed out on a printer. (2001: 21–2)

Babbage borrowed the idea of a programmed machine with punched paper cards from Joseph-Marie Jacquard's mechanical loom. Around 1800, Jacquard invented a loom that was automatically controlled by punched cards. The loom could thus be programmed to weave 'intri-cate figurative images, including Jacquard's portrait' (Manovich, 2001: 22). While many computer historians (e.g. Lévy, 1995) locate the first attempts at building a modern computer to the 1930s, when the German engineer Konrad Zuse built a digital computer in his parents' living room, Babbage's mixing of technologies in the 1830s is an even earlier signif-icant innovation. Manovich identifies five 'principles' of new media. First, new media operate on the basis of *numerical representations*:

(i) A new media object can be described formally (mathematically). For instance, an image of a shape can be described using a mathematical function.
(ii) A new media object is subject to algorithmic manipulation. For instance, by applying appropriate algorithms, we can automatically remove noise from photograph, improve its contrast, locate the edges of the shapes, or change its proportions. In short, *media becomes programmable*. (Manovich, 2001: 27)

Second, new media are based on *modularity*:

The principle can be called the 'fractal structure of new media'. Just as a fractal has the same structure on different scales, a new media object has the same modular structure throughout. Media elements, be they images, sounds, shapes, or behaviours, are represented as collectives of discrete samples (pixels, polygons, voxels, characters, scripts). These elements are assembled into larger-scale objects but continue to maintain their separate identities. (Manovich, 2001: 30)

The modularity means that new media objects are constituted by 'inde-pendent parts', each of which consists of smaller independent parts and so on, down to the elementary components (e.g. pixels or text char-acters). Third, many operations can be automatically retrieved because the elementary components of media can be manipulated in predefined ways. For instance, a long series of digital pictures can be automatically modified in software applications. Mitchell (1992) offers a detailed intro-duction on how digital images can be manipulated in a multiplicity of ways. Fourth, new media offer, as a consequence of the first two prin-ciples, unlimited opportunities for *variability*. 'A new media object is not something fixed once and for all but something that can exist in different, potentially infinite versions,' Manovich argues (2001: 36). For instance, using software programs like Photoshop enables endless oppor-tunities for manipulating images. Fifth and finally, new media produce what Manovich calls *transcoding*, a complicated concept denoting the exchange between what Manovich names the *computer layer*, the totality of technologies, software applications, mathematical algorithms and calculations engaged, computer languages and other resources pertaining to the functioning of computers and computer systems, and the *cultural layer*, the diachronic and synchronic cultures wherein the particular media are located and used. 'Because new media is created on computers, distributed on computers, and stored and achieved on computers,' Manovich exemplifies, 'the logic of the computer can be expected to significantly influence the traditional cultural logic of media; that is, we may expect that the computer layer will affect the cultural layer' (2001: 46). That is, once humans are accustomed to using computers on an everyday basis, terms, images, metaphors, social practices and beliefs embedded in or derived from the *computer layer* will gradually penetrate everyday social life. Commonplace expressions influenced by widely used media such as 'I googled that' (Orlikowski, 2007: 1439), testifying to the significant market penetration of the services provided by Silicon Valley-based firm Google, are representative of what Manovich (2001) calls transcoding.

The five principles of new media are formulated as formal and universal principles. All new media thus share a number of characteristics. For instance, all digital media are discrete, constituted by individual components, share the same digital code, allow for random access, involve the loss of information (e.g. frequencies in the digitalization of music), can be endlessly copied without successive losses of quality and are interactive, that is, the user can interact with the object since it is not fixed but fluid and composed of many tiny entities (e.g. pixels in a picture) (Manovich, 2001: 49). Even though modern computer science is a highly sophisticated domain of technoscience for the layman, in Manovich's (2001) account the computer and new media become intelligible. Beyond all the advanced computer languages, software applications and vast numbers of hardware combinations, the generic principles appear to remain surprisingly stable. Drawing on Saussure's distinction between *la langue* (the systemic nature of language) and *la parole* (its performance, its actual speech), the domain of *la langue* of the computer is an immense territory of code, while its *la parole* becomes possible to apprehend:

All electronic media technologies of the nineteenth and twentieth centuries are based on modifying a signal by passing it through various filters. These include technologies for real-time communication such as the telephone, broadcasting technologies used for mass-distribution of media products such as radio and television, and technologies to synthesize media such as video and audio synthesizers that originate with the instrument designed by Theremin in 1920. (Manovich, 2001: 132)

The same principle applies for computers and other new media. Moreover, Manovich claims that the interfaces of computers are structured like cinema (recall Jonathan Beller's [2006] argument, recounted in Chapter 1, that the present time period is characterized by a 'cinematic mode of production', thus placing cinema at the centre of media). Cinema, the cultural form bringing together sight, sound and movement in one seamless web of representations, is for Manovich the role model for what he calls *Human Computer Interfaces* (HCI): 'Rather than being merely one cultural interface among others, cinema is now becoming *the* cultural interface, a toolbox for all cultural communication, overtaking the printed word' (2001: 86). HCI is central to the actual functioning of the computer and is therefore, in Mark Poster's (2001a: 66–7) formulation, '[a] kind of membrane dividing yet connecting two worlds that are alien to and also dependent on each other':

> With representational machines such as the computer the question of interface becomes especially salient because each side of the human/machine divide now begins to claim its own reality; on the one side of the screen the Newtonian space, on the other, cyberspace. Interfaces of high quality are seamless crossings between the two worlds, thereby facilitating the disappearance of the difference between them and thereby, as well, altering the type of linkage between the two. Interfaces are the sensitive boundary zone of negation between the human and the machinic as well as the pivot of an emerging new set of human/machine relations. (Poster, 2001a: 67)

Summarizing his arguments, Manovich says that the 'visual culture' of a computer age is 'cinematographic in its appearance, digital on the level of its material, and computational (i.e. software driven) in its logic' (2001: 132, emphasis omitted). New media thus operate on three levels: the *cultural level* (where new media mimic cinema), the *material level* (where new media is digitalized) and the *symbolic* or *representational level* (where new media are constituted by computer code and computer languages). The cultural level of new media is important for Manovich because the aesthetics of information processing – Manovich (2001: 217) proposes the concept of 'info-aesthetics' – plays an increasingly central role in contemporary society. In 'info-aesthetics', information and aesthetics merge into a mutually constitutive process situated in the use of new media (Piñeiro, 2007; Case and Piñeiro, 2006).

In Manovich's (2001) analysis, new media are based on five generic principles capturing their material, syntactic and semantic characteristics. In addition, new media are 'encultured' in terms of using HCIs that make sense to humans. The perceptual immersion of cinema, bringing sight, sound and movement together in a productive and meaningful manner, serves as the ideal type for computer interfaces. In this view, there is an increasingly porous line of demarcation between new media and human cognition and action; new media are gradually becoming what computer game programmers call *immersive*, that is, what captures the gamers' attention and makes them forget the distinction between actual and virtual worlds (Zackariasson, Styhre and Wilson, 2006). Computer games are then based on immediacy, the overcoming of the boundary between media and reality. This porous and permeable segment between human and machine is what needs to be carefully examined. Perhaps the most important quality of new, computer-based media versus previous ('old') media is the ability of the viewer/listener/user/gamer to forget they are interacting with a machine rather than a human being or a material object, that is, again, its immediacy. Similar to the *trompe l'oeil* paintings examined by Leppert (1996), the new media are what undermine the cognitive distinction between inside and outside, the actual and the virtual. New media are then the prolongation of a long history, starting perhaps with the use of the *Zograscope* of the mid-eighteenth century (discussed below), of what may be called 'voluntary visual self-deception', that is, the desire to transcend actual visual horizons and enter virtual domains of vision without noticing that is the case.

In summary, media theory is the analysis of how representation (image, text, sound), technology, institutions and practices are turned into functional assemblages operating within and influencing social reality. Media are also not wholly detached from subject-positions and modes of thinking but are instead operating on the level of the very constitution of the subject.

Media and posthumanist thinking

One of the most thought-provoking ideas in the media theory perspective is to approach the human body as being constituted by intersecting material and informational resources. Hayles (1999) speaks of this perspective as being representative of a 'posthumanist discourse' addressed in a number of disciplines, including biology, biochemistry, computer science and emerging domains such as nanotechnology engineering. Hayles (1999: 29) argues that in molecular biology, the human body is regarded as being simultaneously an 'expression of genetic information' and as 'a physical structure'. Hayles says that the same applies to the literary corpus being embodied as physical objects and 'a space of representation'. Hayles refers to the relation between *informational* and *material* components in a particular entity as its *virtuality*: '*Virtuality is the central perception that material objects are interpenetrated by information patterns*' (1999: 13–4, emphasis in the original). In her analysis, Hayles (1999) identifies a series of theoretical frameworks that has made both the virtuality of human bodies and the entities produced by media an object of investigation. For instance, the cybernetic theory framework, first formulated by Norbert Weiner, addressed the informational constitution of the human body:

> In *The Human Use of Human Beings*, he [Norbert Weiner] suggested that human beings are not so much bone and blood, nerve and synapse, as they are patterns of organization. He points out that over the course of a lifetime, the cell composing a human being changes many times over, identity cannot therefore consist in physical continuity ... Consequently, to understand humans, one needs to understand how the patterns of information they embody are created, organized, stored, and retrieved. (Hayles, 1999: 104)

Seen from this point of view, the human body is little more than a passage point for individual cells. Instead it is the capacity of the human body to maintain its structure, its 'organization', and to reproduce the informational content of its ultimate components (e.g. genes, proteins, cells) that is the essence of the body (Kay, 2000; Sarkar, 2006). The materiality of the body is then what appears as ephemeral and transient while information remains fairly stable over the course of the lifetime of the organism. In Lévi-Strauss's (1985: 34) formulation, we have moved from 'homo oeconomicus' to 'homo geneticus' as the dominant metaphor for the human. Lash (2006) talks about the posthumanist discourse advanced by Hayles (1999) as a form of 'neo-vitalism', a rehabilitation of the nineteenth-century idea that life is a process of becoming that needs to be examined in opposition to a 'materialist ontology' (Burwick and Douglass, 1992; Fraser, Kember and Lury, 2005):

> Vitalist or neo-vitalist themes are particularly useful in the analysis of life itself. Here vitalism influenced thinkers such as Donna

Haraway and Katherine Hayles who put things in reverse. They understand not the media in terms of life, but life in terms of media. The study of life becomes the question of 'biomedia'. Thus genetic coding almost seems to be an extension of the coding of media and messages. If media in the age of digital media are increasingly algorithmic or are forms generated by set of instructions, then so are forms of life, by genetic instructions. Thus a mediatic principle or algorithmic principles also structure life. (Lash, 2006: 328)

Bowker (2005: 73) is sceptical about the idea of information being some disembodied, almost ethereal Aristotelian 'substance' circulating freely. Here, '"information" can travel anywhere and be made of anything; sequences in a gene, energy level in an atom, zeroes and ones in a machine, and signals from a satellite are all "information"'. Speaking about 'information mythology', Bowker suggests that 'if everything is information, then a general statement about the nature of information is a general statement about the nature of the universe'. However, the statement that 'everything is information' is not, Bowker (2005: 73) argues, 'a preordained fact about the world' but only 'becomes a fact when we make it so'. The concept of information is thus to some extent mystifying the ultimate matter of being in terms of not being explained *per se* but rather as serving as an *ad hoc* hypothesis. For instance, if life is in essence 'structured information', then information must be explained in greater detail.

The perhaps most well-known and debated example of the active manipulation of the relationship between materiality and information is the increasing development of genetically modified animals in the late 1980s (Haraway, 1997). In 1988, Harvard University became the first institution to patent a genetically modified 'onco-mouse' (which is also protected by a trademark); today there are about 2,000–3,000 types of genetically modified mice in the world (Braidotti, 2006: 101). For Braidotti, such animals are 'biological machine-organism assemblages' transgressing the boundary between nature and culture, materiality and information: 'S/he [the genetically modified animal] is … a cyber-teratological apparatus that scrambles the established codes and thus destabilizes the subject' (2006: 101). Perhaps we are only seeing the beginning of what Paul Virilio calls 'the biomachine' (cited in Der Derian, 1998: 20): 'In the future, just as the geographic world was colonialized by means of transportation or communication, we will have the possibility of a colonialization of the human body by technology,' Virilio predicts.

The other strand of media theory drawing on posthumanist thinking, starting in the hardware rather than the biological organism, is research on artificial intelligence and artificial life (Helmreich, 1998). For some researchers, such as the faculty of the Santa Fe Institute in New Mexico, USA, whose work Helmreich's ethnography gives an account of, media such as the computer are capable of generating lifelike systems obeying principles similar to those of biological life. For others, such as the computer programmer Ellen Ullman (1997), such anthropomorphisms are deceiving and she refers to such ideas as 'projections':

> We call the microprocessor the 'brain'; we say the machine has 'memory'. But the computer is not really like us, it is a projection of a very slim part of ourselves: that portion devoted to logic, order, rule, and clarity. It is as if we took the game of chess and declared it the highest order of human existence. (Ullman, 1997: 89)

Proponents of the emerging field of nanotechnology represent another particular form of technology optimism that hopes for new medical treatments and other applications when new nano-level technology is being developed. Although much of the nanotechnology discourse largely remains 'stuck in the future' in terms of engaging in storytelling about what may eventually come of out the nanotechnology programme (Selin, 2007), it still has some implications for posthumanist thinking. For instance, Milburn (2004) points at the overcoming of epistemological boundaries in nanotechnology thinking:

> The birth of nanotechnology as a scientific discipline provokes the hyperreal collapse of humanistic discourse, punctuating the fragile membrane between real and simulation, science and science fiction, organism and machine, and heralding metamorphic futures and cyborganic discontinuities. In both its speculative-theoretical and applied-engineering modes, nanotechnology unbuilds those constructions of human thought, as well as those forms of human embodiment, based on the secularity of presence and stability – terrorizing presentist humanism from the vantage point of an already inevitable future. (Milburn, 2004: 123)

Milburn says that 'nanologic' is a 'cyborg logic', which means that the separation between biological and technological processes is no longer strictly maintained. The continuous production of proteins in the cell and their intricate relations to the genetic code suggests that biological life *per se* is a kind of machinery continuously reproducing its own materiality. There is thus a recursive relationship between materiality and information that, Milburn says, permits an 'engineering of nanomachines' (2004), that is, nanotechnologies may become part of the tools and processes repairing and reproducing the human body. Seen from this point of view, there is, as suggested by Hansen (2006) a disjunction between 'human embodiment' and the human body: 'Because human embodiment no longer coincides with the boundaries of the human body, a disembodiment of the body forms the condition of possibility for a collective (re)embodiment through technics. The human today is embodied in and through technics' (Hansen, 2006: 95; see also Munster, 2006). For instance, in the pharmaceutical industry – given that we perceive pharmaceutical drugs as a form of technology, an 'informed matter' (Barry, 2005) – proteomics analyses and pharmacogenetics are beginning to open up the possibility of genetically designed drugs created to produce the best medical treatment given the individual patient's gene structure (Rose, 2007; Sowa, 2006; Hedgecoe and Martin, 2003; Hedgecoe, 2006). This is perhaps the most advanced practical application of the theoretical framework formulated by posthumanist thinkers. Future drugs may in fact be designed on the basis of the informational content of the human body. Although the funding of nanotechnology grew from US$116 million in 1997 to US$847 million in 2004 in the USA, from US$126 million in 1997 to US$650 million in 2003 in Western Europe, and from US$120 million in 1997 to US$800 million in 2003 in Japan (Thomas and Ancuña-Narvaez, 2006), the future of nanotechnology largely remains an open field.

Media theory is expanding its perspective into not only examining how media are affecting the body and enabling a variety of perceptions, but also entering the very organism to show the value of recognizing the machine-organism assemblage view of the human body. Materiality and information are then the constitutive components of the biological organism and therefore they need to be theorized as such, what Hayles (1999) calls *virtuality*, the recursive relation between what is embodied and what is informational.

Forms of media: historical overview

Media are constitutive of human societies. The earliest forms of representations, images in caves (Leroi-Gourhan, 1983/1989) and the use of hieroglyphs and symbols in ancient Egypt and Mesopotamia testify to the human need to communicate and document experiences and beliefs. The media that are used in contemporary society, in many cases the bundling of series of media brought together by computer-based technologies, appear most advanced in comparison to these stone-carvings and decorated pieces of wood but their principal and morphological functions are essentially the same; to store and circulate data and information, to communicate, to celebrate individuals or events, or to gain recognition for ideas and beliefs. The chatrooms provided by internet homepages serve the same human needs, *mutatis mutandis*, as the Scandinavian rune-stones erected by the Vikings. At the same time, one must not underrate the effects on perception and cognition brought by media. New media tend to be celebrated as technological breakthroughs but within a generation or so they become naturalized and taken for granted. Today, the wider public has largely forgotten the social and cultural changes brought by the radio receiver because most of us were raised in households equipped with radios. Therefore, an historical overview of new media helps reposition the contemporary media into a broader framework enabling a recognition of the interrelationship between archaic – or to use Michael's (2000) phrase, 'mundane technologies' – and advanced technologies.

Bowker (2005: 26) cites French medieval historian Jacques LeGoff, separating five periods of 'collective memory': (1) oral transmission, (2) written transmissions with tables or indices, (3) simple file cards, (4) 'mechanical writing' and (5) 'electronic sequencing'. The first major media innovation was, of course, the various uses of forms of writing and a widely shared regime of representations. McLuhan (1997: 5) emphasizes the translation of audible sounds into images or signs: 'Writing, in its several modes, can be regarded technologically as the development of new languages. To translate the audible into the visible by phonetic means is to institute a dynamic process that reshapes every aspect of thought, language and society.' McLuhan says that writing brings 'logical analysis' and 'specialism', that is, more advanced and systematic modes of thinking, but also 'militarism and bureaucracy' (1997: 128). Writing represents the birth of the administrative society (see also Goody, 1986). Bolter (1991: 33) emphasizes, similar to Ong (1982), the ability to preserve and circulate human experiences in writing, suggesting that writing is a technology for 'collective memory, for preserving and passing on human experience'. The practice of writing is then one of the first media to be capable of constantly influencing humanity's 'mental life' (Bolter, 1991: 36). One specific form of innovation associated with writing is the establishment of the Greek alphabet – derived from the Phoenician alphabet (Goody, 1987: 46) – wherein vowels were, in contrast to some of the regimes of representations employed in the Middle East, integrated to enable an easier decoding of scriptures. For media theorists like Kittler (1997; 1999), the Greek alphabet is a significant contribution to the advancement of media. Similar to Arabic numbers, much more effectively capturing underlying figures than the clumsy Roman numerals, the Greek alphabet institutes a new mode of thinking and provides new opportunities for media.

The second significant media innovation is the technique of printing, a skill developed in the Renaissance period in the mid-fifteenth century. The birth of printing was brought about by the integration of a series of technological, social and cultural innovations. While the Chinese, who were capable of producing quality paper, may have used books as early as during the Chang dynasty (1765BC–1123BC) (Febvre and Martin, 1997: 71), it took centuries for the Europeans to master the technology. The advancement of paper production, the development of the printing press and an increased demand for books from the emerging bourgeoisie were some of the changes that paved the way for printing, according to the popular account represented by the German goldsmith Johannes Gensfleisch, better known as Johannes Gutenberg, working in the city of Mainz. The advent of printing led to significant changes. For instance, as Eisenstein (1983: 34) points out, 'as learning by reading took on new importance, the role played by mnemonic aids was diminished. Rhyme and cadence were no longer required to preserve certain formulas and recipes.' The scholastic tradition, emphasizing the learning of a few canonical texts (most notably the writings of the Church fathers and Aristotle, see Le Goff [1993]) almost by heart, was gradually displaced by a more restless search for influences. Alexander (2002) discusses the traditional sources of knowledge prior to the modern image of science and scholarly work:

> Traditionally, true knowledge was based on the interpretation of a canon of ancient texts, which included scripture and the corpus of the ancient philosophers and church fathers. The underlying assumption was that all relevant knowledge was already in existence and was contained within prescribed canons. The search for truth, therefore, consisted of the proper application of the wisdom contained within the bounds of these volumes to the problem at hand. If, as was often the case, the canonical texts were in conflict with each other, the difficulties would be resolved through the scholastic practice of disputation. Truth, in other words, was arrived at not through new discoveries but through hermeneutics – the detailed interpretation of authoritative texts. (Alexander, 2002: 99)

Eisenstein (1983: 42) underlines the effects on the work of intellectuals. To consult different books, it was no longer essential to be a wandering scholar. With the birth of printing, scholarly work increasingly became what Eisenstein (1983) calls 'sedentary work', located in single institutions such as monasteries or universities. In addition, scholars were less apt to be engrossed by a single text but started to consult many different texts in a field; 'the era of the glossator and commentator came to an end, and a new "era of intense cross referencing between one book and another began"', Eisenstein (1983: 42) claims. This ability to elaborate on a number of texts led to a new mode of thinking, aimed not primarily at excelling at reporting the ideas or content of a single work in the canon but at comparing ideas and identifying new means by which to approach truth. 'Not only was confidence in old theories weakened, but an enriched reading matter also encouraged the development of new intellectual combinations and permutations,' Eisenstein contends (1983: 43). However, Eisenstein's (1983) belief in a gradual erosion of incumbent thinking and practice conflicts with Febvre and Martin's (1997) account, being more sceptical about the short-term effects of printing:

> Although printing certainly helped scholars in some fields, on the whole it could not be said to have hastened the acceptance of new ideas or knowledge. In fact, by popularising long cherished beliefs, strengthening traditional prejudice and giving authority to seductive fallacies, it could even be said to have represented an obstacle to the acceptance of many new views. Even after new discoveries were made they tended to be ignored and reliance continued to be placed in conventional authorities. (Febvre and Martin, 1997: 71)

In addition, for Vilém Flusser (2002), linear writing brings critical thinking and historical consciousness into human society, but it was not until the invention of printing that this mode of thinking was more evenly distributed in society:

> For most of its course, historical consciousness was the privilege of a small elite, while the vast majority continued to lead a prehistoric, magico-mythical existence. This was so because texts were rare and expensive, and literacy the privilege of a class of scribes and literati. The invention of printing cracked this clerical class open, and it made historical consciousness accessible for the rising bourgeoisie, but it was only during the industrial revolution and through the public primary school system that literacy and historical consciousness can be said to have become common in industrialized countries. (Flusser, 2002: 66)

Printing also brought new ideas about property rights and an ideology emphasizing individual rather than collective contributions to a particular field of enquiry. Around the year 1500, a new regime based on legal protection rather than guild protection was established. Eisenstein reports:

> Once the rights of an inventor could be legally fixed and the problem of preserving unwritten recipes intact was no longer posed, profits could be achieved by open publicity provided new restraints were not imposed. Individual initiative was released from reliance on guild protection, but at the same time new powers were lodged in the hands of a bureaucratic officialdom. (1983: 83)

She continues: 'The new forms of authorship and literary property rights undermined older concepts of collective authority in a manner that encompassed not only biblical composition but also texts relating to philosophy, science, and law' (1983: 85). Among the various and complex social changes brought by printing, a new ideology of science and a new emphasis on individualism at the expense of collectivism was established. The technology of printing brought the core of the scientific ideology and its search for truth, not in a limited number of canonical texts, but in empirical studies and experimental arrangements, thus reinforcing the bourgeoisie ideology of individualism underlying the modern capitalist regime of accumulation and regulation (McCloskey, 2006). Printing is thus a medium at the heart of modernity.

Technologies of perception

While media for writing and printing, emerging in the Renaissance and during the Reformation, may be regarded as components of the infrastructure of media assemblages, more recently (that is, in the eighteenth, nineteenth and twentieth centuries) a number of media mobilizing human perception have been invented (for an overview and demonstration of a series of visual media, see http://www.visual-media.be/history.html). When examining such media, it is important, Gitelman (1999) insists, to recognize the recursive relationship between media (*qua* technological artefact) and culture (the totality of social practice): 'Culture insinuates itself within technology at the same time that technology infiltrates culture,' Gitelman claims (1999: 7). Gitelman is here speaking of an *internalist* and an *externalist* analysis of technology:

> Internalists practice a sort of formalism, attending more narrowly to how things work, the way one telegraph instrument adapted the form

or function of another. Externalists, by contrast, locate things more amid political, economic and cultural contexts. The newer school of social constructivists rejects both thing and context as separate or separable units of analysis. According to this view, an invention succeeds not because 'it works', but rather it is described as 'working' because it succeeds amid prevailing and possibly competitive expectations. Technological function remains something to explain, it does not comprise an explanation in (or of) itself. (Gitelman, 1999: 8)

MacKenzie (1996) warns that the internalist perspective is susceptible to what at times is called 'Whig history', that is, explaining the past on the basis of contemporary conditions and conceiving of historical events as being part of an inevitable progression towards the present state. In such a view, predominant technologies are incapable of being explained because it is simply assumed they were 'intrinsically superior' rather than embedded in contingencies and local conditions:

> Hindsight often makes it appear that the successful technology is simply intrinsically superior, but hindsight – here and elsewhere – can be a misleading form of vision. Historians and sociologists of technology would do well to avoid explaining the success of technology by its assumed intrinsic technical superiority to its rivals. Instead, they should seek, even-handedly, to understand how its actual superiority came into being, while suspending judgment as to whether it is intrinsic. (MacKenzie, 1996: 7).

The externalist view does then emphasize that technologies do not simply work or are appropriated because they function properly or serve a social role but because they are capable of being aligned with dominating political, social and cultural ideas and beliefs. Nye (2006), taking what Gitelman (1999) calls an externalist position and what he himself calls a *contextualist* view, shows that major communication media were originally regarded as 'curiosities' that only came into broader use through their alignment with broader social interests:

> At first, Samuel Morse had trouble convincing anyone to invest in his telegraph. He spent five years 'lecturing, lobbying, and negotiating' before he convinced the US Congress to pay for the construction of the first substantial telegraph line, which ran from Washington to Baltimore. Even after it was operating, he had difficulty finding customers interested in using it. Likewise, Alexander Graham Bell could not find an investor to buy his patents on the telephone, and so he reluctantly

decided to market it himself. Thomas Alva Edison found few commercial applications for his phonograph, despite the sensational publicity surrounding his discovery ... In the mid 1970s, a prototype of the personal computer, when first shown to a group of MIT professors, seemed rather uninteresting to them. They could think of a few uses for it, and they suggested perhaps it would be most useful to shut-ins. In short, the telegraph, the telephone, and phonograph and the personal computer, surely four of the most important inventions in the history of communications, were initially understood as curiosities. (Nye, 2006: 41)

As a consequence, one must broaden the base for the analysis of media and recognize and examine their entanglement with culture, human interests and social relations. Many of the media examined in Gitelman's (1999) edited volume are today forgotten and are at best on display in technology or media museums. However, when they were invented and introduced they were representative of the latest thrusts in science and technology. In fact, as Lightman suggests (2000: 655), 'the results of scientific studies on vision were introduced into popular culture when the optical devices initially used in experiments were converted into forms of popular entertainment'. Theories of perception thus trickled down from the domain of scientific research to the more mundane sphere of entertainment.

Blake (2003) examines the *Zograscope*, a medium capable of providing 3-D images that was one of the first gadget crazes in the period between the mid-1740s and the mid-1750s. In the period, 'zograscopes and zograscope prints appeared regularly in English magazine copy and news paper advertisement, as did hundreds of different engraved, hand-colored images designed for use with the device', Blake says (2003: 1). Being marketed primarily as a source of entertainment for the upper classes and the aristocracy, the Zograscope served the function of one of the first media to exploit the human pleasures of vision – what psychologists would eventually call *scopophilia*. Crary (1990) examines a number of media emerging after the Zograscope such as the *phenakisto-scope*, capable of producing images of movement and invented in the early 1830s by the Belgian scientist Joseph Plateau (Crary, 1990: 107–9). By 1833, phenakistoscopes were sold to the public in London. Other similar media were the *zoetrope*, invented by William G. Horner in 1834, and the *stereoscope*, invented by the German mathematician Simon Stampfer in 1838. The stereoscope was successfully commercialized during the mid-1850s and 1860s (Schiavo, 2003: 113). Although most of these new media have become obsolete and displaced by new, more effective media, the stereoscope has survived as a kid's plaything wherein colourful images can be displayed. The stereoscope also served to help shape the idea of human vision: 'The most significant form of visual imagery in the nineteenth century, with the exception of photographs, was the stereoscope,' Crary claims (1990: 116). These new media were all based on what Virilio (1989) would later call 'the logistics of perception', the structuring and shaping of vision through media. Other media from the nineteenth-century period explored and exploited the faculty of hearing. Stubbs (2003) examines the early development of the telegraph media and what she refers to as the 'telegraph community'. The telegraph succeeded 'semaphore telegraphs', a medium largely forgotten today consisting of a series of geographically distributed towers located every few miles, 'mounted with signaling devices that transmitted in code to observers at each tower equipped with telescopes' (Israel, 1992: 38). The semaphore telegraphs could, their proponents claimed, transmit messages between New York and Washington in 'about twenty-five minutes, and to New Orleans in less than two hours' (Israel, 1992: 38). Still, Samuel Morse's invention, the telegraph, had significant advantages over the semaphore telegraph, inextricably entangled with visual sight, and eventually became one of the determining technologies of the nineteenth century. Stubbs (2003) argues that today, the internet plays the role of being the media enabling new subject-positions and thereby serving as a liberating or even escapist function. For instance, Turkle (1996) speaks of the internet as 'laboratories for the construction of identity' (Stubbs, 2003: 91) and suggests that the internet therefore represents a medium providing opportunities previously unseen. However, Stubbs (2003) shows that the telegraph network built in the USA in the nineteenth century also offered such opportunities for identity construction. Even though she rejects terms such as the 'Victorian internet' (coined by Tom Standage, 1998), the telegraph network enabled new forms of communication:

> A telegraph operator was a member of a community; as many as ten or twelve operators might work on the same telegraph circuit, rapidly transmitting and receiving messages using Morse code. The wire was akin to a party line, as every message transmitted over the wire could be read by all operators. On certain less-tracked rural lines, in the intervals when no official telegraph messages were being sent, operators would routinely have personal conversations with each other over the wire. Given the nature of the technology, it was impossible

to know for certain from what station a given message originated. (Stubbs, 2003: 92)

When the telegraph network was established and used, a new genre of literature, 'telegraph fiction', addressing the 'pleasures and dangers' of the new technology emerged. From the beginning, it was exclusively male operators working on the network but, gradually, female operators were hired by Western Union, the largest American telegraph company. By the end of the 1860s, women, lower paid and 'more docile' than male operators, entered the profession. The telegraph network was based on the faculty of hearing and effectively broke down the distinction between near and far. It also enabled anonymity and offered opportunities for eavesdropping on conversations to take place. It was a medium that for the first time mediated the sound of the voice. Moreover, the telegraphy industry was, Israel (1992) argues, what changed American innovation from being an individual pursuit of skilled local artisans such as smiths, to a full-scale organizational endeavour, located in specific departments and employing various specialists. Israel thus speaks of a 'telegraph industry' that actually preceded the railways as what unified America.

Another significant invention that brought new media was the electrification of the West. From the 1880s and into the twentieth century, European and American cities and even smaller towns were 'electrified' through intensive lighting. By World War I, electricity was established as a central component in a utopian future, ensuring brilliant prospects for civilization (Nye, 1990: 66). Authors in the popular press spoke of electricity as 'white magic' that promised an 'electrical millennium'. Leading social actors saw early the political and cultural significance of electricity and used it to promote political objectives: 'Spectacular lighting had become a sophisticated cultural apparatus. The corporations and public officials who used it could commemorate history, encourage civic pride, simulate natural effects, sell products, highlight public monuments, and edit both natural and urban landscapes' (Nye, 1990: 73). Even though electricity quickly became a commodity, it signified something more than mere profit; 'it helped to define modernity, progress, and physical and social well-being' (Nye, 1990: 141). However, the dominant characteristics of an age are not easily agreed upon and a small but very articulate group of literati longed for a preindustrial past – 'an idealized medieval world of handicraft labor, unalienated social relations, child-like sensuous experience, and ecstatic faith' (Nye, 1990: 142–3). Others, like the perhaps greatest innovator himself, Thomas Alva Edison, 'The

Wizard of Menlo Park', exploited the interest in new technology and were quick to express ideas suitable for the popular press. Edison predicted that electricity would eliminate the distinction between night and day and that it would 'speed up women's mental development, making them the intellectual equals of men'. In addition, constant light might, Edison speculated, lead to the elimination of sleep and, in his later years, he even hinted that he was experimenting with 'electric ways to communicate with the dead' (Nye, 1990: 147). Edison's firm optimism regarding technology, expressed in such spectacular announcements, was not shared by everyone. A certain Bishop Turner representing the African Methodist Church predicted that production of electricity was 'unbalancing air currents, and would lead to floods, hurricanes, and cyclones', and another clergyman predicted that by 1920 'the electricity stored in the earth will come to contact with the heated matter inside and blow the whole world up' (Nye, 1990: 150). The new technology thus engendered both enthusiasm and anxieties (Sconce, 2000). However, as electrified media quickly became widely spread, electric billboards in many colours and shapes were distributed in New York, Boston and Chicago. Among other things, electric lighting changed the night landscape and city skyline and produced an entirely new impression of the city. Perhaps as in no other case, electric lighting is exemplary of McLuhan's (1964) catchphrase 'the media is the message'. Ezra Pound, back from Europe for a visit in 1910, responded positively to the New York night skyline,

> finding it 'the most beautiful city in the world' in the evening. 'It is then that the great buildings lose reality and take on their magical powers. They are immaterial; that is to say one sees but the lighted windows. Square after square of flame, set and cut into the aether. Here is our poetry, for we have pulled down the stars to our will'. (Nye, 1990: 74)

'Intensive lighting seemed to actualise dreams of greatness,' says Nye (1990: 2) – 'it emerged as a glamorous symbol of progress and cultural advancement'. Electricity is then a central feature of what Rem Koolhaas in his *Delirious New York* (1978) would call the 'technology of the fantastic'. Koolhaas discusses how Coney Island, the seaside resort in Brooklyn, New York, became a site of experimentation for the 'the technology of the fantastic'. In Coney Island, various amusement parks such as *Luna Park* and *Dreamland* were built at the end of the nineteenth century. However, representatives of the literati did not immediately appreciate the new forms of spectacle emerging in the American metropolis. In

1906, Maxim Gorky visited New York and Coney Island and reported with great contempt:

> The City, magic and fantastic from afar, now appears an absurd jungle of straight lines of wood, of cheap hastily constructed toyhouses for the amusement of children ... Everything is stripped naked by the dispassionate glare. The glare is everywhere and nowhere is the shadow ... the visitor is stunned; his consciousness is withered by the intense gleam; his thoughts are routed from his mind; he becomes a particle in the crowd. (Maxim Gorky, cited in Koolhaas, 1978: 67–8)

The technology of the fantastic found its laboratory on Coney Island. In the early twentieth century, the technology of the fantastic was transferred to Manhattan, serving as one of the pillars of what Koolhaas calls *Manhattanism*, an ideology of hyperdensity and 'culture of congestion'. The technology of the fantastic enters urban life. In New York City, 42nd Street became its first site, the epicentre of the new electrified society of the spectacle, a position it has maintained ever since.

Cinema and television

The perhaps most immersing medium of the nineteenth and twentieth centuries (with the introduction of sound, a decisive step for the art form and the industry) was cinema (Young, 2003). Hansen (1995) locates cinema within the emerging spectacular society carefully examined by, for instance, Jonathan Crary (1990; 1995), having its roots in the early nineteenth century:

> [T]he cinema appears as part of an emerging culture of consumption and spectacular display, ranging from world expositions and department stores to the more sinister attractions of melodrama, phantasmagoria, wax museums, and morgues, a culture marked by an accelerated proliferation – and, hence, also by an accelerated ephemerality and obsolescence – of sensations, fashions, and styles. (Hansen, 1995: 363)

Cinema thus rested on not only the increasing social and cultural demand for visual entertainment leading to a range of spectacular inventions and public displays, but also on the ability to bundle a range of media and their underlying technologies. The photograph is, of course, the most elementary medium mobilized by cinema, but also the projection technologies and the use of musical instruments such as piano – the early cinema presentations were accompanied by music, illustrating the occurrences on the screen – became part of the media multiplicity. From the very beginning, Singer (1995: 90) says, cinema '[g]ravitated towards an "aesthetics of astonishment", in terms of both form and subject matter'. Cinema is for Singer (1995: 90) the culmination of 'the trend toward vivid, powerful sensation' and thus represented the most advanced form of media until the birth of advanced computer technologies well into the 1970s and 1980s. The social and cultural implications were substantial: Vidler (2000: 100) argues:

> [S]ince the late nineteenth century, film has provided a test case for the definition of modernism in theory and technique. It has also served as a point of departure for the redefinition of the other arts, a paradigm by which the different practices of theater, photography, literature, and painting might be distinguished from each other.

Like no other media, cinema, film and movies (three partially overlapping terms) bring the audience into an experience engaging several human senses. No wonder then that cinema became (after art and music) one of the principal media for propaganda. For instance, the films directed by Leni Riefenstahl in the 1930s, celebrating the forthcoming German third empire, are paradigmatic examples of how politics and media tend to mingle.

It is tempting to assume that television, the media technology forcefully penetrating the private domain at the middle of the twentieth century and ever since playing a central role in social life, is a simple application or modification of the cinema medium. However, technology studies and what Morley (2007) calls 'technoanthropology' show that television in fact shares more qualities with broadcast radio than with cinema. Morley takes a clear externalist stance on the subject matter:

> It is worth remarking that not only was television, in its initial conception, a technology capable of many alternative uses, its gradual introduction to the home was only the result of a long process of debate and anxiety within the nascent television industry itself. (2007: 276)

Representatives of the emerging television industry were concerned about how television, a medium calling for not only audible (like the radio) but also visual attention, could be brought into the structure of everyday family life (Broddy, 2004: 50). For instance, housewives were generally occupied with domestic work and could not spare the time to watch television. In the April 1949 issue of *Sales Management*, a certain Jules Nathan addressed this concern accordingly:

> Radio is an unqualified success during the daytime hours. To a large extent its popularity rests squarely on those factors which may be an insuperable obstacle to video. Women can cook, clean, bake and engage in all the varied mystic rites of the homemaker while keeping a sharp ear out for the last agonies of the radio dramas. Television, alas for the business side of the enterprise, will share the spotlight with no other activities. (Jules Nathan, 'Who will watch daytime television?', *Sales Management*, 1 April 1949, cited in Broddy, 2004: 51)

The 'daytime television concern' was dealt with in two ways. First, the programming of the broadcast was broken up into sequences with commercials enfolded into the programmes, enabling domestic work to be carried out. This fragmented structure was radically different from that of cinema, which was conceived of as what we today would call an immersive medium not tolerating disturbing intermissions and breaks. Second, the architecture of houses was gradually modified, no longer clearly separating the kitchen and the domains where domestic work was conducted and the living room, where the television set was generally located. New doctrines of the architecture of the domestic space gained a foothold. Finally, the domestic sphere increasingly became a domain where leisure time was spent. Previously, especially among the working class, leisure time was spent outdoors (children), in pubs or coffee shops (men), or in bingo halls or similar public places (women), but when television entered domestic life, more time was spent at home. Rather than seeing friends, neighbours and colleagues at the local pub or at the coffee shop, the television spectator became, with the artist Naim June Paik's apt term, a 'stationary nomad' (Morley, 2007: 284), a person experiencing the paradoxical combination of 'a poverty of physical movements and an excess of visual stimulation'. In 1944, an advertisement in *DuMont* magazine promised the television viewer that he – the advertisement features a single man seated in front of his television set – would become 'an armchair Columbus' (cited in Broddy, 2004: 133), thus effectively underlining the dynamic relationship between passivity and active participation incorporated in the television medium. This chimera of movement and participation in society has been grist for the mill for a long series of critical accounts of television, ranging from Raymond Williams's (1990) seminal critique to Pierre Bourdieu's (1996) more recent analysis (for an overview of sociological studies of television, see Grindstaff and Turow, 2006).

The general tendency, historically, was for media to become more and more immersing, thereby undermining the spectator's or user's ability to separate media and reality. In Bolter and Grusin's (1999) terms, processes of immediacy, hypermediacy and remediation occured in tandem. While the instituting of commonly enacted regimes of representations and signs in ancient times may have appeared obscure or even mystical for individuals with fewer capacities for vision and foresight, the cinematic experiences in today's movie theatres (to use the American term) do not demand much from the spectator but the capacity to hear and to look. It is a medium carefully designed to enable a logistics of perception that few spectators can ignore or escape. Media are what enframe everyday life and what determine our condition.

Media and organization

Technology and the influence of the user

The first thing to notice is that all media, from the symbols carved into stones in ancient Assyria through printed books to advanced virtual reality applications, are *technologies*. More specifically, they are technologies designed to store, manipulate, and distribute data. Before moving on to the organizational consequences of media/new media, this curious concept of technology will be examined. Although modern life is thoroughly pervaded by technology, as an analytical category, technology is strangely muted and inarticulate. In his classic essay, 'The Question Concerning Technology', Martin Heidegger said that the essence of technology is nothing technological but is instead what precedes technology, a mode of thinking, an episteme, an attitude, representative of the Western epistemology. Jacques Ellul (1964), expresses similar thoughts when talking about *technics* rather than technology. Dodge and Kitchin (2005) use the term *technicity*, a concept underlining the social implications of technology:

> Technicity refers to the extent to which technologies mediate, supplement, and augment collective life; the extent to which technologies are fundamental to the constitution and grounding of human endeavour; and the unfolding of evolutive power of technologies to make things happen *in conjunction* with people. (Dodge and Kitchin, 2005: 169, emphasis in the original)

The technicity of the focal technology makes it 'contingent, negotiated, and nuanced'; technology is thus what is 'practised' by people 'in relation to historical and geographical context'. In the organization theory literature, Kallinikos has advocated a similar perspective, underlining how technology 'partakes' in the constitution of agents and events:

> Social agents are not disembodied spirits; instead, they are complex ensembles of skills, proclivities, and roles, some of which are brought into being by technology itself ... Technology is not just an exterior force that encroaches upon local, technologically 'unspoiled' contexts, though it may be used that way; most of the time, technology partakes in the constitution of local contexts and agents. (2006a: 144)

On the other hand, as Kallinikos (2005) emphasizes elsewhere, technology also provides a 'platform' where the world is stabilized into predictable relations. This stability is what enables purposeful action. Kallinikos says:

> I will portray technology as a structural form that supports human action in a world beset with contingencies of every sort. Thus viewed, technology emerges as a standardized and closed arrangement of artefacts/processes designed and deployed to produce a minimum platform of predictable relations, in an otherwise shifting and contingent world. (2005: 189)

Also recognizing this two-sided feature of technology, Orlikowski (2000; 1992) advocates, following Anthony Giddens, a structuration theory view of technology wherein institutions, technology and human practices, that is, the totality of the individual co-workers' engagement with a technology, are jointly constitutive of technology: '[T]echnology is physically constructed by actors working in a given context, and technology is socially constructed by actors through the different meanings they attach to it and the various features they emphasize and use' (Orlikowski, 1992: 406). Orlikowski's (1992) empirical study of the use of a computer program in the consulting company Beta suggests that technologies are neither merely tools in the hands of humans, nor capable of determining work, but rather simultaneously influence human action and are affected by their practical use: 'Tools are clearly not instrumental (structuring the production process) they are also normative, as they mediate a shared reality within Beta, producing uniformity and predictability in thought and behavior' (Orlikowski, 1992: 418). Here, technologies are not self-enclosed black boxes (Orlikowski, 2000: 411), ready-made and immutable artefacts, but are strongly affected by their relationship to dominant beliefs and ideologies in the organization. In Perrow's formulation: '[M]ere "things" – equipment, its layout, its ease of operation and maintenance – are shaped by organizational structure and top management interests, and in turn shape operator behavior' (1983: 540). Not only are institutional actors capable of affecting practices, technologies *per se* are also subject to cognitive processes and instituted beliefs and norms. Barley (1990), examining the relationship between radiologists and technicians in the use of CT scanning technology in medical diagnosis work, emphasizes the political embedding of technology:

> Technologies are depicted as implanting or removing skills much as a surgeon would insert a pacemaker or remove a gall bladder. Rarely, however, is the process so tidy. Events subsequent to the introduction of a technology may show that reputedly obsolete skills retain their importance, that new skills surface to replace those that were made redundant, or that matters of skill remain unresolved. In any case, groups will surely jockey for the right to define their roles to their own advantage. (Barley, 1990: 67)

Consequently, human practices are not removed from political interests and individual objectives but are rather shaped and influenced by the purposeful activities of institutional actors (Williams and Edge, 1996; Pentland and Feldman, 2007).

Speaking of technology in a vocabulary fashioned by Gilles Deleuze's philosophy, Wise (1997: 58) suggests that analysts of technology must abandon a modern episteme wherein technologies are 'fixed points', mobilized and used by individuals clearly separated *vis-à-vis* the technology, and think in terms of 'lines, vectors, and assemblages'. For instance, using a journey by train as an example, Wise (1997) emphasizes that the use of a particular technology emerges as an assemblage, as a multiplicity composed of many interrelated parts that cannot be reduced to one another:

> The train is an assemblage within which we may trace the delegation of numerous social actors: the engine driver, the fuel, the track, the wheel, the landscape. The assemblage is not a random configuration but is coded according to particular hegemonies such as the capitalist market, which influences which points will be connected and what the trains will carry ... We will never grasp the assemblage as a whole, nor should that be the objective of the analysis ... Our analysis must resist totality and recognize that vision is partial. (Wise, 1997: 58)

In a vocabulary reminscent of Wise's (1997), Law (2002) speaks of technology – and more specifically, an aircraft defence system – in terms of 'fractional coherence', as what is balancing between being singular and plural: '[a] fractionally coherent subject or object is more than one that balances between plurality and singularity. It is *more than one, but less than many*,' Law says (2002: 3, emphasis in the original). A technology then 'oscillates' between being a unified and coherent object and an assemblage composed of many parts and resources. A similar perspective, seeking to transcend the 'technology-as-artefact' perspective, is advanced by Gartman (2004: 169), saying that sociologists need to abandon their idea of 'the car as a thing, a simple object of production and consumption, and look at it as a system of interlocking social and technical practices that has reconfigured civil society'. Urry (2004), in general defending a sociological analysis based on fluids and flows rather than fixed or semi-stable entities (Urry, 2005), represents a similar view of what he calls the 'system of automobility' constituted by artefacts, infrastructures, social practices and preferences, laws and regulations, ideologies and beliefs, and other social resources constituting a system of personalized mobility.

In summary, one must not assume that users of technology are passive recipients of technology. In fact, they strongly influence, enact, reshape and structure technology (Leonard-Barton, 1988; Lanzara and Patriotta, 2001). On the other hand, technology also affects social relations and individual behaviour (Latour, 1991), thereby rendering technology as emerging in recursive iterations between user and artefact and its broader technological and social ramifications (Pinch and Bijker, 1987; Bijker, 1995; Dobers and Strannegård, 2001; Oudshoorn and Pinch, 2003). Technology is never introduced into social communities as an enclosed and determinate artefact but gradually becomes a social resource through its reworking and continuous adaptation in various settings and communities.

Media at work: from the mundane to cyborgization

In the following, a number of different applications of media and new media pertaining to perception and organizing will be examined (for an overview, see Jackson, Poole and Kuhn, 2002). In doing so, we proceed from the more mundane technologies of 'old media' such as typewriters and filing closets to more recent uses of email and information technology, on to the more spectacular and visionary technologies of virtual reality, providing a more comprehensive 'cyborgization' of the human in terms of the merging of 'wetware' (humans), software and hardware into a technological assemblage capable of producing immersive experiences. Ideally, the uses of overhead projectors, printed books and documents and other forms of 'socially unmarked' and taken-for-granted media should be examined (see Michael, 2000), but, as usual, it is the more advanced and frontline technologies that call for attention. However, it is noteworthy that the more advanced the medium, technology or techno-logical system, the fewer applications there are in contemporary organizations. For instance, virtual reality technologies have caught the human imagination since at least the 1980s, but even today, are still only used primarily by media laboratory researchers and a few users of advanced technological systems used in, for example, the pharmaceutical industry, as a means to represent such concepts as molecules in a 3-D space.

'Old media': media and the historical growth of organizations

Yates's (1989) seminal study of the growth of systematic communication and control in organizations in the nineteenth and twentieth centuries stresses the role of media for the growth of large-scale corporations. In the second half of the nineteenth century, quill pens and bound volumes were displaced by typewriters, stencil duplicators and vertical files, which in turn affected the form and function of communication within the firm. With these new media, new types and 'genres' of communication such as orders, reports, memoranda and meetings developed (Yates, 1989: xv). By 1920, the 'major elements' of modern communication were established in most substantial American firms. Yates argues convincingly that these changes were not additional to or an 'incidental by-product' of the growth of American corporations but in fact was one of the key factors enabling this expansion (Yates, 1989: xvii). In the 1830s, the American railroad industry was established, demanding new forms of coordination and control to operate effectively. In their search for first safety and later on efficiency, railroad managers were pioneers in managerial practice and theory. They anticipated, Yates (1989: 9) agues, the systematic management philosophy in insisting on systematizing procedures and gathering operational information to help facilitating decision-making on a higher level. The principal tool for these approaches was to institute a regular flow of information within the railroad companies. The telegraph was introduced in 1844, enabling long-distance communication, and the use of new technical devices such as the typewriter, carbon paper and duplicators and vertical filing provided new opportunities for storing and circulating information. In 1856 the first aniline dye was invented, providing permanent copies and occasional second copies of the original. Aniline dye 'undoubtedly made press copying a more attractive technology in the second half of the nineteenth century', Yates (1989: 27) notes. The development of new media also operated in tandem with what technology historians and economists call technology push and market pull. For instance, typewriters, which greatly increased the speed and reduced the cost with which written documents would be produced, facilitated written communication. Increased business demands for written documentation increased the demands for even better typewriters, thereby further encouraging technological innovation in the field of media (Yates, 1989: xviii). Moreover, the demand for better communication and information storage, taking the form of an 'organization memory', had significant social implications. Yates argues that a new administrative class of clerical workers developed in the period 1890–1920:

> A whole new class of clerical workers arose to operate the new machines, as well as to take dictation and perform other clerical functions related to the handling of written documents ... In 1890, the US census showed 133,000 people employed in the broader occupational category including stenographers, typists, and secretaries. Such workers continued to flow into business and government in increasing numbers. By 1910 that occupational category had almost tripled to 387,000, and by 1920 it had doubled again to 786,000. (Yates, 1989: 43)

In addition to the growth of what Yates calls 'downward and upward communication' through the organization tiers, new forms of 'horizontal communication' such as 'in-house magazines' were introduced in organizations. The role of these in-house magazines was to distribute information but also to create a sense of shared corporate culture in the increasingly growing corporations. In Yates's account, media is a precursor rather than an effect of large-scale capitalist corporations. The ability to develop, store and circulate information is then one of the principal drivers for the growth of large-scale corporations. Seen from this point of view, our contemporary society, strongly relying on digital media and electronic writing, is by no means radically different from the nineteenth- and twentieth-century corporations. Media remain an indispensable component of the modern firm.

'New media': information and communication technology

There is a massive literature on the use of information and communication technology (ICT) in organizations and this section does therefore not attempt to review this entire corpus of literature. Conferences, journals and academic disciplines are dedicated to the topic of ICT in organizations (see e.g. Avgerou, Ciborra and Land, 2006; Ciborra, 2002; Kallinikos, 2006b). To name a few topics of discussion, there are studies of the implementation of ICT (Prasad, 1993; Heracleous and Barrett, 2001), its use in home-based work (Brocklehurst, 2001), in knowledge sharing (Hayes and Walsham, 2003) and the role of ICT in new so-called 'virtual' organization forms such as virtual corporations, virtual workplaces, or virtual teams (Alexander, 1997; Allcorn, 1997; Boudreau *et al.*, 1998; Davenport and Pearlson, 1998; Jackson, 1999; Black and Edwards, 2000; Cascio, 2000; Maznevsky and Chudoba, 2000; Hughes *et al.*, 2001; Kotorov, 2001; Gibson and Gibbs, 2006). Hughes *et al.*, explain the term virtual organization: '"Virtual" organizational arrangements consists of networks of workers and organizational units linked by information and communication technologies (ICTs), which will flexibly coordinate their activities, and combine their skills and resources in order to achieve common goals' (2001: 49–50). The various forms of virtual organizations are the direct product of the development of advanced ICT: 'Virtual organizations would simply not exist without the advanced information technologies that links their parts together', Boudreau *et al.* contend (1998: 123). For instance, in global virtual product development teams, communication and information-sharing is computer-mediated, making use of a variety of technological applications to share know-how and distribute information (Maznevsky and Chudoba, 2000). However, face-to-face communication is not abandoned altogether but appears to play a central role even when there is an adequate access to media (Gibson and Gibbs, 2006; Krikman *et al.*, 2004). The virtual organization is the outcome of a series of intersecting technological, social and economic changes, underlining the importance of sharing resources between organizational units and compressing product development times through methods such as concurrent engineering. Product development and innovation work are in many cases distributed between organizations in a network organization rather than being located to specific departments (Powell, Koput and Smith-Doerr, 1996; Powell, 1998), thereby raising new demands for effective communication and knowledge-sharing.

It is tempting to conceive of ICT as being a most advanced form of technology, serving to once and for all eliminate a range of administrative and practical concerns and thus release time for more creative or interesting endeavours (Valentine, 2000), but studies of the use of ICT, for instance the day-to-day use of email systems, show that such media in fact produce additional work and concerns regarding the handling of incoming and outgoing mail (Brown and Lightfoot, 2002). ICT is in this respect no different from other technologies, designed to make life easier but in fact not being capable of reducing the number of hours worked (Cowan, 1983). Researchers suggest that email represents a hybrid form of media demanding new social practices and procedures. Lee (1996) argues that email 'stands midway' between the telephone call and the letter:

> As the materiality and formality of the typed letter yield to the immediacy and intimacy of the telephone call, e-mail messages not only contain less contextualizing or background information than the business letter, but also flaunt informal vocabulary, phonetic spellings, and colloquial sentence structures. Appropriately enough, considering that cyberspace is quite literally neither here nor there, correspondence in this virtual community uses codes reflecting both orality and literacy. (Lee, 1996: 277)

The email thus represents a new form of media demanding certain routines, ethics and rhetorical skills. Lee (1996: 279) says that the nearest comparable social practice is oral communication, but email is, in fact, a form of 'virtual conversation', which in itself produces a number of concerns and ambiguities. For instance, should emails be stored and filed or are they to be regarded as verbal utterances, literally vanishing into thin air once they have been sent? Email here plays the ambiguous role of being both an infrastructure for communication (a medium in its original sense of the term) and a textual or symbolic and material message. Therefore the use of email cannot be taken for granted or remain socially unmarked. Edenius and Styhre (2006) examined how email users classified and structured their emails and found that the day-to-day handling of incoming and outgoing email was not a trivial matter but involved significant work and tradeoffs between objectives.

In summary, ICT is a 'new' media drawing on social practices of classification and categorization developed in substantially older information and communication technologies. Even though the remediation of images, sounds and texts in the new ICT is introduced by its proponents as being capable of more effectively handling a range of administrative and managerial activities – which in fact it actually does – it does not solve all such concerns. Media enframe the activities (e.g. written communication) and locate them in a specific technological setting (e.g. the email system), but such enframing does not once and for all solve how to classify and store the emails or prescribe for how long emails should be stored. Proponents of media inscribe them with qualities that provide integrated and coherent solutions to administrative and managerial concerns. However, no media *per se* are capable of offering such sets of ready-made solutions to contingent and situated concerns. Media are used in local and contextual settings, and must therefore be what Mol (2002) calls *enacted*; their use must be determined in correspondence with users and their objectives. No medium is an island, but it can be stabilized by what Pickering (1995), with a colourful metaphor, calls the 'mangle of practice'.

Media and surveillance

Another domain of research wherein forms of media play an increasingly important role in organizations is in the various integrated technological systems providing surveillance of public spheres and workplaces. Theorists such as Lyon (1994) and Bogard (1996) have examined the social, political, economic and philosophical implications of the rise of the 'surveillance society'. Moreover, the technology theorist Paul Virilio (1989) speaks of 'endo-colonialization' – the colonialization of the interior instead of the outside – in a situation where military technology is gradually penetrating civil society to control and monitor citizens. This is for Virilio a situation of 'total war' – military technology is present everywhere in our everyday lives. For instance, Davis (1990) argues that significant parts of Los Angeles are now monitored by surveillance technologies, thus being endo-colonialized by media and transforming the city into a 'war zone'. For these theorists, the alarming growth rate of surveillance technologies is a major political concern posing new threats to personal integrity and open society. Somewhat paradoxically, proponents of surveillance technologies often advocate the use of such media in terms of actually being an asset to open society. Such debates can be expected to continue in the future as new more advanced technoscientific media are developed and introduced.

In the workplace, surveillance technologies are, in a similar manner, becoming a naturalized part of many organizations. Ball (2005) defines surveillance in the following way:

> Surveillance is the practice of gathering and sorting data with the explicit purpose of influencing and managing the data target. This interpellates many modern organizational processes and the networks of actors and institutions involved: consumer monitoring through loyalty cards, credit scoring and geo-demographic profiling; workforce monitoring through various recruitment practices, email and

internet usage, keystroke monitoring, access control and performance management. (Ball, 2005: 90)

Surveillance practices emerge, in this definition, in many forms and in many settings. What they share is the underlying practice of visuality, enacting an object of inspection and analysis. Numerous studies of surveillance practices in the workplace show that employees respond to such managerial initiatives in a variety of ways, ranging from protests and confrontations to more subtle forms of resistance such as joking and irony (Sewell and Barker, 2006; McGail, 2002; Mason *et al.*, 2002; Kinnie, Hutchinson and Purcell, 2000; Sewell, 1998). Forms of surveillance may appear in a mediated form, based on technologies controlling the process of work or the output from a production process (e.g. the number of received calls in a call-centre) or may be socially embedded, in many cases grounded in the idea of peer-surveillance or team-based control. For instance, in the case of Japanese management methods and, more specifically, the practice of Total Quality Management (TQM), a range of empirical studies of TQM implementations pointed at the 'intensification of work' and the increased reliance on 'peer pressure' (Graham, 1994; 1995; Wilkinsson, Morris and Munday, 1995). Surveillance is a form of managerial control based on visuality and inspection, which may or may not be mediated.

Organizing on the internet

A third mediated domain influencing organizing is the internet. The internet is a thoroughly debated and examined technological medium that has no less than revolutionized contemporary lives (Poster, 2001b). The internet is unique, DiMaggio *et al.* (2001: 308) argue, because it integrates both different 'modalities of communication' such as 'reciprocal interaction, broadcasting, individual reference-searching, group discussions, person/machine interaction' and different kinds of content (e.g. text, video, visual images, audio) in a single medium. DiMaggio *et al.* (2001) predict that the internet will alter social relations even more than previous mass media such as radio and television. The internet virtually exploded in the 1990s: in 1995, only 25 million or 3 per cent of Americans had ever used the internet. In 1999, 55 million Americans used internet on a typical day. In 1995, there were roughly 20,000 websites and, in 2000, there were more than 10 million (DiMaggio *et al.*, 2001: 308). The internet quickly become a major social factor in contemporary everyday life; it has become the infrastructure *par excellence* in what Castells (1996) calls the 'network society'.

In 1945, Vannevar Bush, one of the architects behind what president Dwight Eisenhower referred to as the 'military-industrial complex' in the USA and a former dean and vice-president at MIT, wrote an essay for *The Atlantic Monthly* wherein he speculated about a 'future device' called a 'memex', a 'memory extender', where all personal documents and files could be retrieved in a matter of seconds: 'A memex is a device in which an individual stores all his books, records, and communication, and which is mechanized so that it may be consulted with exceeding speed and flexibility. It is an enlarged intimate supplement to his memory' (Bush, 1945/2001: 149). Bush continues:

> If the user wishes to consult a certain book, he taps its code on the keyboard, and the title page of the book promptly appears before him, projected onto one of his viewing positions. Frequently used codes are mnemonic, so that he seldom consults his code book; but when he does, a single tap of a key projects it for his use. (1945/2001: 150)

Vannevar Bush's ideas about the memex are today widely recognized as the inspiration for the development of hypertext on the internet (Coyne, 1999: 65). The access to information, know-how, services and entertainment has increased rapidly since the mid-1990s when the internet became a concern for the broader public. However, like any medium, the internet has social, cultural and economic ramifications. For instance, as Turkle (1996) shows, the internet may provide opportunities for alternative or complementary subject-positions and may broaden the scope of the human experience. The ability to transcend one's self is one of the most persist themes in the media literature. Katherine Hayles here associates new media with religious experiences in the Middle Ages: 'Perhaps not since the Middle Ages have the fantasies of leaving the body behind been so widely dispersed through the population, and never has it been so strongly linked with existing technologies' (cited in Mosco, 2004: 97). However, like any media, from the early visual technologies such as the stereoscope, to radio, television and today's internet homepages, media may be used to represent selected parts of or specific perspectives on social reality (Williams, 1990; Bourdieu, 1996). Just as Renaissance or Flemish paintings portray social reality in an idiosyncratic and highly selective manner, so may television and the internet provide edited and manipulated images and sound excerpts that cannot be accepted simply as uncomplicated representations of reality. For instance, in his controversial analysis of the Gulf War in the early 1990s, *The Gulf War Did Not Take Place*, Baudrillard (1995) declares the advent of the 'TV war', a war directed, edited and broadcast as a specific form of televised 'entertainment' (or more adequately as what has been called 'edutainment' or 'infotainment'). As Manovich (2001) notes, any new media are operating on basis of digitalized entities providing opportunities for endless manipulation and interactivity. Thus, media and new media are making us rearticulate the question of truth (Lévy, 1998).

The internet has naturally been appropriated by organizations and companies as an arena for both commerce and trade and for maintaining contact with customers, suppliers and, ultimately, the wider public. For instance, the field of e-trade has established itself as a domain of research (see e.g. Amit and Zott, 2001) and virtually all major corporations offer advanced internet services and information on homepages and on joint industry sites. The management of firms and organizations is also structured around intranets designed in accordance with the same principles as the 'external' homepages (Newell *et al.*, 2000). Documents and reports can be downloaded and accounting systems, human resource management systems and so forth are made easily accessible through the intranet services. In many industries where new product development work is organized in project form, project co-workers structure and coordinate their activities on project homepages. In other cases, it is external customers and users that are targeted in what Zammuto *et al.* (2007) call 'mass collaboration'. For instance, Nielsen (2005) studied how the pharmaceutical company AstraZeneca employed an internet homepage to monitor and keep in touch with asthma patients, finding that the project remained viable for a while but that some groups involved, like the medical doctors and GPs, did not fully believe in the idea and felt sidestepped in the process, thereby ultimately undermining the use of the internet. In some industries, the internet opens up more comprehensive re-evaluation of the core competencies employed and the nature of the industry. For instance, in mass-media news companies a change of focus from 'printed paper' as the central product to an emphasis on the production, editing and distribution of information into various media have been observed (Mazza and Pedersen, 2004). In this change of perspective, journalists no longer produce a newspaper but rather create the information that can be piped in many directions and into many settings. The focus has thus changed from the artefact (i.e. the newspaper) to the journalistic production of information. In addition, the journalist's role as the privileged figure in the news flow has been complemented by a stronger focus on interactivity. Fredberg (2003) shows that news companies use their homepages to maintain ongoing interactive exchanges with their readers. The readers here become 'co-producers' in terms of being engaged in web polls, encouraged to sub-mit their own pictures and messages, and to create their own webpages. While some commentators regard such initiatives as actually strength-ening democracy and giving voice to previously silenced groups, others regard these tendencies in the mass media as gradually undermining the opportunities for qualified and professional journalistic work, thereby slowly displacing critical investigations of the activities and decisions of office-holders and authorities with celebrity-spotting contests and other frivolous forms of light entertainment (Poster, 2001b; Mulder, 2006), in what Grindstaff and Turow (2006: 109) call 'plebeian public spheres'.

Another interesting thing to notice about the internet is that while it is surrounded by an air of modernity and is generally portrayed as the state-of-the-art technology representing absolutely contemporary aesthetics, views and beliefs anchored in traditional thinking are not abandoned overnight. For instance, speaking from a gender theory perspective, Gus-tavsson and Czarniawska (2004) demonstrate that female avatars on the internet largely reproduce traditional views of women in terms of their roles, positions and embodied appearance. Instead of undermining con-ventional gender roles, the internet, a medium often claimed to be at the forefront of contemporary culture, reinforces and reproduces gendered society through its representation of what are supposedly taken-for-granted roles of women. Conventional images of embodiment and gen-der are thus reproduced in new media (Wajcman, 2004; Lupton, 1995).

Virtual reality and its practical uses

In the 1970s and 1980s, the emerging cyberspace literature pioneered by William Gibson brought a great deal of interest in a variety of computer-generated media (Shields, 2003; Wise, 1997). An extensive academic literature waxes enthusiasm over this genre, anticipating a society where the distinction between actual and virtual realities becomes permeable and porous. Theoretically, the concept of the *cyborg*, the 'cybernetic organism' sketched by Norbert Weiner in his introduction to his new science of cybernetics, *Cybernetics, or Control and Communication in the Animal Machine,* first published in 1948, has been introduced to capture meaningful interaction between human and machine (Thomas, 1995; Balsamo, 1995; Wood, 1999; Hayles, 2006). Donna Haraway's (1991) introduction of the term in gender theory discourse, in particular, has been much debated and referenced by feminist theorists (e.g. Lykke and Braidotti, 1996). As perhaps no other research project, virtual reality media seek to transform the theoretical concept of the cyborg to an actual human experience. The most advanced and visionary of the various projects initiated on the basis of this scenario is the research on virtual reality technology. Steuer (1992: 73) says that the common view of virtual reality is to point at 'a particular collection of technological hardware, including computers, head-mounted displays, headphones, and motion-sensing gloves'. However, Steuer claims that such an 'object-centered view of technology' (1992: 74) is not entirely relevant for the understanding of what virtual reality technology seeks to accomplish: '[V]irtual reality refers to an experience, rather than a machine. This definition thereby shifts the locus of virtual reality from particular hardware packages to the perceptions of an individual,' Steuer (1992: 79) argues. Bolter (1996) agrees with Steuer's emphasis on perceptual experience as the central process of virtual reality and locates virtual reality in a long-standing tradition beginning, perhaps, with perspective painting in Renaissance Italy:

> Virtual reality belongs in the tradition that begins at least as early as perspective painting in the Italian Renaissance and includes photography, cinema, and television. Like these earlier examples, virtual reality is a technology of illusion, whose purpose is to convince the viewer that he or she is occupying the same visual spaces as the object in view. (Bolter, 1996: 113)

Virtual reality (VR) is not only to be examined as a technological apparatus but also as a culturally and socially embedded medium.

Zettl offers the following definition of virtual reality:

> A computer-generated three-dimensional image and stereo sound that displays events (objects and environments) and that is interactive with the user. In this case, interactivity means that we change from mere observers or viewers to event participants. As such, we exercise some control over the event display. (1996: 86)

Furthermore, Steuer lists a number of definitions of virtual reality such as Coates's (1992), saying that 'virtual reality is electronic simulations of environments via head-mounted eye goggles and wired clothing enabling the end user to interact in realistic three-dimensional situations' (1992: 74). The central construct in the VR project is then not the technology *per se* but rather the *human experience* generated in computer-mediated settings. Steuer here emphasizes the concept of *presence*:

> The key to defining virtual reality in terms of human experience rather than technological hardware is the concept of *presence*. Presence can

be thought of as the experience of one's physical environment: it refers not to one's surroundings as they exist in the physical world, but to perception of those surroundings as mediated by both automatic and controlled mental processes ... *Presence is defined as the sense of being in an environment.* (Steuer, 1992: 75, emphasis in the original)

In contrast to presence, the sensuous and cognitive experience of being in a physical environment, the concept of *telepresence* denotes a similar human experience in a computer-mediated milieu: '*Telepresence is defined as the experience of presence in an environment by means of a communication medium.* In other words, *presence* refers to the *natural* perception of an environment, and *telepresence* refers to the *mediated* perception of an environment' (Steuer, 1992: 75, emphasis in the original). In the production of telepresence and human experiences mimicking that of dwelling in physical environments, a number of central concepts operationalized in the VR discourse are introduced. The two central categories are *vividness* and *interactivity*, which in turn can be broken down into subcategories. '*Vividness*', Steuer writes, 'refers to the ability of technology to produce a sensorially rich mediated environment ... *Interactivity*, refers to the degree to which users of a medium can influence the form content of the mediated environment' (1992: 80). Vividness is created through the manipulation of two parameters, *breadth*, referring to 'the number of sensory dimensions simultaneously presented', and *depth*, referring to 'the resolution within each of these perceptual channels' (Steuer, 1992: 81). Similarly, interactivity is operationalized into *speed*, 'the rate at which input can be assimilated into the mediated environment', *range*, 'the number of possibilities for action at any given time', and *mapping*, 'the ability of a system to map its controls to changes in the mediated environment in a natural and predictable manner'. Vividness and interactivity are then the two main parameters shaping the human experience of telepresence generated by the virtual reality medium. Proponents of virtual reality dream about one day being able to construct a computer-mediated system where the interacting human cannot fully separate actual and virtual reality, and Steuer (1992: 84) speculates about a future 'perceptual Turing test' proving the fickle line of demarcation between actual reality and computer-mediated realities. The term used to capture such inclusive experiences of telepresence is *immersive*. Biocca (1992: 25) explains:

Immersive is a term that refers to the degree to which a virtual environment submerges the perceptual system of the user in virtual stimuli.

The more the system captivates the senses and blocks out stimuli from the physical world, the more the system is considered immersive.

The more immersive a computer-mediated environment is, the more 'real' it appears for the user. This 'quest for the real' is expressed in terms of mathematical algorithms and coded language. The graphic computer expert Alvy Ray Smith famously claimed that 'graphic reality' could be defined as 'as 80 million polygons *per second*' (Bolter and Grusin, 1999: 119; also cited by Biocca, 1992: 61). This is an estimate of a virtual reality that has been widely debated and reflected upon. Will there be opportunities for generating such hyperreal representations standing the 'perceptual Turing test'? Even though Steuer (1992) is eager to broaden the scope of the discourse from technological artefacts and software programming to include human perception, the materiality of VR systems cannot be ignored. Biocca (1992) examines the immediate and physical integration of the human body with a series of ocular, 'electrotactile' and electromechanical devices:

> The process of creating a strong sense of presence begins by coupling the sensory organs of the user to output devices of the computer. The output devices are orchestrated by one of more computers to generate convincing simulation of the look, feel, and sound of another environment, a virtual reality, the eyes, ears, hands, and inner proprioceptive senses receive electromechanical stimuli that attempt to simulate a world pressing upon the senses. (Biocca, 1992: 27)

The photographs of VR systems featured in Biocca's text show the opportunities for a cyborgization of the human body. Gloves, goggles, helmets and other technical devices constitute an apparatus that at best is fascinating, at worst outright terrifying. As in few other discourses and scientific projects, the VR media undermine the line of demarcation between man and machine, between flesh and steel, wires and software. Even today it remains visionary in its ambition to release humans from their brute and immediate materiality and open up new computer-mediated terrains.

The use of VR media in organizations is, to date, relatively limited but there are some examples of how advanced computer-mediated environments can be used to simulate real situations. For instance, in surgery, VR has, since it was introduced in 1991, been used to simulate operations (Gallagher and Cates, 2004). It is estimated that medical errors cause 44,000–94,000 deaths annually in the USA, and, Gallagher and Cates (2004: 1538) argue, 'many medical errors are caused by human factors associated with invasive image-guided techniques' such as arthroscopy, laparoscopy and flexible endoscopy. Research shows that training in a VR environment enabled 'significantly fewer' operative errors than the standard-trained reference group. In another study, the VR-trained group made six times fewer operative errors and worked 30 per cent faster that the reference group (Gallagher and Cates, 2004: 1538). Prentice (2005), studying the use of simulation in surgery training, argues that surgeons develop a "'somato-conceptual" intelligence', (p. 857), a form of embodied knowledge derived from the interaction between the surgeon's hands and the patient's body: 'With years of practice,' Prentice says, 'surgeons learn to use tools as extensions of their bodies. Technique becomes fully embodied and, therefore, largely unconscious, when all proceeds smoothly' (2005: 856). The simulated 'body objects', a 'silicon second nature' (Helmreich, 1998), must therefore be 'articulated' graphically and 'haptically' – capable of feeding sensory information into the hands of the practising surgeon – so that humans can understand them, and mathematically, so computers can understand them (Prentice, 2005: 847). The problem is, though, that bodies are always multiple (Mol, 2002), capable of being expressed from complementary perspectives (Prasad, 2005). For instance, the female pelvis is expressed differently by a gynaecologist and an orthopaedist, and it therefore requires a 'digital articulation' by specialists from two surgical disciplines (Prentice, 2005: 851). In addition, in order to provide an adequate surgery training experience, the haptic interface must be capable of simulating the 'fleshiness' of the human body. The simulated body is thus an *ersatz* resource standing in for actual human bodies: Prentice concludes:

> Surgical knowledge can be thought of as the interface of a surgeon's hands and a patient's body, as it exists in practice. Whether taught by a simulator or by another surgeon, the surgeon's knowledge becomes his or her ability to sculpt the anatomical model from highly variable patient bodies. (2005: 861; see also Johnson, 2007)

In a study of the use of Magnetic Resonance Imaging (MRI) in health care practice, Prasad (2005) speaks of *cyborg visuality* in cases where the 'body multiple' is reproduced in new 'images of the body'. Even though these images are constituted by bits of information that can be subject to human manipulation, this 'new visuals regime' does not abandon the idea of *realism*. Rather, MR images '[p]roduce different reconfigurations of the body, each of which provide a partial perspective of the body and together they constitute the MR radiological gaze', Prasad says

(2005: 310). MRI offers alternative images of the body that both enable new understanding of the patient's health situation and produce the body multiple. MRI is thus a 'vision-machine' that enframes and shapes human perception.

Another domain where VR techniques are used is in new drug development and, more specifically, in what is called 'virtual screening', to detect molecules that can be further explored; this is known as 'lead optimisation' in new drug development (Eckert and Bajorath, 2007; Walters, Stahl and Murcko, 1998). Since synthesis chemists engaging in identifying promising molecules operate in what Walters, Stahl and Murcko (1998) call a 'virtual chemistry space', including some 10 to the power of 100 possible molecules, there is a great need to reduce this number. Virtual screening means that technologies are used to automatically examine a library of molecules in a 2-D setting to identify potentially interesting molecules. Selected molecules are then further examined through 3-D visualization technologies. Even through virtual screening is capable of reducing the number of investigated molecules, there are significant methodological concerns regarding this gradual reduction and the method is consequently debated in the pharmaceutical industry (see e.g. Oprea, 2002).

Other applications of virtual reality technologies include its contribution to computer-aided design (CAD), an application that has been implemented, according to some studies (Whyte and Bouchlaghem, 2002), with a not altogether satisfying result, or, on the contrary, according to others (Baba and Nobeoka, 1998; Boland, Lyytinen and Yoo, 2007), has been very successful. In summary, VR has found a number of applications where it may be fruitfully exploited in the future. Still, research conducted by social scientists, not representing vested interests in the technology or the technology-optimism characterizing the field, points at a long series of technological, social and behavioural challenges that need to be overcome before VR technology can be appropriated on a broad front (Hindmarch, Heath and Fraser, 2006).

Media, perception and organizing

Media are today, as Friedrich Kittler says, what 'determine our condition'; they are what structure, shape, reinforce, alter and modify our perception. At times, media help to distribute information over short distances, as in the case of emails being sent within an office. In other cases, media are what fundamentally structure and shape work. The American architect Frank O. Gehry claims he cannot design his buildings without the support of the computer (Bennis, 2003: 81; Boland,

Lyytinen and Yoo, 2007). Gehry thus inhabits a worklife fundamentally determined by media; they are constitutive of his professional life world, one may say. While media are capable of remediating texts and speech in email systems, word-processing software programs, voice mail services and so forth, they are also capable of remediating images and sounds. More specifically, as, for instance, Derrida points out (Derrida and Stiegler, 2002), media collapse the distinction between text and image and increasingly operate on the basis of hieroglyphics and pictograms. Text and image merge in the use of new media. In organizations, media play a central role as what structure and amplify perception; there is, as suggested by Nietzsche and later in Bourdieu, no 'purity' or 'immaculate perception' in the mediated perception but the signal is always being enframed by the media. For critics like Virilio, an outspoken follower of Merleau-Ponty, the widespread use of such 'vision machines' is a major concern in contemporary society. Perception is, for Virilio, no longer what resides in the human body but what is produced elsewhere, in the interface between man and machine. 'Today, we are no longer truly *seers* [*voyants*] of our world, but merely *reviewers* [*revoyants*], the tautological repetition of the same, at work in our mode of production (i.e. individual production), is equally the work in our mode of perception,' Virilio argues (2005: 37, emphasis in the original). Perception is today in the hands of machines and media. Against eschatological views of an increasingly mediated future one may position the many benefits and immediate effects of these human–media assemblages; the ability to circulate and share information, the increased security and precision in social services, the improved performance in, for instance, surgery work and so forth. There is little value in extreme positions either deifying or vilifying media because media are not inherently good or bad. Technology optimists are prone to believe, we learn from sceptics like Coyne (1999), May (2002) and Mosco (2004), that media will make us come to the end of a range of human concerns and limitations and that media *per se* will enable amazing things to happen. On the contrary, technology critics such as Virilio insist on seeing media and technology as what may or may not pose a substantial and real threat to a series of entrenched social virtues and liberties. A tempered view of media, operating between rosy enthusiasm and bleak dystopian scenarios probably offers the best predictions on how media will develop human society and, more specifically, perception in organization. We also learn from history that predicting social and technological changes is a complicated matter. He or she who engages in such endeavours always runs the risk of being wrong and thereby eventually becoming a laughing stock in the future (like the Decca record company executive Dick Rowe who turned down The Beatles, famously claiming that 'guitar bands are on the way out'). Still, there is reason to believe that we will spend our lives in an economy increasingly based on 'fluff' rather than 'stuff' (Lanham, 2006), that is, where symbols, images and, ultimately, Lanham argues, attention are what matter. If Lanham (2006) and other proponents of an *attention economy* are right in their predictions, beneath all the iconoclastic and speculative formulations, that the 'political economy of attention' is what will shape our future, then one may argue in favour of a more or less straight line from the mid-nineteenth-century research on perception and attention to contemporary society, where attention plays the role of being the scarce resource *par excellence*. However, if one does not want to ascribe the whole future to one single concept model – which seems to be a reasonable, non-reductionist position – at least the concept of perception, underlying attention, remains a central human faculty and organizational resource in the new millennium.

Summary and conclusion

In this chapter the concept of media has been examined as what is capable of 'remediating' images and sounds as well as texts. Such a remediation structures and orders perception in organization and therefore it is of central importance for everyday organizational life. Media theory is a multi- or transdisciplinary field of research engaging scholars from the social sciences, the humanities and the technical and mathematical sciences. While there are significant differences between these theoretical and methodological positions, the literature shares a concern for understanding or even explaining the central features of media. Media are then not solely bundles of interrelated technologies but constitute assemblages including humans 'in the flesh', hardware and software. Organizations, increasingly mediated, demonstrate a broad range of uses and applications of media, from the more mundane circulation of data and information in email systems to virtual reality-generated simulations of surgical operations. Underlying this heterogeneous use of media is the faculty of perception; to use media is to engage one or a few of the human senses. The mediated organizational life is one of continuous perception, of ongoing oscillations between cognition and perception, effectively bridging the external world of events and occurrences and the internal world of cognitive and embodied responses. Perception is a membrane connecting the two worlds.

5
Perception and Organizing: Beyond the Text

Introduction

In this final chapter some lingering questions will be brought back into discussion and some concluding remarks will be articulated. The dominant idea pursued in this book is that instead of following what has been called the linguistic turn in philosophy and the social sciences to the bitter end and conceiving of social reality, including organization, organizing and managerial practices, as being exclusively linguistic in nature, one should take into account and recognize the concept of perception, that is, humans' sensual relationship with the external world – most notably vision and audible capacities – and emphasize that perception also plays a central role for organization. Human beings not only rely on their cognitive capacities to orient themselves in everyday life; they also see, hear, smell, touch and taste their way through social life and this human condition is, it is argued here, not sufficiently attended to in the organization literature. The other main idea discussed is that human perception is a situated and contingent capacity, embedded in new orientations in philosophy and scientific research interests in the nineteenth century. This fascinating period of time – the formative years of modern, urban life, if you will – was also the period where organization theory and managerial concerns was first clearly articulated. In a number of places in this text, an unambiguous causal linearity between these two events has been rejected or at least rendered problematic. The relationship between the two events can be a source of speculation and investigation elsewhere; here their temporal proximity is noted. The three preceding chapters have examined art, music and media, and have sought to present these domains of investigation and research as highly complex domains integrating various disciplinary perspectives and theoretical orientations. However, in their own idiosyncratic ways, these concepts influence perception in organization through their capacity to exploit human attention. 'Art, music, media' are then organizational resources that deserve to be examined not as marginal or decorative social resources (as in the arts and music) or black-boxed and naturalized infrastructures (as in the case of media). Human beings inhabit a world where art and images, music and sounds, media and technologies of representation constantly intervene in their existence. Perception is not what is complementary or additional to day-to-day workings in organizations, but operates throughout everyday life in organizations.

Beyond the text: Text versus image?

One lingering concern when operating with dual categories such as text/nontext (i.e. image, sound, etc.) is how to understand such a distinction, the very separation between text and image: what does it mean to say that something is non-text? Can texts be understood without images? For instance, in the linguistics of Ferdinand de Saussure (1959), an image of the referent serves as the signified that the signifier denotes. The entire sign (that is, in the commonplace formula Sign = Signifier/Signified) is thus incomprehensible without images of referents. Needless to say, the relationship between text and image is part of the *philosophia perennis* and a major aporia in philosophy. Still, a theorist like Vilém Flusser (2000; 2002) (discussed in Chapter 2) provides some interesting ideas regarding the relationship between text and image. Speaking of photography, Flusser (1983/2000: 7) outlines two major human inventions, that of 'the invention of linear writing' and that of 'the invention of technical images' (e.g. photography in the nineteenth century). Prior to the invention of linear writing, humans had recourse to images to communicate. Images are, Flusser (1983/2000: 8) argues, of necessity 'connotative'; they are ambiguous complexes of symbols and are therefore 'spaces open for interpretation'. Elsewhere Flusser (2002: 15) speaks of 'three forms of communication': 'those that order the symbols in linear sequences (the diachronical ones); those that order them in surfaces (the plain synchronic ones); and those that order them in space (the tridimensional synchronical ones)'. Spoken languages and the alphabet are of the first type; Chinese writings and paintings of the second type; theatre and architecture are of the third type. For Flusser (2002), the three types can be variously combined. For instance, television is 'a complex combination of diachronicity and plain synchronicity'. Flusser (2002: 22) distinguishes more generally between *linear codes* and *surface codes* and suggests that the former are becoming less important for most people today and that reliance on surface codes means that one needs to master new ways of decoding:

> We must follow the written text if we want to get at its message, but in a picture we may get at the message first, and then try to decompose it. And this points to the difference between the one-dimensional line and the two-dimensional surface: the one aims at getting somewhere; the other is there already, but may reveal how it got there. This difference is one of temporality, and involves the present, the past, and the future. (Flusser, 2002: 22)

In linear communication, the message is brought forward in the very reading of the text; in surface codes, the message is 'already there' but reveals little of its meaning. In Flusser's (2000) view, images are 'mediations between the world and human beings'; images make the world comprehensible but as soon as that happens, images, in fact, 'come between the human and the world': 'They [images] are supposed to be maps but they turn into screens: Instead of representing the world, they obscure it until human beings' lives finally become a function of the images they create,' Flusser says (2000: 9–10). This leads to what Flusser calls 'idolatry'; human beings 'cease to decode images and instead project them, still encoded, into the world "out there"'. The image is then what precedes the world and is commonly regarded as truer than life itself. With the invention of linear writing,* a long-standing 'struggle' between image and text is established' – a struggle of what Flusser calls 'historical consciousness against magic'. With linear writing comes the capacity for conceptual thinking, which, Flusser says, 'consisted of abstracting lines from surfaces'. He continues:

> [W]ith the invention of writing, human beings took one step further back from the world. Texts do not signify the world; they signify the images they tear up. Hence, to decode texts means to discover the images signified by them. The interpretation of texts is to explain

---

* Burns (1989: 12) suggests the following periods for the emergence of writing: 'The first written documents in Sumeria date from the second half of the fourth millennium BC, in Egypt from the early third, in Mohenjodaro and Harappa on the Indus and in Crete from the early second millennium BC.' However, the skill of writing has proven to disappear during periods of decline, for instance in Greece during 1200BC–900BC (Burns, 1989: 51). The history of writing is thus not devoid of disruptive events and detours.

images, while that of concepts is to make ideas comprehensible. In this way, texts are a metacode of images. (1983/2000: 11)

Seen from this point of view, texts are abstractions of the images, which in turn are representations of the world. Borgmann (1999) similarly emphasizes that alphabetic writing, contrary to pictographic writing, corresponding to Flusser's 'plain synchronic communication' (e.g. Chinese writing), is capable of shielding off the world in all its density and imposing a particular logical structure, that of sequence and linearity, onto the world:

> Pictographic writing ... lifts particular kinds of things out of the web of reality and language and sets them down distinctively in pictographs. But no matter how many hundreds or thousand of things, events, and signs were singled out and fixed in such writing, there remained a dense and inexhaustible context of further objects, processes, and relations. Alphabetic writing, on the contrary, suggests that reality is structured all the way down, and at bottom is composed of a small number of meaningless, but well-defined, elements. (Borgmann, 1999: 61)

Flusser also recognizes that such conceptual thinking is only capable of capturing a subset of the information in the image: '[W]hen we translate image into concept, we decompose the image – we analyze it. We throw, so to speak, a conceptual point-net over the image, and capture only such meanings as did not escape through the meshes of the net' (2002: 28). From a historical perspective, this implies that images – 'surface codes' such as 'frescoes and mosaics, tapestries and church windows' (Flusser, 2002: 36) – played a central role in European thinking for a long period after the institution of linear writing. However, with the invention of printing, linear writing began to undermine the status of the image. When conceptual thinking is established, the previous regime of 'idolatry' is displaced by 'textolatry', the 'the faithfulness of texts' – a doctrine that scholasticism and religious fundamentalism but also social science doctrines such as Marxism adhere to. It is the text that needs to be carefully decoded and understood; texts *per se* are of central importance and bearers of universal truths. The invention of 'technical images' (i.e. the daguerrotype and eventually the photograph) in the nineteenth century brought for, the first time, opportunities for what Flusser calls 'third order abstractions'. Just as texts were used to abstract and decode original images, thereby rendering them more archaic than texts and the principal vehicle for thinking, the technical images are abstractions of the third order: 'They abstract from texts which abstract from traditional images which themselves abstract from the concrete world' (Flusser, 2000: 14). Photography is, therefore, as was discussed in Chapter 2, a major human invention in parity with the invention of linear writing. Technical images are, however, not capable of 'speaking for themselves' – the ideology of *res ipsa loquitur* is overturned. Quite the contrary, they are themselves what need to be explained and a principal mistake is to believe that they unambiguously represent social reality. In Flusser's (2000; 2002) account of text and images from a historical and anthropological perspective, the relationship between text and image is a dynamic and fluid one; text and images are used both to obscure and clarify social reality and it is fundamentally complicated for us moderns to sort out for ourselves whether text and images are in fact capable of representing social conditions or if they, as in Niklas Luhmann's (2000) analysis of journalism and media, operate in a self-regulating and autopoietic system separated from broader society. It may be argued that Flusser's (2000; 2002) thinking is speculative, poorly embedded in historical and anthropological studies, and incapable of providing any conclusive arguments, but his thinking is, in fact, seeking to formulate a theory of images that recognizes the uses of texts and writing as what precedes and enframes the production of technical images such as photographs. For Flusser, confusing the relationship between text and images is the major fallacy of new media.

One of the noteworthy implications from Flusser's (2002) discussion is that organization theory needs to address the increased emphasis on surface codes in everyday worklife. Historically, verbal interaction and written instruction have dominated organizational life, but new media bringing together audible, visual and even tactile competencies are employed more widely. What is of specific importance is the combination of linear and surface codes in organizing, for instance, in the use of email, which is an example of a hybrid medium blending written and oral communication and increasingly involving internet-based hypertext resources. Perception and organization are here entangled in new and perhaps unpredicted ways, producing new opportunities but also new challenges for everyday organizing. Ultimately, there is no conclusive distinction between linguistic resources (text, narratives, etc.) and images and sounds in organizations. Linguistic resources and perception are complementary rather than mutually exclusive categories.

Perception and organizing

'The loudspeaker's electrical amplification of the voice', Kwinter (2001: 20) writes, 'made possible the staging of vast, live aural spectacles, the amassing of unprecedented crowds of people, which gave literal and palpable expression to the concept of "mass culture" and "mass movement".' This is a strong case for both perception and media when it comes to their organizational implications. Organization is the outcome from social practices involving both material and intangible, social resources (Orlikowski, 2007). In this book, the concept of perception has been emphasized as a central human capacity being relatively undertheorized in comparison to, for instance, linguistic and narrative perspectives on organizations. Verbal and written communication are indispensable components of any organization, but the ability to see, hear, smell, taste and touch also matter considerably. Organization members speak and write, but they also use their five senses in their day-to-day lives. Organizational lives are embodied and draw on perceptual capacities. Therefore, the relationship between perception and organization deserves some theoretical attention and empirical study. In the first chapter, it was shown that the scientific research on perception, and more specifically, the concept of attention, and the development of more systematic managerial methods emerge at a similar point in time, namely at the end of the first half of the nineteenth century. However, it is not suggested that these two domains of research – one philosophical and laboratory-based and one more or less derived from the practical experience of engineers and managers in their work – are causally related. If there is one single driving force behind these two domains of thought and practice, it is the dawning modernity of the European industrialized states. The quick urbanization in many European countries in the nineteenth century produced a new interest in the way individuals perceive and pay attention in their daily life. In modern life, as Georg Simmel suggested, human perception is coming short; the modern urban dweller can no longer apprehend and process all the sense-impressions encountered. With modern society, perception and attention becomes a social and human resource worth exploring in detail.

The history of modern management and the growth of modern organizations is a story of how to structure, influence and indeed shape human perception, that is, to optimize attention. Early management writers such as Charles Babbage, Andrew Ure and, eventually, Frederick Winslow Taylor and his disciples all emphasized more or less explicitly the importance of human perception and attention. If there is one single factor that connects Taylor's *Principles of Scientific Management* (1913) and contemporary internet companies like Google, an exemplary organization in the attention economy, it is their joint interest in understanding how people pay attention in their day-to-day lives. For several writers (e.g. Beller, 2006; Lanham, 2006; Davenport and Beck, 2001), attention is one of the single most important scarce resources in today's economy. Attention is what is entangled with human perception, the ability to see, hear, smell, touch and taste. In this book, it is primarily the visual and auditory human capacities that have been discussed. In the two chapters addressing art and music, seeing and hearing and listening have been examined as important organizational resources that strongly affect everyday life in organizations. In the section 'Art and organization', the concept of art is examined as not only an outcome from organized activities but also, in turn, influencing and affecting organizations. Arts management is, for instance, a field of research and practice wherein the connections between art and organization are studied. Art here plays the role of a metonym for visual perception; art strongly shapes and influences human perception and therefore it serves potentially as a resource in organizations (Styhre and Eriksson, 2008). In the section of the second chapter, 'Music and organization', music plays a similar metonymic role *vis-à-vis* auditory perception. Music is in itself of necessity based on certain organizational principles, formulated in terms of rhythm, timbre, harmony and so forth, but it is also developed, used and circulated in organizations. One may work in the music industry or one may use music in everyday work but, in both cases, music is a form of auditory experience that produces certain social effects. In the fourth chapter, the capacity to see and hear is examined as what is restructured and reorganized, that is, *remediated*, under the influence of media. Media – both 'new media' and not quite so new ones – are here regarded as having the capacity to influence and structure human perception. For instance, cinema produces the experience of movement through showing a series of consecutive images at high speed. Media are here conceived of as the totality of technologies, devices and tools, capable of producing new means of perception. In contemporary society and in everyday work in organizations, media strongly influence human perception; we speak and listen to friends and colleagues over telephone connections, we find ourselves watching computer screens almost daily, and so forth. Media are bound up with perception. Media, in other words, serve as what Heidegger called the *Gestell*, the 'enframing' of everyday perception in contemporary life. Therefore, discussing perception in organizations demands that the concept of media is addressed in one way or another. Media, as emphasized by various media theorists and media writers, not only convey data from an external, unambiguous social or natural reality, but are in fact capable of manipulating such images infinitely and almost effortlessly. For instance, a photograph may be modified and transformed in a variety of ways in the common off-the-shelf programs that accompany most computer purchases today. Human perception is then no longer 'authentic' or primordial but is increasingly mediated.

This book does not seek to present any decisive theory regarding the relationship between organization and perception. Instead, the discussion of art, music and media aim at opening a series of black boxes and to point out how art, music, media, human perception and organization are connected in a variety of ways. Music, for instance, is both organized *per se*, constitutes an industry and is a component, historical studies show, of the managerial arsenal aimed at reducing fatigue and boredom and creating motivated and productive workers. The book is also written with the ambition to inspire additional empirical and theoretical work in the field where perception and organization intersect. A number of empirical studies in arts management, the music industry and of the general use of media in organizations and firms have pointed at interesting aspects of how human perception and organizing are related and co-dependent. Continuing this tradition of empirical research may open up more elaborate theoretical discussion on how perception and organization have developed historically and how they relate to one another in contemporary organizations. To move 'beyond the text' – the subtitle of this chapter – here means that organization researchers may conceive of organizations as not only embedded in verbal and written communication and formal documentation – captured by the metonym 'the text' – but also, arguably, the outcome of human perception and the use of social, organizational and human resources such as art, music and media. To 'move beyond the text' is to recognize the value and complexity of human perception and to recognize it as a valuable source for organization theory. For instance, as Kwinter (2001) suggested, the mediated voice distributed by the loudspeaker is one of the driving forces behind modernity. When seen from this perspective, in hindsight and after decades or even centuries of experience from a particular medium, the connection between human perception and organization is rather unsurprising. The trick is just to naturalize or defamiliarize such a theoretical perspective, that is, to see connections between what is either taken for granted or more or less ignored.

Summary and conclusion

In this book, the following arguments have been put forth:

- The concept of perception generated new interest in the first half of the nineteenth century. This was also the period where organization theory and management as a practice and political programme emerged. Rather than postulating a linear causality between these two historical events, they can be more loosely assumed to be derived from a shared source. If nothing else, the concept of *attention* is put forth as a central social problem worthy of proper examination in the two fields of investigation.

- In comparison to the literature taking the linguistic turn in the social sciences seriously, conceiving of organization as embedded in the use of language in discourse, narratives and conversations, the relationship between perception and organizing is relatively little explored and theorized in organization theory and management studies.

- Perception is a term used in a series of scholarly disciplines and theoretical enterprises, including the social sciences, philosophy, clinical psychology and psychoanalysis, and the humanities. The term denotes the human use of the five senses and the ability to see, hear, smell, taste and touch the 'external world' (a term here used within citation marks since, as for instance Merleau-Ponty emphasizes, the line of demarcation between the body and the external world becomes problematic when examining perception as ontological and epistemological category).

- While the ability to smell, taste and touch is by no means irrelevant to organization theory – the entire food industry, for example, is arguably based on such human faculties – visuality and the capacity to perceive sounds plays a central role in most organizational activities. In order to understand these two perceptual skills and their uses in organization, concepts such as art and music may be invoked.

- Rather than assuming that vision and auditory perception are socially unmarked and uncomplicated, the literature on art and music, notwithstanding the substantial heterogeneity of these literary corpuses, shows that both art and music are social categories shaping and playing with human perception. Perception is never pure and unaffected by previous experiences but is always 'staged' as what embodies formal training, socially and economically embedded preferences and tastes, and previous experiences. Perceiving art and music never occurs in some isolated social space but instead draws on a variety of social resources and conditions. In addition, what counts as art and music is in itself a highly contested topic, of necessity embedded in complex social processes and negotiations. Therefore, there is no 'innocent' or 'immaculate perception'; to use Lacan's expression, the gaze of the Other always interpenetrates our vision.

- Media are assemblages including technology, regimes of representation and means of inscription strongly affecting perception in contemporary society. Media thus structure, order and enframe perception in organizations. Perception of art and music in real-life settings is already determined by a range of individual and social conditions and idiosyncrasies, and mediated perception adds another dimension to the act of seeing and hearing. Media provide immense opportunities for manipulating the signals producing images or sounds and thus perception is never 'finished' but is in a continuous state of reorganization. Media thus constitute another layer capable of reinforcing, enhancing or distorting perception. Mediated perception is what determines our condition in contemporary society.

- In summary, seeing and hearing are central human faculties, debated from the beginning of philosophy. Heraclitus's fragments address the hierarchy of the human senses and today human perception is what co-mingles with media and technology. However, rather than assuming that media may serve as fully fledged vision machines displacing and rendering human perception obsolete, the co-evolution and coexistence of human perception and media may enable new opportunities. For instance, the virtual reality-generated simulations of surgical operations used in medical training is one example of how human perception and media can be fruitfully aligned and brought into harmony. However, media cannot be expected to solve all kinds of human concerns and problems, simply because media are tools in the hands of humans rather than being external to social interests and concerns. Media are not animated and self-perpetuating forces but are what we humans can make use of, more or less effectively.

- At the bottom line, it is suggested that perception should be more closely examined as a central human resource in organizations and firms. The intersection of perception and organizing is a field of great interest from both a theoretical and practical perspective.

Perhaps the future will bring an increased theoretical and practical interest in perception and organizing – *qui vivra verra*.

Bibliography

Aaseth, Espen (2003) We all want to change the world: The ideology of innovation in digital media, in Liestøl, G., Morrison, A., Rasmussen, Terje, eds, *Digital Media Revisited*, Cambridge and London: MIT Press, pp. 415–39.

Adler, Nancy (2006) The arts and leadership: Now then we can do anything, what will we do?, *Academy of Management Learning and Education*, 5(4): 486–99.

Adorno, Theodore W. (1934/1978) On the fetish-character in music and the regression of listening, in Arato, Andrew and Gebhardt, Eike, eds, (1978), *The Essential Frankfurt School Reader*, New York: Urizen Books, pp. 270–99.

Adorno, Theodore W. (1953/2003) *Philosophy of Modern Music*, trans. Anne G. Mitchell and Wesley W. Blomster, New York and London: Continuum.

Adorno, Theodore W. (1997) *Aesthetic theory*, Ed. by Gretel Adorno and Rolf Tiedemann, Trans. by Robert Hullot-Kentor, London and New York: Continuum.

Alan, David (2006) Effects of popular music in advertising on attention and memory, *Journal of Advertising Research*, 46(4): 434–44.

Alexander, Amir R. (2002) *The Voyages of Discovery and the Transformation of Mathematical Practice*, Stanford: Stanford University Press.

Alexander, Marcus (1997) Getting to grips with the virtual organization, *Long Range Planning*, 30(1): 122–4.

Allcorn, Seth (1997) Parallel virtual organizations, *Administration and Society*, 29(4): 412–40.

Amit, Raphael and Zott, Christoph (2001) Value creation in e-business, *Strategic Management Journal*, 22: 493–520.

Archimbaud, Michel (1993) *Francis Bacon: In conversation with Michel Archimbaud*, London: Phaidon.

Arian, Edward (1971) *Bach, Beethoven, and Bureuacracy: The case of the Philadelphia Orchestra*, The University of Alabama Press.

Aristotle (1986 edn) *De Anima*, London: Penguin.

Aristotle (1998 edn) *Politics*, Indianapolis and Cambridge: Hackett.

Arnaud, Gilles (2003) A coach or a couch? A Lacanian perspective on executive coaching and consulting, *Human Relations*, 56(9): 1131–54.

Assad, Maria L. (1999) *Reading with Michel Serres: An encounter with time*, Albany: State University of New York Press.

Attali, Jacques (1985) *Noise: The political economy of music*, trans. B. Massumi, Manchester: Manchester University Press.

Avgerou, Chrisanthi, Ciborra, Claudio and Land, Frank, eds (2006) *The Social Study of Information and Communication Technology: Innovations, actors, and contexts*, Oxford and New York: Oxford University Press.

Baba, Yasunori and Nobeoka, Kentaro (1998) Towards knowledge-based product development: The 3-D CAD model of knowledge creation, *Research Policy*, 26(6): 643–59.

Babbage, C. (1833) *On the Economy of Machinery and Manufactures*: London: Charles Knight.

Bakhtin, Michail (1968) *Rabelais and His World*, Bloomington: Indiana University Press.

Bakhtin, M.M. (1981) *The Dialogical Imagination: Four essays*, trans. Caryl Emerson and Michael Holquist, Austin: University of Texas Press.

Ball, Kirstie (2005) Organization, surveillance and the body: Toward a politics of resistance, *Organization*, 12(1): 89–108.

Balsamo, Anne (1995) Form of technological embodiment: reading the body in contemporary culture, in Featherstone, Mike and Burrows, Roger, eds, *Cyberspace/cyberbodies/cyberpunk: Cultures of technological representations*, London: Sage.

Barenboim, Daniel and Said, Edward W. (2002) *Parallels and Paradoxes: Explorations in music and society*, New York: Pantheon Books.

Barley, Stephen R. (1990) The alignment of technology and structure through roles and networks, *Administrative Science Quarterly*, 35: 61–103.

Barry, Andrew (2005) Pharmaceutical matters: The invention of informed materials, *Theory, Culture and Society*, 22(1): 51–69.

Barthes, Roland (1981) *Camera Lucida*, trans. by Richard Howard, London: Vintage.

Bataille, Georges (1945/1992) *On Nietzsche*, New York: Paragon House.

Bataille, Georges (1973/1985) *Literature and Evil*, London: Marion Boyars.

Baudrillard, Jean (1995) *The Gulf War Did Not Take Place*, Sidney: Power Publications.

Baudrillard, Jean (1998) *The Consumer Society: Myths and Structures*, Thousand Oaks, London and New Delhi: Sage.

Becker, Howard S. (1982) *Art Worlds*, Berkeley, Los Angeles and London: University of California Press.

Belfiore, Eleaonora (2002) Art as a means of alleviating social exclusion: Does it really work? A critique of instrumental policies and social impact studies in the UK, *International Journal of Cultural Policy*, 8(1): 91–106.

Beller, Jonathan (2006) *The Cinematic Mode of Production: Attention Economy and the Society of the Spectacle*, Duke Hanover: Dartmouth College Press.

Belova, Olga (2006) The event of seeing: A phenomenological perspective on visual sense-making, *Culture and Organization*, 12(2): 93–107.

Benjamin, Walter (1973) The work of art in the age of mechanical reproduction, in Benjamin, W., *Illuminations*, London: Fontana Press.

Benjamin, Walter (1999) *The Arcades Project*, trans. Howard Eiland and Kevin McLaughlin, Cambridge: Belknap Press.

Bennis, Warren (2003) Frank Gehry: Artist leader, and 'neotenic', *Journal of Management Inquiry*, 12(1): 81–7.

Benson, Barbara Elna (1945) *Music and Sound Systems in Industry*, New York and London: McGraw-Hill.

Bentham, Jeremy (1995 edn) *The Panopticon Writings*, London: Verso.

Berger, John (1972) *Ways of Seeing*, London: Penguin.

Bergson, Henri (1920/1975) *Mind-energy: Lectures and essays*, Trans. by H. Wildon Carr, Westport & London: Greenwood Press.

Berkeley, George (1709/2004) From *An Essay Towards a New Theory of Vision*, in Schwatz, Robert, ed. (2004), *Perception*, Oxford and Malden: Blackwell, pp. 18–23.

Berkeley, George (1709/2007) *An Essay Towards a New Theory of Vision*, London: Kessinger Publishing.

Bernard, Jonathan W. (1987) *The Music of Edgard Varèse*, New Haven and London: Yale University Press.

Bijker, Wiebe E. (1995) *Of Bicycles, Bakelites, and Bulbs: Toward a theory of sociotechnical change*, Cambridge and London: MIT Press.

Bijsterveld, Karin and Schulp, Marten (2004) Breaking into a world of perfection: Innovation in today's classical musical instruments, *Social Studies of Science*, 34(5): 649–74.

Biocca, Frank (1992) Virtual reality technology: A tutorial, *Journal of Communication*, 42(4): 23–74.

Black, Janice A. and Edwards, Sandra (2000) Emergence of virtual or network organizations: Fad or feature, *Journal of Organization Change Management*, 13(6): 567–76.

Blake, Erin C. (2003) Zograscopes, virtual reality, and the mapping of polite society in eighteenth-century England, in Gitelman, Lisa and Pingree, Geoffrey B., eds, *New media*, Cambridge and London: MIT Press, pp. 1–30.

Blumenberg, Hans (1993) Light as a metaphor for truth: At the preliminary stage of philosophical concept formation, in Levin, David Michael, ed., *Modernity and the Hegemony of Vision*, Berkeley, Los Angeles and London: University of California Press, pp. 30–62.

Blumer, Herbert (1969) *Symbolic Interactionism: Perspective and method*, Berkeley: University of California.

Bode, Matthias (2006) 'Now that's what I call music': An interpretative approach to music in advertising, *Advances in Consumer Research*, 33: 580–5.

Boden, Deindre (1994) *The Business of Talk: Organizations in action*, Cambridge: Polity Press.

Bogard, William (1996) *The Simulation of Surveillance: Hypercontrol in telematic societies*, Cambridge: Cambridge University Press.

Boje, David M. (1991) The storytelling organization: a study of story performance in an office supply firm, *Administrative Science Quarterly*, 36: 106–26.

Boje, David. M. (2001) Carnivalesque resistance to global spectacle: A critical postmodern theory of public administration, *Administrative Theory and Practice*, 23(3): 431–58.

Boland, Richard J., Lyytinen, Kalle and Yoo, Youngjin (2007) Wakes of innovation in project networks: The case of digital 3-D representation in architecture, engineering, and construction, *Organization Science*, 18(4): 631–47.

Bolter, Jay David (1991) *Writing Space: The computer, hypertext, and the history of writing*, Hillsdale, Hove and London: Lawrence Erlbaum.

Bolter, Jay David (1996) Virtual reality and the redefinition of self, in Strate, Lance, Jacobson, Ronald, Gibson, Stephanie, B., eds (1996) *Communication and Cyberspace: Social interaction in an electronic environment*, Cresskill, NJ: Hampton Press, pp. 105–19.

Bolter, Jay David & Grusin, Richard (1999) *Remediation. Understanding new media*, Cambridge & London: The MIT Press.

Boorsma, Miranda (2002) Art marketing and the societal functioning of the arts: The case of the subsidised dramatic arts in the Netherlands, *International Journal of Cultural Policy*, 8(1): 65–74.

Boorsma, Miranda (2006) A strategic logic for arts marketing: Integrating customer value and artistic objectives, *International Journal of Cultural Policy*, 12(1): 73–92.

Borges, Jorge Luis (1999) The postulation of reality, in Borges, Jorge Luis (1999) *Selected non-fiction*, Weinberger, Eliot, ed., London: Penguin, pp. 59–64.

Borgmann, Alfred (1999) *Holding on to Reality: The nature of information at the turn of the new millennium*, Chicago and New York: University of Chicago Press.

Boudreau, Marie-Claude, Loch, Karen D., Robey, Daniel and Straud, Dietmar (1998) Going global: Using information technology to advance the competitiveness of the virtual transnational organization, *Academy of Management Executive*, 12(4): 120–8.

Bourdieu, Pierre (1977) *Outline of a Theory of Practice*, Cambridge: Cambridge University Press.

Boudieu, Pierre (1984) *Distinction*, London: Routledge and Kegan Paul.

Bourdieu, Pierre (1990) *The Logic of Practice*, Cambridge: Polity Press.

Bourdieu, Pierre (1991) *Language and Symbolic Power*, Cambridge: Polity Press.

Bourdieu, Pierre (1993) *The Field of Cultural Production: Essays on art and literature*, ed. Randall Johnson, Cambridge: Polity Press.

Bourdieu, Pierre (1996) *On Television*, New York: New Press.

Bourdieu, Pierre (2004) *The Science of Science and Reflexivity*, Chicago and London: University of Chicago Press.

Bourdieu, Pierre (2005) *The Economic Structures of Society*, Cambridge: Polity Press.

Bourdieu, Pierre and Haake, Hans (1995) *Free Exchange*, Cambridge: Polity Press.

Bourdieu, Pierre and Wacquant, Loic J.D. (1992) *An Invitation to Reflexive Sociology*, Chicago and London: University of Chicago Press.

Bowen, David E. and Stiehl, Caren (1992) Sweet music: Grateful employees, grateful customers, 'grate' profits, *Journal of Management Inquiry*, 1(2): 154–6.

Bowker, Geoffrey (2005) *Memory Practices of the Sciences*, Cambridge and London: MIT Press.

Bowker, Geoffrey C. and Leight Star, Susan (1999) *Sorting Things Out: Classification and its consequences*, Cambridge and London: MIT Press.

Braidotti, Rosi (2006) *Transpositions: On Nomadic Ethics*, Cambridge and Malden: Polity Press.

Brewis, Joanna and Linstead, Stephen (2000) *Sex, Work and Sex Work*, London and New York: Routledge.

Brighton, Andrew (2000) Francis Bacon's modernism, *Critical Quarterly*, 42(1): 137–42.

Broch, Hermann (1933/1968) Notes on the problem of kitsch, in Dorfles, Gillo, (1968), *Kitsch: An anthology of bad taste*. London: Studio Vista, pp. 49–76.

Brocklehurst, Michael (2001) Power, identity and new technology homework: Implications for 'new forms' of organizing, *Organization Studies*, 22(3): 445–66.

Broddy, William (2004) *New Media and Popular Imagination: Radio, television, and digital media in the United States*, Oxford and New York: Oxford University Press.

Brown, Steven D. (2002) Michel Serres: Science, translation and the logic of the parasite, *Theory, Culture and Society*, 19(3): 1–27.

Brown, Steven D. (2004) Parasitic logic, *Journal of Organization Change Management*, 17(4): 383–95.

Brown, Steven D. and Lightfoot, Geoffrey (2002) Presence, absence, and accountability: E-mail and the mediation of organizational memory, in Woolgar, Steve, ed., *Virtual Society? Technology, cyberbole, reality*, Oxford and New York: Oxford University Press.

Bruner, Jerome (1986) *Actual Minds, Possible Worlds*, Cambridge: Harvard University Press.

Bruner, Jerome, (1990), *Acts of meaning*, Cambridge: Harvard University Press.

Brunsson, Nils (2006) *Mechanisms of Hope: Maintaining the dream of the rational organization*, Copenhagen: Copenhagen Business School Press; Malmö: Liber; Oslo: Universitetsforlaget.

Bryman, Alan (2004) *The Disneyization of Society*, London, Thousand Oaks and New Delhi: Sage.

Bryson, Norman (1988) The gaze in the expanded field, in Foster, Hal, ed., *Vision and Visuality*, New York: New Press, pp. 86–113.

Burke, Edmund (1998) *A Philosphical Enquiry into Our Ideas of the Sublime and the beautiful*, Oxford and New York: Oxford University Press.

Burns, Alfred (1989) *The Power of the Written Word: the role of literacy in the history of Western civilization*, New York: Peter Lang.

Burrows, Roger and Gane, Nicholas (2006) Geodemographics, software and class, *Sociology*, 40(5): 793–812.

Burwick, Frederick and Douglass, Paul, eds (1992) *The Crisis in Modernism: Bergson and the vitalist controversy*, Cambridge: Cambridge University Press.

Bush, Vannevar (1945/2001) As we may think, in Packer, Randall and Jordan, Ken, eds. (2001), *Multimedia: From Wagner to virtual reality*, New York: W.W. Norton, pp. 135–53.

Callon, Michel (2002) Writing and (re)writing devices tools for managing complexity, in Law, John and Mol, Annemarie, eds., *Complexities: Social studies of knowledge practices*, Durham and London: Duke University Press.

Carr, Adrian and Downs, Alexis (2004) Transitional and quasi-objects in organization studies: Viewing Enron from the object relations world of Winnicott and Serres, *Journal of Organization Change Management*, 17(4): 352–64.

Cascio, Wayne F. (2000) Managing a virtual workplace, *Academy of Management Executive*, 14(3): 81–90.

Case, Peter and Piñeiro, Erik (2006) Aesthetic, performativity and resistance in the narrative of computer programming community, *Human Relations*, 59(6): 753–82.

Castells, M. (1996) *The Information Age: Economy, Society and Culture, Vol. 1: The Rise of the Network Society*, Oxford: Blackwell.

Cavanaugh, J. Michael and Prasad, Pushkala (1994) Drug testing as symbolic managerial action: In response to 'A case against workplace drug testing', *Organization Science*, 5(2): 267–71.

Caves, Richard E. (2000) *Creative Industries*, Cambridge and London: Harvard University Press.

Chandler, A.D. (1977) *The Visible Hand: The Managerial Revolution in American Business*, Cambridge: Harvard University Press.

Chang, Jeff (2003) *Can't Stop, Won't Stop: A history of the hip-hop generation*, New York: Picador.

Cho, Theresa S. and Hambrick, Donald C. (2006) Attention as the mediator between top management team characteristics and strategic change: The case of airline deregulation, *Organization Science*, 17(4): 453–69.

Chung, Chuihua Judy, Inaba, Jeffrey, Koolhaas, Rem and Leong, Sze Tsung, eds (2001) *Harvard Design School Guide to Shopping*, Köln: Taschen.

Ciborra, Claudio (2002) *The Labyrinths of Information: Challenging the wisdom of systems*, Oxford and New York: Oxford University Press.

Clark, Kenneth S. (1929) *Music in Industry*, New York: National Bureau for the Advancement of Music.

Clayson, Alan (2002) *Edgard Varèse*, London: Sanctuary.

Clegg, Stewart, Kornberger, Martin and Rhodes, Carl (2004) Noise, parasites and translation: Theory and practice in management consulting, *Management Learning*, 35(1): 31–44.

Cohen, Michael D., March, James G., Olsen, Johan P. (1972) A garbage can model of organizational choice, *Administrative Science Quarterly*, 17: 1–25.

Cooren, François (2004) Textual agency: How texts do things in organizational settings, *Organization*, 11(3): 373–93.

Corbett, M. (2003) Sound organization: A brief history of psychosonic management, *Ephemera*, 3(4): 265–76.

Cowan, Ruth Schwartz (1983) *More Work for Mother: The ironies of household technology from the open hearth to the microwave*, New York: Basic Books.

Cowell, Henry (2006) The joys of noise, in Cox, Christoph and Warner, Daniel, eds, *Audio Cultures: Readings in modern music*, New York and London: Continuum, pp. 22–4.

Coyne, Richard (1999) *Technoromanticism: Digital narrative, holism, and the romance of the real*, Cambridge and London: MIT Press.

Cox, Christoph and Warner, Daniel, eds (2006) *Audio Cultures: Readings in modern music*, New York and London: Continuum.

Crary, Jonathan (1990) *Techniques of the Observer: On vision and modernity in the nineteenth century*, Cambridge and London: MIT Press.

Crary, Jonathan (1995) Unbinding vision: Manet and the attentive observer in the late nineteenth century, in Carney, Leo and Schwartz, Vanessa R., eds, *Cinema and the Invention of Modern Life*, Berkeley: University of California Press, pp. 46–71.

Crary, Jonathan (1999) *Suspensions of Perception: Attention, spectacle, and modern culture*, Cambridge and London: MIT Press.

Croce, Benedetto (1995) *Guide to Aesthetics*, trans. Patrick Romanell, Indianapolis and Cambridge: Hackett.

Cuff, Dana (1991) *Architecture: The story of practice*, Cambridge: MIT Press.

Cunliffe, Ann L., Luhman, John T. and Boje, David M. (2004) Narrative temporality: Implications for organizational research, *Organization Studies*, 25(2): 261–86.

Cusick, Suzanne G. (1998) Feminist theory, music theory and the mind/body problem, in Krims, Adam, ed., *Music/ideology: Resisting aesthetic*: Amsterdam: G+B Arts International, pp. 37–55.

Cyert, Richard M. and March, James G. (1963) *A Behavioral Theory of the Firm*, Englewood Cliffs: Prentice-Hall.

Czarniawska, Barbara (1997) *Narrating the Organization: Dramas of institutional identity*, Chicago and London: University of Chicago Press.

Dane, Erik and Pratt, Michael G. (2007) Exploring intuition and its role in managerial decision making, *Academy of Management Review*, 32(1): 33–54.

Daston, Lorraine (1999) Objectivity and the escape from perspective, in Biagioli, Mario, ed., *The Science Studies Reader*, London and New York: Routledge, pp. 110–23.

Daston, Loraine and Galison, Peter (2007) *Objectivity*, New York: Zone Books.
Davenport, Thomas and Pearlson, Keri (1998) Two cheers for the virtual office, *Sloan Management Review*, 39(3): 51–65.
Davenport, Thomas H. and Beck, John C. (2001) *The Attention Economy: Understanding the new currency of business*, Boston: Harvard University Press.
Davis, Mike (1990) *City of Quartz: Excavating the future in Los Angeles*, London and New York: Verso.
Davis, Mike (2006) *Planet of Slums*, London: Verso.
Davismoon, Stephen (2004) The transmutation of the old with the new in the modernist vision of Edgard Varèse, *Contemporary Music Review*, 23(2): 45–58.
Debord, G. (1977) *Society of the Spectacle*, Detroit: Black & Red.
De Landa, Manuel (1991) *War in the Age of Intelligent Machines*, New York: Zone Books.
Deleuze, Gilles (1966/1988) *Bergsonism*, New York: Zone Books.
Deleuze, Gilles (1991) *Empiricism and Subjectivity: An essay on Hume's theory of human nature*, New York: Columbia University Press.
Deleuze, Gilles (2003) *Francis Bacon: The logic of sensation*, London and New York: Continuum.
Deleuze, Gilles (2004) *Desert islands and other texts, 1953–1994*, ed. By David Lapoujade, trans. by Michael Taormina, New York & Los Angeles: Semiotext[e].
Deleuze, Gilles (2006) *Two Regimes of Madness: Texts and interviews 1975–1995*, trans. Ames Hodgs and Mike Taormina, New York and Los Angeles: Semiotext(e).
Deleuze, Gilles and Guattari, F. (1994) *What is Philosophy?*, New York: Columbia University Press.
Dennis, Simone (2007) *Police Beat: The emotional power of music in police work*, Youngstown: Cambria Press.
DeNora, Tia (2000) *Music in Everyday Life*, Cambridge: Cambridge University Press.
Der Derian, James, ed. (1998) *The Virilio Reader*, Oxford: Blackwell.
Derrida, Jacques (1987) *The Truth in Painting*, trans. Bennington, Geoff and McLeaod, Ian, Chicago and London: University of Chicago Press.
Derrida, Jacques and Stiegler, Bernard (2002) *Echographies of Television: Filmed interviews*, trans. Jennifer Bajorek, Cambridge: Polity press.
Dewey, John (1934/1987) *Art as Experience*, Carbondale & Edwardsville: Southern Illinois University Press.
DiMaggio, Paul (1987) Classification in Art, *American Sociological Review*, 52(4): 440–55.
DiMaggio, Paul, Hargittai, Eszter, Neuman, W. Russell and Robinson, John P. (2001) Social implications of the internet, *Annual Review of Sociology*, 27: 307–36.
Dobers, Peter & Strannegård, Lars (2001) Loveable networks — A story of affection, attraction and treachery, *Journal of Organization Change Management*, 14(1): 28–49.
Dodge, Martin and Kitchin, Rob (2005) Code and the transduction of space, *Annals of the American Geographers*, 95(1): 162–80.
Dokic, Jérôme (1998) Music, noise, silence: Some reflections on John Cage, *Angelaki*, 3(2): 103–12.
Donnellon, Anne (1996) *Team Talk: Listening between the lines to improve team performance*, Boston: Harvard Business School Press.
Dorfles, Gillo, ed. (1968) *Kitsch: An anthology of bad taste*. London: Studio Vista.
Du Gay, Paul (2000) *In Praise of Bureaucracy*, London: Sage.

Duhem, Pierre (1996) *Essays in the History and Philosophy of Science*, trans. and ed. Roger Ariew and Peter Barker, Indianapolis and Cambridge: Hackett.

Eagleton, Terry (1990) *The Ideology of the Aesthetics*, Oxford and Cambridge: Blackwell.

Eco, Umberto (1957/2006) The poetics of the open work, in Cox, Christoph and Warner, Daniel, eds, *Audio Cultures: Readings in modern music*, New York and London: Continuum, pp. 167–75.

Eckert, Hanna and Bajorath, Jürgen (2007) Molecular similarity analysis in virtual screening: foundations, limitations and novel approaches, *Drug Discovery Today*, 12(5–6): 225–33.

Edenius, Mats and Styhre, Alexander (2006) Knowledge management in the making: Using Balanced Scorecard and e-mail systems, *Journal of Knowledge Management*, 10(3): 86–102.

Edenius, Mats and Yakhlef, A. (2007) Space, vision, and organizational learning: The interplay of incorporating and inscribing practices, *Management Learning*, 38(2): 193–210.

Eisenstein, Elizabeth (1983) *The Printing Revolution in Early Modern Europe*, Cambridge: Cambridge University Press.

Elias, Norbert (1991/1993) *Mozart: Portrait of a genius*, trans. Edmund Jephcott, Cambridge: Polity Press.

Ellul, Jacques (1964) *The Technological Society*, New York: Vintage.

El-Sawad, Amal and Korczynski, Marek (2007), Management and Music: The Exceptional Case of the IBM Songbook, *Group and Organization Management*, 32(1): 79–108.

Elsbach, Kimberly D. (2006) *Organizational Perception Management*, Mahwah and London: Lawrence Erlbaum.

Entwhistle, Joanna and Racamora, Agnès (2006) The field of fashion materialized: A study of London Fashion Week, *Sociology*, 40(4): 735–51.

Evens, Adam (2005) *Sound Ideas: Music, machines and experiences*, Minneapolis and London: University of Minnesota Press.

Everett, Anna (2003) Digitextuality and click theory: Theses on convergence media in the digital age, in Everett, Anna and Caldwell, John T., eds, *New Media: Theories and practices of digitextuality*, New York and London: Routledge, pp. 3–28.

Ewenstein, Boris and Whyte, Jennifer K. (2007a) Visual representations as 'artifacts of knowing', *Building Research and Information*, 35(1): 81–9.

Ewenstein, Boris and Whyte, Jennifer (2007b) Beyond words: Aesthetic knowledge and knowing in organizations, *Organization Studies*, 28(5): 689–708.

Febvre, Lucien and Martin, Henri-Jean (1958/1997) *The Coming of the Book: The impact of printing 1450–1800*, trans. David Gerard, London and New York: Verso.

Fine, Gary Alan (1996) *Kitchens: The culture of restaurant work*, Berkeley, Los Angeles and London: University of California Press.

Fink, Bruce (1995) *The Lacanian Subject: Between language and jouissance*, Princeton: Princeton University Press.

Fitzgerald, Paula and Ellen, Pam Scholder (1999) Scents in the marketplace: Explaining a fraction of olfaction, *Journal of Retailing*, 75(2): 243–62.

Fleming, Peter (2005) 'The kindergarten cop': paternalism and resistance in a high-commitment workplace, *Journal of Management Studies*, 42(6): 1469–89.

Flusser, Vilém (1983/2000) *Towards a Philosophy of Photography*, London: Reaktion.

Flusser, Vilém (2002) *Writings*, ed. by Andreas Ströhl, trans. Erik Eisel, Minneapolis and London: University of Minnesota Press.

Foucault, Michel (1967) *Madness and Civilization*, London: Routledge.

Foucault, Michel (1972) *An Archaelogy of Knowledge*, London: Routledge.

Foucault, Michel (1973) *The Birth of the Clinic*, London: Routledge.

Foucault, Michel (1977) *Discipline and Punish*, New York: Pantheon.

Frank, Thomas (1997) *The Conquest of Cool: Business culture, counterculture and the rise of hip consumerism*, Chicago and London: University of Chicago Press.

Fraser, Miriam, Kember, Sarah and Lury, Celia (2005) Inventive life: Approaches to a new vitalism, *Theory, Culture and Society*, 22(1): 1–14.

Fredberg, Tobias (2003) Interface Strategies: Internet and the business of large Swedish newspapers, PhD thesis, Dept. of Technology Management and Economics, Chalmers University of Technology, Gothenburg, Sweden.

Freud, Sigmund (1955) The Uncanny, in *The Standard Edition of the Complete Psychological Works of Sigmund Freud*, Strachey, J., ed., Vol. 17, An Infantile Neurosis and Other Works, pp. 218–56.

Freud, Sigmund (1940/2003) *An Outline of Psychoanalysis*, London: Penguin.

Gabriel, Yannis (2000) *Storytelling in Organizations: facts, fictions, and fantasies*, Oxford: Oxford University Press.

Gabriel, Yannis, ed. (2004) *Myths, stories, and organizations: Premodern narratives of our time*, Oxford and New York: Oxford University Press.

Gadamer, Hans-George (1960/1975) *Truth and Method*, London: Sheed and Ward.

Gallagher, A. and Cates, C. (2004) Virtual reality training for the operating room and cardiac catheterisation laboratory, *The Lancet*, 364: 1538–40.

García, Beatriz (2004) Urban regeneration, arts programming, and major events: Glasgow 1990, Sydney, 2000 and Barcelona 2004, *International Journal of Cultural Policy*, 10(1): 103–18.

Garfinkel, H. (1967) *Studies in Ethnomethodology*, Englewood Cliffs: Prentice-Hall.

Garlin, Francis V. and Owen, Katherine (2006) Setting the tone with the tune: A meta-analytic review of the effects of background music in retail settings, *Journal of Business Research*, 59: 755–64.

Gartman, David (2004) Three ages of the automobile: the cultural logics of the car, *Theory, Culture and Society*, 21(4/5): 169–95.

Gay, Peter (1984) *The Bourgeois Experience: Victoria to Freud: Vol. 1: Education of the senses*, New York and Oxford: Oxford University Press.

George, Nelson (1998) *Hip Hop America*, London: Penguin.

Gibson, Christina B. and Gibbs, Jennifer L. (2006) Unpacking the concept of virtuality: The effects of geographic dispersion, electronic dependence, dynamic structure, and national diversity in team innovation, *Administrative Science Quarterly*, 51: 451–95.

Gibson, James J. (1950) *The Perception of the Visual World*, Boston: Houghton Mifflin.

Gibson, Lisanne (2002) Managing the people: Art programs in the American depression, *Journal of Arts Management, Law, and Society*, 31(4): 279–91.

Gilbreth, Frank B. (1911) *Motion study: A method for increasing the efficiency of the workman*, NewYork: Van Nostrand.

Gitelman, Lisa (1999) *Scripts, grooves, and writing machines: Representing technology in the Edison era*, Stanford. Stanford University Press.

Gitelman, Lisa (2003) Souvenir foils: On the status of print at the origin of recorded sound, in Gitelman, Lisa and Pingree, Geoffrey B., eds, *New Media, 1740–1915*, Cambridge and London: MIT Press, pp. 157–74.

Gitelman, Lisa (2006) *Always Already New: Media, history and the data of culture*, Cambridge and London: MIT Press.

Gitelman, Lisa and Pingree, Geoffrey B., eds (2003) *New Media, 1740–1915*, Cambridge and London: MIT Press.

Goehr, Lydia (1998) *The Quest for Voice: On music, politics, and the limits of philosophy*, Oxford: Clarendon Press.

Goffman, Erwin (1959) *The Presentation of Self in Everyday Life*, New York: Doubleday Anchor.

Goldhill, Simon (1996) Refracting classic vision: Changing cultures of viewing, in Brennan, Teresa and Jay, Martin, eds, *Vision in Context: Historical and contemporary perspectives on sight*, New York and London: Routledge, pp. 17–28.

Gombrich, E.H. (1960) *Art and Illusion: A study in the psychology of pictorial representation*, London: Phaidon.

Goodwin, Charles (1994) Professional vision, *American Anthropologist*, 96(3): 606–33.

Goodwin, Charles (1995) Seeing in depth, *Social Studies of Science*, 25: 237–74.

Goody, Jack (1986) *The Logic of Writing and the Organization of Society*, Cambridge: Cambridge University Press.

Goody, Jack (1987) *The Interface Between the Written and the Oral*, Cambridge: Cambridge University Press.

Goody, Jack (1997) *Representations and Contradictions: Ambivalences towards images, theatre, fiction, relics and sexuality*, Oxford and Malden: Blackwell.

Graham, Gerald H., Unruh, Jeanne and Jennings, Paul (1990) The Impact of Nonverbal Communication in Organizations: A survey of perceptions, *The Journal of Business Communication*, 28(1): 45–62.

Graham, L. (1994) How Does the Japanese Model Transfer to the United States? A View from the Line, in Elger, T. and Smith, C., eds, *Global Japanization – The transnational transformation of the labour process*, London: Routledge.

Graham, L. (1995) *On the Line at Subaru-Isuzu: The Japanese Model and the American Worker*, Ithaca: ILR Press.

Greffe, Xavier (2004) Artistic work in the digital age, *Journal of Arts Management, Law, and Society*, 34(1): 79–94.

Grindstaff, Laura and Turow, Joseph (2006) Video cultures: Television sociology in the 'New TV' age, *Annual Review of Sociology*, 32: 103–25.

Grosz, Elizabeth (1990) *Jacques Lacan: A feminist introduction*, London and New York: Routledge.

Grosz, Elizabeth (2005) *Time Travels: Feminism, nature, power*, Durham: Duke University Press.

Guillén, Mauro F. (1994) *Models of Management: Work, authority, and organization in a comparative perspective*, Chicago and London: University of Chicago Press.

Guillén, Mauro F. (1997) Scientific management's lost aesthetic: Architecture, organization, and the taylorized beauty of the mechanical, *Administrative Science Quarterly*, 42: 682–715.

Guillén, Mauro F. (2006) *The Taylorized Beauty of the Mechanical: Scientific management and the rise of modernist architecture*, Princeton and London: Princeton University Press.

Gunning, Tom (1995) Tracing the individual body: Photography, detectives, and early cinema, in Carney, Leo and Schwartz, Vanessa R., eds, *Cinema and the Invention of Modern Life*, Berkeley: University of California Press, pp. 15–45.

Gustavsson, Eva and Czarniawska, Barbara (2004) Web woman: the on-line of corporate and gender images, *Organization*, 11(5). 651–70.

Guve, Bertil Gonzàlez (2007) Aesthetics of financial judgments: On risk capitalists' confidence, in Guillet de Monthoux, Pierre, Gustafsson, Claes and Sjöstrand, Sven-Erik, eds, *Aesthetic Leadership: Managing fields of flow in art and business*, Basingstoke: Palgrave Macmillan, pp. 128–40.

Habermas, J. (1987) *The Theory of Communicative Action: Vol 2: Life World and System: A Critique of Functionalist Reason*, Cambridge: Polity Press.

Hackman, W.D. (1989) Scientific instruments; Models of brass and aids to discovery, in Gooding, David, Pinch, Trevor and Schaffer, Simon, eds, *The Uses of Experiments: Studies in the natural sciences*, Cambridge, New York and Melbourne: Cambridge University Press, pp. 31–65.

Hall, Duncan (2001) *'A pleasant change from politics': Music and the British labour movement between the wars*, Cheltenham: New Clarion Press.

Hamilton, Andy (2007) *Aesthetic and Music*, New York and London: Continuum.

Hancock, Philip (2005) Uncovering the semiotics in organizational aesthetics, *Organization*, 12(1): 29–50.

Hansen, Mark B.N. (2004) *New Philosophy for New Media*, Cambridge and London: MIT Press.

Hansen, Mark B.N. (2006) Media theory, *Theory, Culture and Society*, 23(2–3): 297–306.

Hansen, Miriam Bratu (1995) America, Paris, the Alps: Kracauer (and Benjamin) on cinema and modernity, in Carney, Leo and Schwartz, Vanessa R., eds, *Cinema and the Invention of Modern Life*, Berkeley: University of California Press, pp. 362–402.

Hansen, Morten T. and Haas, Martine R. (2001) Competing for attention in knowledge markets: Electronic document dissemination in a management consulting company, *Administrative Science Quarterly*, 46(1): 1–28.

Haraway, Donna (1989) *Primate Visions: Gender, race, and nature in the modern world of science*, New York and London: Routledge.

Haraway, Donna J. (1991) *Simians, Cyborgs, and Women: The Reinvention of Nature*, London: Free Association Books.

Haraway, Donna (1997) *Modest=Witness@Second=Millenium. FemaleMan©=Meets= OncoMouse™*, London: Routledge.

Hardy, Cynthia (2001) Researching organizational discourse, *International Studies of Management and Organization*, 31(3): 25–47.

Hardy, Cynthia and Philips, Nelson (1999) No joking matter: Discursive struggle in the Canadian refugee system, *Organization Studies*, 20(1): 1–24.

Harrison, Julia (1997) Museums as agencies of neocolonialism in a postmodern world, *Studies in Cultures, Organizations and Societies*, 3: 41–65.

Hassard, John and Parker, Martin (1993) *Postmodernism and Organizations*, London, Thousand Oaks and New Delhi: Sage.

Hayes, Niall and Walsham, Geoff (2003) Knowledge sharing and ICTs: A Relational Perspective, in Easterby-Smith, Mark and Lyles, Marjorie A. (2003) *Handbook of Organization Learning and Knowledge Management*, Oxford and Malden: Blackwell, pp. 54–77.

Hayles, N. Katherine (1999) *How we became posthuman: Virtual bodies in cybernetics, literature, and informatics,* Chicago and London: The University of Chicago Press.

Hayles, N. Katherine (2002) W*riting Machines,* Cambridge and London: MIT Press.

Hayles, N. Katherine (2005) *My Mother was a Computer: Digital subjects and literary texts,* Chicago and London: University of Chicago Press.

Hayles, N. Katherine (2006) Unfinished work: From cyborg to cognisphere, *Theory, Culture and Society,* 23(7–8): 159–66.

Hedgecoe, Adam (2006) Pharmacogenetics as alien science: Alzheimer's disease, core sets and expectations, *Social Studies of Science,* 36(5): 723–52.

Hedgecoe, Adam and Martin, Paul (2003) The drug don't work: Expectations and the shaping of pharmacogenetics, *Social Studies of Science,* 33(3): 327–64.

Heidegger, Martin (1977) *The Question Concerning Technology and Other Essays,* New York: Harper and Row.

Heikkinen, Merja (2005) Administrative definitions of artists in the Nordic model of state support for artists, *International Journal of Cultural Policy,* 11(3): 325–40.

Helmholtz, Herman von (1968) Concerning the perception in general, in Helmholtz, Herman von, *Helmholtz on Perception: Its physiology and development,* ed. Richard M. Warren and Roslyn P. Warren, New York: John Wiley, pp. 169–203.

Helmholtz, Hermann von (2004) From *Treatise on Physiological Optics,* in Schwatz, Robert, ed., *Perception,* Oxford and Malden: Blackwell, pp. 42–9.

Helmreich, Stefan (1998) *Silico Second Nature: Culturing artificial life in a digital world,* Berkeley, Los Angeles and London: University of California Press.

Hennion, Antoine (2002) Music lovers: Taste as performance, *Theory, Culture and Society,* 18(5): 1–22.

Heracleous, Loizos and Barrett, Michael (2001) Organization change as discourse: Communicative actions and deep structures in the context of information technology implementation, *Academy of Management Journal,* 44(4): 755–78.

Hindmarch, Jon, Heath, Christian and Fraser, Mike (2006) (Im)materiality, virtual reality and interaction: Grounding the 'virtual' in studies of technologies in action, *The Sociological Review,* 54(4): 795–817.

Hochschild, Arlie R. (1983) *The Managed Heart,* Berkeley: University of California Press.

Holquist, Michael (2003) Dialogism and aesthetics, in Gardiner, Michael E., ed., (2003), *Mikhail Bakhtin, Vol. 1,* London, Thousand Oaks & New Delhi: Sage, pp. 367–85.

Homer, Sean (2005) *Jacques Lacan,* London and New York: Routledge.

Hooper, Giles (2006) *The Discourse on Musicology,* Aldershot and Burlington: Ashgate.

Hopper, Trevor and Macintosh, Norman (1998) Management accounting numbers: Freedom or prison – Geneen versus Foucault, in McKinlay, Alan and Starkey, Ken, eds, *Foucault, Management and Organization Theory,* London, Thousand Oaks and New Delhi: Sage.

Horning, Susan Schmidt (2004) Engineering the performance: Recording engineers, tacit knowledge and the art of controlling sound, *Social Studies of Science,* 34(5): 703–31.

Hughes, Everett Cherrington (1958) *Men and Their Work,* Glencoe, IL: Free Press.

Hughes, John A., O'Brien, Jon, Randall, Dave, Rouncefield, Mark and Tolmie, Peter (2001) Some 'real' problems on 'virtual' organization, *New Technology, Work and Employment*, 16(1): 49–64.

Hume, D. (1992 edn) *Treatise of Human Nature*, Buffalo: Prometheus Books.

Israel, Paul (1992) *From Machine Shop to Industrial Laboratory: Telegraphy and the changing context of American innovation, 1830–1920*, Baltimore and London: Johns Hopkins University Press.

Jackson, Michèle H. and Poole, Marshall Scott and Kuhn, Tim (2002) The social construction of technology in studies of the workplace, in Lievrouw, Leah A., and Livingstone, Sonia, eds, *Handbook of New Media: Social shaping and consequences of ICT*, London, Thousand Oaks and New Delhi: Sage, pp. 236–53.

Jackson, Paul, ed. (1999) *Virtual Working: Social and Organizational Dynamics*, London: Routledge.

Jaër, Muriel (2004) 'To be modern is to be natural' – Your voice even resonates in me, Varèse, *Contemporary Music Review*, 23(1): 59–65.

James, William (1950) *Principles of Psychology*, Vol. 1, London: Dover.

James, William (1996) *A pluralistic universe*, Lincoln & London: University of Nebraska Press.

Jay, Martin (1988) Scopic regimes of modernity, in Foster, Hal, ed., *Vision and Visuality*, New York: New Press, pp. 3–23.

Jay, Martin (1996) Vision in context: Reflection and refractions, in Brennan, Teresa and Jay, Martin, eds, *Vision in Context: Historical and contemporary perspectives on sight*, New York and London: Routledge, pp. 1–12.

Jay, Martin (2002) Cultural relativism and the visual turn, *Journal of Visual Culture*, 1(3): 267–78.

Johnson, Ericka (2007) Surgical simulations and simulated surgeons: Reconstituting medical practices and practitioners in simulations, *Social Studies of Science*, 37: 585–608.

Jones, Keith (2005) Music in factories: A twentieth-century technique for control of the productive self, *Social and Cultural Geography*, 6(5): 723–44.

Jordanova, Ludmilla (1989), *Sexual Visions: Images of gender in science and medicine between the eighteenth and twentieth centuries*, London: Harvester Wheatsheaf.

Julier, Guy (2000) *The Culture of Design*, London, Thousand Oaks and New Delhi: Sage.

Kallinikos, Jannis (2005) The order of technology: Complexity and control in a connected world, *Information and Organization*, 15(3): 185–202.

Kallinikos, Jannis (2006a) Farewell to constructivism: Technology and context-embedded action, in Avgerou, Chrisanthi, Ciborra, Claudio and Land, Frank, eds, *The Social Study of Information and Communication Technology: Innovations, actors, and contexts*, Oxford and New York: Oxford University Press, pp. 140–61.

Kallinikos, Jannis (2006b) *The Consequences of Information: Informational implications of technological change*, Cheltenham: Edward Elgar.

Kant, Immanuel (1781/1952) *The Critique of Judgment*, trans. James Creed Meredith, Oxford: Clarendon Press.

Kant, Immanuel (1763/1960) *Observations on the Beautiful and the Sublime*, trans. John T. Goldthwaite, Berkeley and Los Angeles: University of California Press.

Kasson John F. (1976) *Civilizing the Machine: Technology and republican values in America, 1776–1900*, New York: Grossman.

Kavanaugh, Donncha (2004) Ocularcentrism and its others: A framework for metatheoretical analysis, *Organization Studies*, 25(3): 445–64.

Kay, Lily E. (2000)*Who Wrote the Book of Life? A history of the genetic code*, Stanford and London: Stanford University Press.

Keenoy, T., Oswick, C. and Grant, D. (1997) Organizational Discourses: Text and Context, *Organization*, 4(2): 147–57.

Khatri, Naresh and Ng, H. Alvin (2000) The role of intuition in strategic decision making, *Human Relations*, 53(1): 57–86.

Kinnie, Nik, Hutchinson, Sue and Purcell, John (2000) 'Fun and surveillance': The paradox of high commitment management in call centres, *International Journal of Human Resource Management*, 11(5): 967–85.

Kittler, Friedrich (1990) *Discourse Networks 1800/1900*, trans. Michael Metteer and Chris Cullens, Stanford: Stanford University Press.

Kittler, Friedrich A. (1997) *Essays. Literature, media, information systems*, ed. John Johnston, Amsterdam: G+B Arts International.

Kittler, Friedrich (1999) *Gramophone, Film, Typewriter*, trans. Geoffrey Winthrop-Young and Michael Wutz, Stanford: Stanford University Press.

Kittler, Friedrich (2006) Thinking colours and/or machines, *Theory, Culture and Society*, 23(7–8): 39–50.

Koolhaas, Rem (1978) *Delirious New York*, New York: Monticelli Press.

Korczynski, Marek (2007) Music and meaning on the factory floor, *Work and Occupation*, 34(3): 253–89.

Korczynski, M. and Jones, Keith (2006) Instrumental music? The social origin of broadcast music in British factories, *Popular Music*, 25(2): 145–64.

Korczynski, M., Pickering, Michael, Robertson, Emma and Jones, Keith (2005) We sang ourselves through that war: Women, music and factory work in World War Two, *Labour History Review*, 70(2): 185–214.

Korthagen, Fred A.J. (2005) The organization in balance: Reflection and intuition as complementary processes, *Management Learning*, 36(3): 371–87.

Kotorov, Rodoslav P. (2001) Virtual organization: Conceptual analysis of the limits of its decentralization, *Knowledge and Process Management*, 8(1): 55–62.

Koyré, Alexandre (1965) *Newtonian Studies*, Cambridge: Harvard University Press.

Kracauer, Siegfried (1995) Photography, in *The Mass Ornament: Weimar essays*, trans. Thomas Y. Levin, Cambridge and London: Harvard University Press, pp. 47–64.

Kramer, Lawrence (1990) *Music as Cultural Practice, 1800–1900*, Berkeley, Los Angeles and Oxford: University of California Press.

Kramer, Lawrence (1995) *Classical Music and Postmodern Knowledge*, Berkeley, Los Angeles and London: University of California Press.

Kramer, Lawrence (2002) *Musical Meanings: Toward a critical theory*, Berkeley, Los Angeles and Oxford: University of California Press.

Krämer, Sybille (2006) The cultural techniques of time axis manipulation: On Friedrich Kittler's conception of media, *Theory, Culture and Society*, 23(7–8): 93–109.

Krikman, Bradley L., Rosen, Benson, Tesluk, Paul E. and Gibson, Christina B. (2004) The impact of team empowerment on virtual team performance: The moderating role of face-to-face interaction, *Academy of Management Journal*, 47(2): 175–92.

Krims, Adam (1998) Introduction: Postmodern musical poetics and the problem of 'close reading', in Krims, Adam, ed., *Music/ideology: Resisting aesthetic*: Amsterdam: G+B Arts International, pp. 1–14.

Kristeva, Julia (1982) *Power of Horrors: An essay on abjection*, trans. Leon S. Roudiez, New York: Columbia University Press.

Kundera, Milan (1988) *The art of the novel*, trans. by Linda Asher, New York: Grove Press.

Kwinter, Sanford (2001) *Architecture of Time: Towards a theory of the event in modernist culture*, Cambridge and New York: MIT Press.

Lacan, Jacques (1989) *Écrits: A selection*, London and New York: Routledge.

Lacan, Jacques (1998) *The Four Fundamental Concepts of Psychoanalysis: The seminars of Jacques Lacan, Book XI*, trans. Alan Sheridan, New York and London: W.W. Norton.

Landow, George P. (2006) *Hypertext 3.0: Critical theory and new media in an era of globalization*, Baltimore: Johns Hopkins University Press.

Lanham, Richard (2006) *The Economics of Attention: Style and substance in the age of information*, Chicago and London: University of Chicago Press.

Lanza, Joseph (1994) *Elevator Music: A surreal history of Muzak, Easy-listening, and other moodsong*, New York: St Martin's Press.

Lanzara, Giovan Francesco and Patriotta, Gerardo (2001) Technology and the courtroom: An inquiry into knowledge making in organizations, *Journal of Management Studies*, 38(7): 943–71.

Lash, Scott (2006) Life (Vitalism), *Theory, Culture & Society*, 23(2–3): 323–9.

Latour, Bruno (1988) The Enlightenment without the critique: A word on Michel Serres's philosophy, in Griffith, J., ed., *Contemporary French Philosophy*, Cambridge: Cambridge University Press.

Latour, Bruno (1991) Technology is society made durable, in Law, John, ed., *A Sociology of Monsters: Essays on power, technology and domination*, London and New York: Routledge.

Law, John (2002) *Aircraft Stories: Decentering the object in technoscience*, Durham: Duke University Press.

Lazzarato, Maurizio (2007) Machines to crystallize time: Bergson, *Theory, Culture and Society*, 24(6): 93–122.

Lee, Judith Yaross (1996) Charting the codes of cyberspace: A rhetoric of electronic mail, in Strate, Lance, Jacobson, Ronald, & Gibson and Stephanie, B., eds, (1996) *Communication and cyberspace: Social interaction in an electronic environment*, Cresskill, NJ: Hampton Press, pp. 275–96.

Lefebvre, Henri (1991) *The Production of Space*, Oxford: Blackwell.

Lefebvre, Henri (2004) *Rhythmanalysis: Space, time and everyday life*, trans. Stuart Elden and Gerald Moore, London and New York: Athlone Press.

Le Goff, Jacques (1988) *Your Money or Your Life: Economy and religion in the Middle Ages*, New York: Zone Books.

Le Goff, Jacques (1993) *Intellectuals in the Middle Ages*, Oxford and Cambridge: Blackwell.

Leidner, Robin (1993) *Fast Food, Fast Talk: Service work and the routinization of everyday life*, Berkeley: University of California Press.

Lena, Jennifer C. (2006) Social context and musical content of rap music, 1979–1995, *Social Forces*, 85(1): 479–95.

Leonard-Barton D. (1988), Implementation as Mutual Adoption of Technology and Organization, *Research Policy*, 17: 251–67.

Leppert, Richard (1993) *The Sight of Sound: Music, representation, and the history of the body*, Berkeley, Los Angeles and London: University of California Press.

Leppert, Richard (1996) *Art and the Committed Eye: The cultural foundations of imaginary*, Boulder: Westview Press.

Leppert, Richard and McClary, Susan, eds (1987) *Music and Society: The politics of composition, performance and reception*, Cambridge: Cambridge University Press.

Leroi-Gourhan, André (1989) *The Hunters of Prehistory*, trans. Claire Jacobson, New York: Atheneum.

Letiche, Hugo (2004) 'Talk' and Hermès, *Culture and Organization*, 10(2): 143–61.

Leupin, Alexandre (1991) Introduction; Voids and knots in knowledge and truth, in Leupin, Alexandre, ed., *Lacan and the Human Sciences*, Lincoln and London: University of Nebraska Press.

Levin, David Michael (1993) Introduction, in Levin, David Michael, ed., *Modernity and the Hegemony of Vision*, Berkeley, Los Angeles and London: University of California Press, pp. 1–29.

Lévi-Strauss, Claude (1979) *Myth and Meaning: Cracking the Code of Meaning*, New York: Shocken Books.

Lévi-Strauss, Claude (1985) *The View from Afar*, trans. Joachim Neugroshel and Phoebe Hoss, Oxford: Blackwell.

Lévy, Pierre (1995) The invention of the computer, in Serres, Michel, Ed., (1995), *A History of Scientific Thought*, Oxford: Blackwell.

Lévy, Pierre (1998) *Becoming virtual: reality in the digital age*, Trans. by Robert Bononno, New York and London: Plenum Trade.

Lightman, Bernard (2000) The visual theology of Victorian popularizers of science. From reverent eye to chemical retina, *Isis*, 91(4): 651–80.

Lindqvist, Katja (2003) Exhibition Enterprising: Six cases of realization from idea to institution, PhD Thesis, Stockholm University: School of Business.

Linstead, Alison and Brewis, Joanna (2004) Beyond boundaries: Towards fluidity in theorizing and practice, *Gender, Work and Organization*, 11(4): 430–54.

Linstead, Stephen (2006) Exploring culture with *The Radio Ballads*: using aesthetics to facilitate change, *Management Decision*, 44(4): 474–85.

Linstead, S. and Höpfl, H., ed. (2000) *The Aesthetics of Organization*, London, Thousand Oaks and New Delhi: Sage.

Littlefield, Richard (1998) The silence of frames, in Krims, Adam, ed., *Music/ideology: Resisting aesthetic*: Amsterdam: G+B Arts International, pp. 213–31.

Lock, Charles (2003) Carnival and incarnation. Bakhtin and Orthodox theology, in Gardiner, Michael E., ed., *Mikhail Bakhtin, Vol. 1*, London , Thousand Oaks and New Delhi: Sage, pp. 285–99.

Luhmann, Niklas (2000a) *The reality of the mass media*, Cambridge: Polity Press.

Luhmann, Niklas (2000b) *Art as a social system*, trans by Eva M. Knodt, Stanford: Stanford University Press.

Lupton, Deborah (1995) The embodied computer/user, in Featherstone, Mike and Burrows, Roger, eds, *Cyberspace/cyberbodies/cyberpunk: Cultures of technological representations*, London: Sage.

Lykke, Nina and Braidotti, Rosi (1996) *Between Monsters, Goddesses and Cyborgs: Feminist Confrontations with Science, Medicine, and Cyberspace*, London: Zed Books.

Lynch, Michael (1985) *Art and artifact in Laboratory science. A study of shop work and shop talk in a research laboratory*, London: Routledge & Kegan Paul.

Lynch, Michael (1988) The externalized retina: Selection and mathematization in the visual documentation of objects in the life sciences, in Lynch, Michael and Woolgar, Steve, eds (1990), *Representation in Scientific Practice*, Cambridge and London: MIT Press, pp. 153–86.

Lyon, David (1994) *The Electronic Eye: The rise of surveillance society*, Cambridge: Polity Press.

Lyotard, Jean-François (1988) *The Differend*, Minneapolis and London: University of Minnesota Press.

Lyotard, Jean-François (1991) *The Inhuman,* Cambridge: Polity Press.

Lyotard, Jean-François and Thébaud, Jean-Loup (1985) *Just Gaming*, Minneapolis: University of Minnesota Press.

MacDonald, Malcolm (2003) *Varèse: Astronomer in sound*, London : Kahn & Averill.

Mack, Kathy S. (2007) Senses of seascapes: Aesthetics and the passion of knowledge, *Organization*, 14(3): 373–90.

MacKenzie, Donald (1996) *Knowing Machines: Essays on technical change*, Cambridge: MIT Press.

Macnaughton, Jane (2007) Art in hospital spaces: the role of hospitals in an aestheticised society, *International Journal of Cultural Policy,* 13(1): 86–101.

Maitlis, Sally (2005) The social processes of organizational sensemaking, *Academy of Management Journal*, 48(1): 21–49.

Manovich, Lev (2001) *The Language of New Media*, Cambridge and London: MIT Press.

March, James G. (1994) *A Primer on Decision Making*, New York: Free Press.

March, James G. and Olsen, Johan P. (1976) *Ambiguity and Choice in Organizations*, Oslo: Universitetsforlaget.

Marotto, Mark, Roos, Johan and Victor, Bart (2007) Collective virtuosity in organizations: A study of peak performance in an orchestra, *Journal of Management Studies*, 44(3): 388–413.

Markeley, Robert, ed. (1996) *Virtual Realities and their Discontents*, Johns Hopkins University Press.

Martin, Patricia Yancey (2005) *Rape Work. Victims, gender, and emotions in organization and community context*, London and New York: Routledge.

Marx, Leo (1964) *The Machine in the Garden: Technology and the pastoral ideal in America*, New York and Oxford: Oxford University Press.

Mason, David, Button, Graham, Lankshear, Gloria and Coates, Sally (2002) Getting real about surveillance and privacy at work, in Woolgar, Steve, ed., *Virtual Society? Technology, cyberbole, reality*, Oxford and New York: Oxford University Press.

Massumi, Brian (2002) *Parables of the Virtual: Movement, affect, sensation*, Durham and London: Duke University Press.

May, Christopher (2002) *The Information Society: A sceptical view*, Cambridge: Polity Press.

Maznevsky, Martha L. and Chudoba, Katherine M. (2000) Bridging space over time: Global virtual team dynamics and effectiveness, *Organization Science*, 11(5): 473–92.

Mazza, Carmelo and Pedersen, Jesper Strannegaard (2004) From press to E-media? The transformation of an organizational field, *Organization Studies*, 25(6): 875–96.

McClary, Susan (1987) Talking politics during the Bach year, in Leppert, Richard and McClary, Susan, eds, *Music and Society: The politics of composition, performance and reception*, Cambridge: Cambridge University Press, pp. 13–62.

McClary, Susan (1991) *Feminine Endings: Music, gender and sexuality*, Minneapolis and Oxford: University of Minnesota Press.

McClary, Susan (2006) Rap, minimalism, and structures of time in late twentieth-century culture, in Cox, Christoph and Warner, Daniel, eds, *Audio Cultures: Readings in modern music*, New York and London: Continuum, pp. 289–98.

McCloskey, Deirdre N. (2006) *The Bourgeois Virtues: Ethics for an age of commerce*, Chicago and London: University of Chicago Press.

McGail, Brian A. (2002) Confronting electronic surveillance: Desiring and resisting new technologies, in Woolgar, Steve, ed., *Virtual Society? Technology, cyberbole, reality*, Oxford and New York: Oxford University Press.

McGivern, Gerry and Ferlie, Ewan (2007) Playing tick-box games: Interrelating defences in professional appraisal, *Human Relations*, 60(9): 1361–85.

McLuhan, Marshall (1962) *The Gutenberg Galaxy: The making of typographic man*, London: Routledge and Kegan Paul.

McLuhan, Marshall (1964) *Understanding Media*, New York: Signet Books.

McLuhan, Marshall (1997) *Media Research: Technology, art and communication*, Amsterdam: G+B Arts.

McMillan, Ann (2004) Celebrated villages: Edgard Varèse 1883 1965, *Contemporary Music Review*, 23(1): 3–9.

McNair, Brian (2002) *Striptease Culture*, London and NewYork: Routledge.

Menger, Pierre-Michel (1999) Artistic labour markets and careers, *Annual Review of Sociology*, 25: 541–74.

Merleau-Ponty, Maurice (1962) *Phenomenology of Perception*, London and New York: Routledge.

Merleau-Ponty, Maurice (1964a) Bergson in the making, in *Signs*, trans. Richard C. McCleary, Chicago: Northwestern University Press, pp. 182–91.

Merleau-Ponty, Maurice (1964b) *The Primacy of Perception and Other Essays on Phenomenological Psychology, the Philosophy of Art, History and Politics*, trans. James M. Edie, Chicago: Northwestern University Press.

Merleau-Ponty, Maurice (1968) *The Visible and the Invisible*, Evanston: Northwestern University Press.

Merleau-Ponty, Maurice (1974a) Indirect language and the voices of silence, in *Phenomenology, Language and Sociology: Selected essays of Maurice Merleau-Ponty*, ed. John O'Neill, London: Heineman, pp. 36–80.

Merleau-Ponty, Maurice (1974b) On the phenomenology of language, in *Phenomenology, Language and Sociology: Selected essays of Maurice Merleau-Ponty*, ed. John O'Neill, London: Heinemann, pp. 81–94.

Merleau-Ponty, Maurice (1993a) Cézanne's doubt, in *The Merleau-Ponty Aesthetics Reader: Philosophy and painting*, Evanston: Northwestern University Press, pp. 59–75.

Merleau-Ponty, Maurice (1993b) Eye and mind, in *The Merleau-Ponty Aesthetics Reader: Philosophy and painting*, Evanston: Northwestern University Press, pp. 121–49.

Merleau-Ponty, Maurice (1948/2004) *The World of Perception*, trans. Oliver Davis, London and New York: Routledge.

Meyer, J.W. and Rowan, B. (1992) Institutionalized organizations: Formal structure as myth and ceremony, in Meyer, J.W. and Scott, W.R., *Organizational Environments: Ritual and Rationality*, London: Sage.

Michaels, Mike (2000) *Reconnecting Culture, Technology and Nature: From society to heterogeneity*, London and New York: Routledge.

Milburn, Colin (2004) Nanotechnology in the age of posthuman engineering: Science fiction as science, in Hayles, N. Katherine, ed., (2005), *Nanoculture: Implications of the new technoscience*, Bristol: Intellect, pp. 109–29.

Miller, Henry (1945) *The Airconditioned Nightmare*, New York: New Direction Books.

Mitchell, William J. (1992) *The Reconfigured Eye: Visual truth in the post-photographic era*, Cambridge and London: MIT Press.

Mody, Cyrus C.M. (2005) The sounds of silence: Listening to laboratory practice, *Science Technology and Human Values*, 30(2): 175–98.

Mol, Annemarie (2002) *The Body Multiple: Ontology in medical practice*, Durham: Duke University Press.

Moore, Don A., Tetlock, Philip E., Tanlu, Lloyd and Bazerman, Max H. (2006) Conflict of interest and the case of auditor independence: Moral seduction and strategic issue cycling, *Academy of Management Review*, 31(1): 10–29.

Morley, David (2007) Television: not so much a visual medium, more a visual subject, in Morley, David, *Media, Modernity and Technology: The geography of the new*, London and New York: Routledge, pp. 273–92.

Mosco, Vincent (2004) *The Digital Sublime: Myth, power and cyberspace*, Cambridge and London: MIT Press.

Mowitt, John (1987) The sound of music in the era of its electronic reproducibility, in Leppert, Richard and McClary, Susan, eds, *Music and Society: The politics of composition, performance and reception*, Cambridge: Cambridge University Press, pp. 173–97.

Mulder, Arjen (2006) Media, *Theory, Culture and Society*, 23(2–3): 289–96.

Mulvey, Laura (1989) Visual pleasures and narrative cinema, in Mulvey, Laura, *Visual and Other Pleasures*, London: Macmillan, pp. 14–26.

Munster, Anna (2006) *Materializing New Media: Embodiment in information aesthetics*, Hanover: Dartmouth College Press.

Münsterberg, Hugo ([1913] 1998) *Psychology and Industrial Efficiency*, Boston: Houghton Mifflin.

Murningham, Keith J. and Conlon, Donald E. (1991) The dynamics of intense work groups: A study of British string quartets, *Administrative Science Quarterly*, 36: 165–86.

Nelson, Ted (1974/2001) Computer lib/Dream machines, in Packer, Randall and Jordan, Ken, eds (2001), *Multimedia: From Wagner to virtual reality*, New York: W.W. Norton, pp. 154–66.

Newell, Sue, Scarborough, Harry, Swan, Jacky and Hislop, Donald (2000) Intranets and knowledge management: De-centred technologies and the limits of technological discourse, in Prichard, Craig, Hull, Richard, Chumer, Mike and Willmott, Hugh, eds, *Managing Knowledge: Critical investigations of work and learning*, New York: St Martin's Press.

Nicolini, Davide (2007) Studying visual practices in construction, *Building Research and Information*, 35(5): 576–80.

Nielsen, Henriette Langstrup (2005) Linking Healthcare: An inquiry into the changing performances of web-based technology for asthma monitoring, PhD thesis, Department of Organization and Industrial Sociology, Copenhagen Business School.

Nietzsche, Friedrich (1997) *Untimely meditations*, ed. by Daniel Breazeale, Trans. by R.J. Hollingdale, Cambridge: Cambridge University Press.

Nightingale, Paul (1998) A cognitive model of innovation, *Research Policy*, 27: 698–709.

Nixon, Sean (2005) *Advertisement Culture*, London, Thousand Oaks and New Delhi: Sage.

Nye, David E. (1990) *Electrifying America: Social meanings of a new technology, 1880–1940*, Cambridge: MIT Press.

Nye, David E. (1994) *American Technological Sublime*, Cambridge and London: MIT Press.

Nye, David (2004) Electricity and signs, in Schwartz, Vanessa R. and Przyblyski, Jeannene M., eds, *The Nineteenth-century Visual Culture Reader*, London and New York: Routledge, pp. 211–17.

Nye, David E. (2006) *Technology Matters: Questions to live with*, Cambridge and London: MIT Press.

Ocasio, William (1997) Towards an attention-based view of the firm, *Strategic Management Journal*, Special issue on Organizational and competitive interactions, 18: 187–206.

O'Conner, Ellen (1999) Minding the Workers: The Meaning of 'Human' and 'Human Relations' in Elton Mayo, *Organization*, 6(2): 223–46.

Ong, W.J. (1982) *Orality and Literacy: The Technologizing of the Word*, London: Routledge.

Oprea, Tudor Ionel (2002) Virtual screening in lead discovery: A viewpoint, *Molecules* 7: 51–62.

Orlikowski, Wanda J. (1992) The duality of technology: Rethinking the concept of technology in organizations, *Organization Science*, 3(3): 398–427.

Orlikowski, Wanda J. (2000) Using technology and constituting structures: A practice lens for studying technology in organizations, *Organization Science*, 11(4): 404–28.

Orlikowski, Wanda J. (2007) Sociomaterial practices: Exploring technology at work, *Organization Studies*, 28(9): 1435–48.

Orlikowski, Wanda J. and Iacono, C. Suzanne (2001) Research commentary: Desperately seeking the 'IT' in IT research – A call to theorizing the IT artifact, *Information Systems Research*, 12(2): 121–34.

Osbourne, Thomas (2003) Against 'creativity': A philistine rant, *Economy and Society*, 32(4): 507–25.

Oswick, Cliff, Keenoy, Tom W. and Grant, David (2000) Discourse, organizations and organizing: Concept, objects and subjects, *Human Relations*, 53(9): 1115–23.

Oudshoorn, Nelly and Pinch, Trevor, eds (2003) *How Users Matter: The co-construction of users and technologies*, Cambridge and London: MIT Press.

Ouellette, Fernand (1968) *Edgard Varèse*, trans. Derek Coltman, New York: Orion Press.

Pape, Gerard (2004) Varèse the visionary, *Contemporary Music Review*, 23(2): 19–25.

Pasveer, Bernike (2006) Representing or mediating; A history and philosophy of X-ray images in medicine, in Pauwels, Luc, ed., *Visual Cultures of Science: Rethinking representational practices in knowledge building and science communications*, Hanover: Dartmouth College Press, pp. 41–62.

Patriotta, Gerardo (2003) *Organization Knowledge in the Making: How firms create, use, and institutionalise knowledge*, Oxford and New York: Oxford University Press.

Pentland, Brian T. (2000) Will auditors take over the world? Programs, techniques, and verification of everything, *Accounting, Organization and Society*, 25: 307–12.

Pentland, Brian T. and Feldman, Martha S. (2007) Narrative networks: Patterns of technology and organization, *Organization Science*, 18(5): 781–95.

Perrow, Charles (1983) The organizational context of human factors engineering, *Administrative Science Quarterly*, 28: 521–41.

Peters, Tom J. and Waterman, Robert H. (1982) *In Search of Excellence*, New York: Harper & Row.

Peterson, Richard A. and Anand, N. (2004) The production of culture perspective, *Annual Review of Sociology*, 30: 311–34.

Piaget, Jean (1950/2001) *The Psychology of Intelligence*, London and New York: Routledge.

Pickering, Andrew (1995) *The Mangle of Practice: Time, agency, and science*, Chicago and London: University of Chicago Press.

Pinch, Trevor J. and Bijker, Wiebe E. (1987) The social construction of facts and artifacts: Or how the sociology of science and the sociology of technology might benefit one another, in Bijker, Wiebe E., Hughes, Thomas P. and Pinch, Trevor J., eds, *The Social Construction of Technological Systems: New directions in the sociology and history of technology*, Cambridge and London: MIT Press, pp. 17–50.

Piñeiro, Erik (2007) Aesthetics at the heart of logic: On the role of beauty in computing innovation, Guillet de Monthoux, Pierre, Gustafsson, Claes and Sjöstrand, Sven-Erik, eds, *Aesthetic Leadership: Managing fields of flow in art and business*, Basingstoke: Palgrave Macmillan, pp. 105–27.

Pinnington, Ashly and Morris, Timothy (2002) Transforming the architect. Ownership from the archtype change, *Organization Studies*, 23(2): 189–210.

Polanyi, M. (1958) *Personal Knowledge: Toward a post-critical philosophy*, Chicago: University of Chicago Press.

Polkinghorne, Donald E. (1988) *Narrative Knowing and the Human Sciences*, Albany: State University of New York Press.

Pollard, S. (1965) *The Genesis of Modern Management: A study of the industrial revolution in Great Britain*, London: Edward Arnold.

Porcello, Thomas (2004) Speaking of sound: Language and the professionalization of sound-recording engineers, *Social Studies of Science*, 34(5): 733–58.

Porter, Theodore M. (1995) *Trust in Numbers: The pursuit of objectivity in science and public life*, Princeton: Princeton University Press.

Poster, Mark (2001a) *The Information Subject: Essays*. Amsterdam: G+B Arts.

Poster, Mark (2001b) *What's the Matter with the Internet*, Minneapolis: University of Minnesota Press.

Powell, Walter W. (1998) Learning from Collaboration: knowledge and networks in the biotechnology and pharmaceutical industries, *California Management Review*, 40(3): 228–40.

Powell, Walter W., Koput, Kenneth W. and Smith-Doerr, Laurel (1996) Interorganizational collaboration and the locus of innovation: Networks of learning in biotechnology, *Administrative Science Quarterly*, 41: 116–45.

Power, M. (1994) The audit society, in Hopwood, A.G. and Miller, P., eds, *Accounting as Social and Institutional Practice*, Cambridge: Cambridge University Press.

Power, Michael (2004) Counting, control and calculation: Reflection on measuring and management, *Human Relations*, 57(6): 765–83.

Prasad, Amit (2005) Making images/making bodies: Visibility and disciplining through magnetic resonance imaging (MRI), *Science, Technology and Human Values*, 30(2): 291–316.

Prasad, Pushkala (1993) Symbolic process in the implementation of technological change: A symbolic interactionist study of work computerization, *Academy of Management Journal*, 36(6): 1400–29.

Prentice, Rachel (2005) The anatomy of surgical simulations: The mutual articulation of bodies in and through the machine, *Social Studies of Science*, 35(6): 837–66.

Prichard, Craig, Korczynski, Marek and Elmes, Michael (2007) Music at work: An introduction, *Group and Organization Management*, 32(1): 4–21.

Radano, Ronald (1989) Interpreting muzak: Speculation on the musical experience in everyday life, *American Music*, 7(4): 448–60.

Radick, Gregory (2003) R.L. Garner and the rise of the Edison phonograph in evolutionary philology, in Gitelman, Lisa and Pingree, Geoffrey B., eds, *New Media, 1940–1915*, Cambridge and London: MIT Press, pp. 175–206.

Rafaeli, Anat, Dutton, Jane, Harquail, Celia V. and Mackie-Lewis, Stephane (1997) Navigating by attire: The use of dress by female administrative employees, *Academy of Management Journal*, 40(1): 9–45.

Rajagopal, Arvind (2006) Imperceptible perceptions in our technological modernity, in Chun, Wendy Hui Kyong and Keenen, Thomas, eds, *New Media, Old Media: A history and theory reader*, New York and London: Routledge, pp. 277–86.

Rappaport, Erika D. (1995) 'A new era of shopping': The promotion of women's pleasure in London's West End, 1909–1914, in Carney, Leo and Schwartz, Vanessa R., eds, *Cinema and the Invention of Modern Life*, Berkeley: University of California Press, pp. 130–55.

Reeves, Terrie C., Duncan, W. Jack, and Ginter, Peter M. (2001) Motion Study in Management and the Arts: A Historical Example, *Journal of Management Inquiry* 10(2): 137–49.

Rehn, Alf and Sköld, David (2005) I love the dough; Rap lyrics as a minor economic literature, *Culture and Organization*, 11(1): 17–31.

Rheinberger, Hans-Jörg, (1997) *Toward a history of epistemic things: Synthesizing proteins in the test tube*, Stanford: Stanford University Press.

Rhodes, Carl (2001) D'Oh: *The Simpsons*, popular culture, and the organizational carnival, *Journal of Management Inquiry*, 10(4): 2374–83.

Rhodes, Carl (2007) Outside the Gates of Eden: Utopia and Work in Rock Music, *Group and Organization Management*, 32(1): 22–49.

Risset, Jean-Claude (2004) The liberation of sound, art-science and the digital domain: Contacts with Edgard Varèse, *Contemporary Music Review*, 23(2): 27–54.

Ritzer, George (1997) *Postmodern Social Theory*, New York: McGraw-Hill.

Ritzer, George (1998) *The McDonaldization Thesis*, London: Sage.

Ritzer, George (2005) *Enchanting a Disenhanted World: Revolutionizing the means of consumption*, 2nd edn, Thousand Oaks: Pine Forge Press.

Robertson, Emma, Korczynski, Marek and Pickering, Michael (2007) Harmonious relations? Music at work in the Rowntree and Cadbury factories, *Business Horizon*, 49(2): 211–34.

Roodhouse, Simon (2006) The unreliability of cultural management information: Defining the visual arts, *Journal of Arts Management, Law, and Society*, 36(1): 48–65.

Ropo, Arja and Parviainen, Jaana (2001) Leadership and bodily knowledge in expert organizations: Epistemological rethinking, *Scandinavian Journal of Management*, 17: 1–18.

Rose, Nikolas S. (2007) *The Politics of Life Itself: Biomedicine, Power and Subjectivity in the Twenty-First Century*, Princeton and Oxford: Princeton University Press.

Rosen, Michael (1985) Breakfast at Spiro's dramaturgy and dominance, *Journal of Management*, 11(2): 31–48.

Rosen, Michael (2000) You asked for it. Christmas at the bosses' expense, in Rosen, Michael, *Turning Words, Spinning Worlds. Chapters in organizational ethnography*, Amsterdam: Harwood.

Roth, Wolff-Michael (2005) Making classifications (at) work: Ordering practices in science, *Social Studies of Science*, 35(4): 581–621.

Russo, Mary and Warner, Daniel (2006) Rough music, futurism and postpunk industrial noise bands, in Cox, Christoph and Warner, Daniel, eds, *Audio Cultures: Readings in modern music*, New York and London: Continuum, pp. 47–54.

Russolo, Luigi (1986) *The Art of Noises*, trans. Barclay Brown, New York: Pendragon Press.

Said, Edward W. (1991) *Musical Elaborations*, New York: Columbia University Press.

Sanders, Teela (2004) Controllable laughter: Managing sex work through humour, *Sociology*, 38(2): 273–91.

Sarkar, Sahotra (2006) From genes as determinants to DNA as resource: Historical notes on development and genetics, in Neumann-Held, Eva M. and Rehmann-Sutter, Christoph, eds, *Genes in Development; Re-reading the molecular paradigm*, Durham and London: Duke University Press, pp. 77–95.

Saussure, F. de (1959) *Course in General Linguistics*, London: Peter Owen.

Saxenian, AnnaLee (1994) *Regional Advantage: Culture and competition in Silicon valley and Route 128*, Cambridge and London: Harvard University Press.

Schafer, R. Murray (2006: 34) The music of the environment, in Cox, Christoph and Warner, Daniel, eds, *Audio Cultures: Readings in modern music*, New York and London: Continuum, pp. 29–39.

Schatzki, Theodore R. (2002) *The Site of the Social: A philosophical account of the constitution of social life and change*, University Park, PA: Pennsylvania State University Press.

Schatzki, Theodore R., Knorr Cetina, Karin and Savigny, Eike von, eds (2001) *The Practice Turn in Contemporary Theory*, London and New York: Routledge.

Schiavo, Laura Burd (2003) From phantom image to perfect vision: Physiological optics, commercial photography, and the popularization of the stereoscope, in

Gitelman, Lisa and Pingree, Geoffrey B., eds, *New Media, 1740–1915*, Cambridge and London: MIT Press, pp. 113–38.

Schiller, Friedrich (1795/2004) *On the Aesthetic Education of Man*, Mineola: Dover.

Schivelbusch, Wolfgang (1986) *The Railway Journey: The industrialization and perception of time and space in the 19th century*, Leamington Spa: Berg.

Schopenhauer, Arthur (1995) *The World as Will and Idea*, London: Everyman.

Schwartz, Vanessa R. and Przyblyski, Jeannene M., eds (2004) *The Nineteenth-century Visual Culture Reader*, London and New York: Routledge.

Sconce, Jeffrey (2000) *Haunted Media: Electronic presence from telegraphy to television*, Durham and London; Duke University Press.

Selin, Cynthia (2007) Expectations and the emergence of nanotechnology, *Science, Technology and Human Values*, 32(2): 196–220.

Serres, Michel (1982) *The Parasite*, Baltimore: Johns Hopkins University Press.

Serres, Michel (1995a) *Angels: A modern myth*, Paris and New York: Flammarion.

Serres, Michel (1995b) *Genesis*, Ann Arbor: University of Michigan Press.

Sewell, Graham (1998) The discipline of teams: The control of team-based industrial work through electronic and peer surveillance, *Administrative Science Quarterly*, 43: 397–428.

Sewell, Graham and Barker, James R. (2006) Coercion versus care: Using irony to make sense of organizational surveillance, *Academy of Management Review*, 31(4): 934–61.

Shapin, Steven (1994) *A Social History of Truth: Civility and science in seventeenth-century England*, Chicago and London: Chicago of University Press.

Shenhav, Yehouda (1999) *Manufacturing Rationality. The engineering foundation of the managerial revolution*, Oxford and New York: Oxford University Press.

Shepherd, John (1987) Music and male hegemony, in Leppert, Richard and McClary, Susan, eds, *Music and Society: The politics of composition, performance and reception*, Cambridge: Cambridge University Press, pp. 151–72.

Shields, Rob (2003) *The Virtual*, London and New York: Routledge.

Shklovsky, Viktor ([1929] 1990) *Theory of prose*, trans. by Benjamin Sher., Elmwood Park: Dalkey Archive Press.

Shusterman, Richard (2006) Aesthetics, *Theory, Culture and Society*, 23(2–3): 237–52.

Sicca, Luigi Maria (2000) Chamber music and organization theory: Some typical organizational phenomena seen under the microscope, *Studies of Cultures, Organizations and Societies*, 6: 145–68.

Simmel, Georg (1971) The metropolis and mental life, in *On individuality and social forms, Selected writings*, Levine, D.A., ed., Chicago: The University Press of Chicago, pp. 324–39.

Simmel, Georg (1916/2005) *Rembrandt: An essay in the philosophy of art*, trans. Alan Scott and Helmut Straubmann, London and New York: Routledge.

Simondon, Gilbert (1964/1992) The genesis of the individual, in Crary, Jonathan & Kwinter, Sanford, eds., (1992), *Incorporations*. New York: Zone Books, pp. 297–319.

Sinclair, Marta and Ashkanasy, Neal M. (2005) Intuition: Myth or decision-making tool?, *Management Learning*, 36(3): 353–70.

Sinclair, Upton (1906/2006) *The Jungle*, London: Penguin.

Singer, Ben (1995) Modernity, hyperstimulus, and the rise of the popular sensationalism, in Carney, Leo and Schwartz, Vanessa R., eds, *Cinema and the Invention of Modern Life*, Berkeley: University of California Press, pp. 72–99.

Sommerlund, Julie (2006) Classifying microorganisms: The multiplicity of classifications and research practices in molecular microbial ecology, *Social Studies of Science*, 36(6): 909–28.

Sontag, Susan (1966) Against interpretation, in Sontag, Susan, *Against Interpretation and Other Essays*, New York: Farrar, Straus & Giroux.

Sontag, Susan (1973) *On Photography*, New York: Farrar, Straus & Giroux.

Sowa, Yoshihiro (2006) Present state and advances in personalized medicine: Importance of the development of information service systems for the public, *Quarterly Review*, 18, National Institute of Science and Technology Policy, Japan (available at www.nistep.go.jp/achiev/ftx/eng/stfc/stt018e/qr18pdf/STTqr1801.pdf, accessed 9 March 2007).

Spinoza, B. (1994) *Ethics*, London: Penguin.

Standage, Tom (1998) *The Victorian Internet: The remarkable story of the telegraph and the nineteenth century's online pioneers*, London: Weidenfeld & Nicolson.

Star, Susan Leigh and Bowker, Geoffrey C. (2002) How to infrastructure, in Lievrouw, Leah A. and Livingstone, Sonia, eds, *Handbook of New Media: Social shaping and consequences of ICT*, London, Thousand Oaks and New Delhi: Sage, pp. 151–62.

Sterne, Jonathan (1997) Sounds like the mall of America: Programmed music and the architectonics of commercial space, *Ethnomusicology*, 41(1): 22–3.

Steuer, Jonathan (1992) Defining Virtual Reality: Dimensions determining telepresence, *Journal of Communication*, 42(4), 73–93.

Stivers, Richard (1999) *Technology as Magic: The triumph of the irrational*, New York: Continuum.

Stockhausen, Karlheinz (2006) Electronic and instrumental music, in Cox, Christoph and Warner, Daniel, eds, *Audio Cultures: Readings in modern music*, New York and London: Continuum, pp. 370–80.

Strati, Antonio (1999) *Organization and Aesthetics*, London, Thousand Oaks and New Delhi: Sage.

Stross, Randall (2007) For the 2008 race, Google is a crucial constituency, *New York Times*, 2 December 2007.

Stubbs, Katherine (2003) Telegraphy's corporeal fictions, in Gitelman, Lisa and Pingree, Geoffrey B., eds, *New Media, 1740–1915*, Cambridge and London: MIT Press, pp. 91–112.

Styhre Alexander (2007) Against the antagonist view of professionals-managers relationships: The case of the culture industry, *Human Resource Development International*, 10(4): 401–16.

Styhre, Alexander and Eriksson, Michael (2008) Bring in the arts and get the creativity for free: A study of the *Artists in Residence* project, *Creativity and Innovation Management*, 17(1): 47–57.

Subotnik, Rose Rosengard (1996) *Deconstructive Variations: Music and reason in Western society*, Minneapolis and London: University of Minnesota Press.

Sudnow, David (1978) *Ways of the Hand: The organization of improvised conduct*, Cambridge: Harvard University Press.

Sylvester, David (1980) *Interviews with Francis Bacon 1952–1979*, 2nd edn, London: Thames & Hudson.

Taylor, Steven S. and Hansen, Hans (2005) Finding form: Looking at the field of organizational aesthetics, *Journal of Management Studies*, 42(6): 1211–31.

Taylor, Timothy D. (2001) *Strange Sounds: Music, Technology and Culture*, London and New York: Routledge.

Thomas, David (1995) Feedback and cybernetics: Reimaging the body in the age of the cyborg, in Featherstone, Mike and Burrows, Roger, eds, *Cyberspace/cyberbodies/cyberpunk: Cultures of technological representations*, London: Sage.

Thomas, Tom C. and Acuña-Narvaez, Rachelle (2006) The convergence of biotechnology and nanotechnology: Why here, why now?, *Journal of Commercial Biotechnology*, 12(2): 105–10.

Tomlinson, Gary (1993) *Music in the Renaissance Magic: Towards historiography of others*, Chicago and London: University of Chicago Press.

Traweek, Sharon (1988) *Beamtimes and Lifetimes: The world of high energy physicists*, Cambridge and London: Harvard University Press.

Treleaven, Lesley (2004) A knowledge-sharing approach to organization change: A critical discourse analysis, in Tsoukas, Haridimos and Mylonopoulos, Nikolaus, eds, *Organization Knowledge Systems: Knowledge, learning and dynamic capabilities*, Basingstoke and New York: Palgrave, pp. 154–80.

Trethewey, Angela (1999) Disciplined Bodies: Women's Embodied Identities at Work, *Organization Studies*, 20(3): 432–50.

Trieb, Marc (1996) *Space Calculated in Seconds: The Philips pavillon, Le Corbusier, Edgard Varèse*, Princeton: Princeton University Press.

Tsoukas, Haridimous (2005) *Complex Knowledge: Studies in organizational epistemology*, Oxford and New York: Oxford University Press.

Turkle, Sherry (1996) *Life on the Screen: Identity in the age of the Internet*, London: Weidenfeld & Nicolson.

Tyler, Melissa and Abbott, Pamela (1998) Chocs away: Weight watching in the contemporary airline industry, *Sociology*, 32(3): 433–50.

Tyler, Melissa and Taylor, Steve (1998) The exchange of aesthetics: Women's work and 'the gift', *Gender, Work and Organization*, 5(3): 165–71.

Ullman, Ellen (1997) *Close to the Machine: Technophilia and its discontents*, San Francisco: City Lights.

Ure, Andrew (1835/1967) *The Philosophy of Manufacturers*, London: Frank Cass & Co.

Urry, John (2004) The 'system' of automobility, *Theory, Culture and Society*, 21(4/5): 25–39.

Urry, John (2005) The complexities of the global, *Theory, Culture and Society*, 22(5): 23–54.

Valentine, Jeremy (2000) Information technology, ideology and governmentality, *Theory, Culture and Society*, 17(2): 21–43.

Van Delinder, Jean (2005) Taylorism, managerial control strategies, and the ballets of Balanchine and Stravinsky, *American Behavioral Scientist*, 48(11): 1439–52.

Veblen, Thorstein (1904) *The Theory of the Business Enterprise*, New York: Schreiber.

Vidler, Anthony (2000) *Warped Space: Art, architecture, and anxiety in modern society*, Cambridge and London: MIT Press.

Virilio, Paul (1989) *War and Cinema: The logistics of perception*, trans. Patrick Camiller, London and New York: Verso.

Virilio, Paul (2002) *Desert Screen: War at the speed of light*, London and New York: Continuum.

Virilio, Paul (2003) *Art and Fear*, trans. Julie Rose, London and New York: Continuum.

Virilio, Paul (2005) *Negative Horizon*, London and New York: Continuum.

Vygotsky, Lev (1978) *Mind in Society: The development of higher psychological processes*, ed. Michael Cole, Vera John-Steiner, Sylvia Scribner and Ellen Souberman, Cambridge and London: Harvard University Press.

Wagner, Richard (1849/2001) Outlines of the artwork of the future, in Packer, Randall and Jordan, Ken, ed. (2001), *Multimedia: From Wagner to virtual reality*, New York: W.W. Norton, pp. 2–9.

Wajcman, Judy (2004) *Technofeminism*, Cambridge and Malden: Polity.

Walkowitz, Judith (2004) Urban spectatorship, in Schwartz, Vanessa R. and Przyblyski, Jeannene M., eds, *The Nineteenth-century Visual Culture Reader*, London and New York: Routledge, pp. 205–10.

Walters, W. Patrick, Stahl, Matthew T. and Murcko, Mark A. (1998) Virtual screening – An overview, *Drug Discovery Today*, 3: 160–78.

Warneke, Georgia (1993) Ocularcentrism and social criticism, in Levin, David Michael, ed., *Modernity and the Hegemony of Vision*, Berkeley, Los Angeles and London: University of California Press, pp. 287–308.

Weber, Max (1958) *The Rational and Social Foundations of Music*, trans. Don Martindale, Johannes Riedel and Gertrude Neuwirth, Carbondale: Southern Illinois University Press.

Weick, K.E. (1979) *The Social Psychology of Organizing*, New York: McGraw-Hill.

Weick, Karl E. and Sutcliffe, Kathleen M. (2006) Mindfulness and the quality of organizational attention, *Organization Science*, 17(4): 514–24.

Weiner, Norbert (1948) *Cybernetics, or Control and Communication in the Animal Machine*, New York: John Wiley

Weiss, Gilbert and Wodak, Ruth, eds (2003) *Critical Discourse Analysis: Theory and interdisciplinarity*, Basingstoke and New York: Palgrave.

Westwood, Robert (2007) The staging of humour; Organizing and managing comedy, in Westwood, Robert and Rhodes, Carl, eds (2007) *Humour, Work and Organization*, London and New York: Routledge, pp. 271–98.

White, Hayden, (1978), *Tropics of Discourse: Essays in cultural criticism*, Baltimore & London: Johns Hopkins University Press.

White, Hayden (1987) *The Content of Form: Narrative discourse and historical representation*, Baltimore and London: Johns Hopkins University Press.

White, Michael (2007) Who'll stop the ring tones?, *New York Times*, 18 November 2007.

Whitehead, Alfred North (1927) *Symbolism: Its meaning and effects*, New York: Fordham University Press.

Whyte, Jennifer and Bouchlaghem, Dino (2002) Implementation of VR systems: A comparison between the early adoption of CAD and current uptake of VR, *Construction Innovation*, 2:(3): 13.

Whyte, Jennifer K., Ewenstein, Boris, Hales, Michael and Tidd, Joe (2007) Visual practices and the objects used in design, *Building Research and Information*, 35(1): 18–27.

Wilkinsson, B, Morris, J. and Munday, M. (1995) The iron fist and the velvet Glove: Management and organization in Japanese manufacturing transplants in Wales, *Journal of Management Studies*, 32(6): 819–30.

Williams, Raymond (1974/1990) *Television: Technology and Cultural Form*, 2nd edn, London and NewYork: Routledge.

Williams, Robin and Edge, David (1996) The social shaping of technology, *Research Policy*, 25: 865–99.

Wise, J. Macgregor (1997) *Exploring Technology and Social Space*, Thousand Oaks, London and New Delhi: Sage.

Wodak, Ruth, ed. (1997) *Gender and Discourse*, London, Thousand Oaks and New Delhi: Sage.

Wolf, Michael J. (1999) *The Entertainment Economy: How mega-media forces are transforming our lives*, London: Penguin.

Wood, Martin (1999) Cyborg: A design for life in the borderlands, *Emergence*, 1(3): 92–104.

Wren, Daniel A. (1972) *The Evolution of Management Thought*, New York: Ronald Press Company.

Yalch, Richard and Spangenberg, Eric (1990) Effects of store music on shopping behavior, *Journal of Consumer Marketing*, 7(2): 55–63.

Yates, JoAnne (1989) *Control Through Communication*, Baltimore and London: Johns Hopkins University Press.

Young, Paul (2003) Media on display: A telegraphic history of early American cinema, in Gitelman, Lisa and Pingree, Geoffrey B., eds, *New Media, 1740–1915*, Cambridge and London: MIT Press, pp. 229–64.

Zackariasson, Peter, Styhre, Alexander and Wilson, Tim (2006) Phronesis and creativity: Knowledge work in video game development, *Creativity and Innovation Management*, 15(4): 419–29.

Zammuto, Raymond F., Griffith, Teri L., Majchrzak, Ann, Dougherty, Deborah J. and Faraj, Samer (2007) Information technology and the changing fabric of organization, *Organization Science*, 19(5): 749–62.

Zembylas, Tasos (2004) Art and public conflict: Notes on the social negotiation of the concept of art, *Journal of Arts Management, Law, and Society*, 34(2): 119–31.

Zettl, Herbert (1996) Back in Plato's cave: Virtual reality, in Strate, Lance, Jacobson, Ronald, Gibson, Stephanie, B., eds, *Communication and Cyberspace: Social interaction in an electronic environment*, Cresskill, NJ: Hampton Press, pp. 83–94.

Ziarek, Krzysztof (2004) *The Force of Art*, Stanford: Stanford University Press.

Žižek, Slavoj (1995) *The Metastases of Enjoyment*, London: Verso.

Zolberg, Vera L. (1990) *Constructing a Sociology of the Arts*, Cambridge: Cambridge University Press.

Index